Mrs Gustav Holst

An Equal Partner?

by

Philippa Tudor

Circaidy Gregory Press

Copyright information

Text copyright © 2022 Philippa Tudor. This edition, copyright © 2022 Kay Green t/a Circaidy Gregory Press. All rights reserved. No part of this publication may be reproduced, stored in a retrieval system, rebound or transmitted in any form or for any purpose without the prior written permission of the author and publisher. This book is sold subject to the condition that it shall not be lent, resold, hired out or otherwise circulated without the publisher's prior consent in any form or binding other than that in which it is here published.

Front cover: Painting of Isobel in the music room at 10 The Terrace, Barnes, by Millicent Lisle Woodforde (Holst Victorian House), reproduced with permission.

Back cover: Portrait of Isobel by Prior Conway (James Brown) 1914, privately owned, reproduced with permission.

ISBN 9781910841594

Printed in the UK by
Catford Print

Published March 2022
by
Circaidy Gregory Press
Creative Media Centre,
45 Robertson St, Hastings,
Sussex TN34 1HL

Circaidy Gregory Press

Isobel in the living room at 10 The Terrace, Barnes, painted by Millicent Lisle Woodforde
(Holst Victorian House)

Acknowledgements

I express my deep gratitude to the large number of people who have helped and supported me during my research into Isobel's life, which started in January 2012. They are too numerous to name all of them individually, but those whom I have bothered repeatedly include: the late Graham Lockwood, former Chairman of the Holst Birthplace Trust, and Laura Kinnear, Curator of Holst Victorian House Cheltenham; Elaine Andrews, Learning Resources Centre Manager at Morley College; Sarah Batchelor, Assistant Librarian, Royal College of Music; Elen Curran, former Archivist, and Barbara Kley, former Head of Music, James Allen's Girls' School, Dulwich; Holst scholar Alan Gibbs; Michael Goatcher, whose multiple kindnesses included interviewing people in Thaxted who remembered Isobel and her daughter; Roland Goslett, whose generous assistance included sharing insights from his conversations with Sebastian Brown; Holst scholar Raymond Head; Bruno Lima, film maker; Colin Matthews; Tim McGee, author of the biography of Gustav's pupil Clare Mackail, who generously shared his copies of the 18 surviving letters from Clare to Isobel or Imogen; Judith Ratcliffe, Archivist, Britten Pears Arts, and colleagues and volunteers at Aldeburgh; Christopher Scheer, Associate Professor of Musicology at Utah State University; Michael Short, author of the outstanding biography *Gustav Holst: the man and his music*; and John Wellingham, who studied with Imogen Holst at Dartington and gave me permission to use one of the photos in his collection.

Gustav Holst's nephew Theodore von Holst (1935–2018), the son of his half-brother Max von Holst, kindly corresponded with me about his impressions of life in the von Holst household when Adolph von Holst's four sons were growing up. The late Peter King shared his memories of Isobel, and Sybil King, founder of the Thaxted Society, provided further insights into members of the Holst family. Sylvia Heath (née Putterill) corresponded with her own and her mother's memories of the Holsts at Thaxted). Philip Oliver, great nephew of Vally Lasker, shared his childhood and family memories of her, and generously gave me permission to use material relating to his great aunt.

Alan Gibbs and Raymond Head, both of whom have written much about Gustav Holst and his music over many years, read earlier drafts of this book and made helpful corrections and suggestions, including for further study. I am most grateful to them for sharing their expertise. Publisher Kay Green has also gone above and beyond with successive iterations.

The genesis of this book was a fundraising talk I gave for the Holst Birthplace Museum (now Holst Victorian House) in 2015, for which I produced an associated short book entitled *Gustav Holst's Other Half*. The present book benefited greatly from contributions and ideas from the informed audience at Cheltenham.

My husband, David Beamish, has helped in numerous ways, including compiling Isobel's family tree and the index.

Contents

1. Forgotten Wives — 1
2. Life before Imogen — 11
   - Isobel's family — 11
   - Gustav's family — 14
   - The Hammersmith Socialist Society and club activity — 16
3. Early married life — 27
4. Family life in Barnes and Thaxted — 35
5. War Work and the Planets Suite — 53
6. Fame and its Aftermath — 69
7. Gustav and Isobel in their Fifties — 87
8. Life after Gustav — 103

Epilogue: An Equal Partner? — 115
Appendix 1: The family tree of Isobel Holst née Harrison — 121
Appendix 2: Isobel Holst's key dates and home addresses — 122
Bibliography — 123
  - Manuscript sources — 123
  - Printed sources — 124
  - Sound recording — 126
  - Television — 127
  - Typescripts — 127
Index — 128

Illustrations

Front cover: Painting of Isobel in the music room at 10 The Terrace,
    Barnes, by Millicent Lisle Woodforde (Holst Victorian House)
Frontispiece: Painting of Isobel in the living room at 10 The Terrace,
    Barnes, by Millicent Lisle Woodforde (Holst Victorian House)

Isobel in the music room at Monk Street, near Thaxted (Holst Victorian House)	1
Isobel (Holst Victorian House)	11
Isobel and Gustav on honeymoon in Berlin, 1903 (Holst Victorian House)	27
Portrait photograph of Imogen and Isobel by Lizzie Caswall Smith (Holst Victorian House)	35
Isobel and Nora Day outside the music room of Monk Street cottage (Britten Pears Arts HOL/2/11/14/3)	52
Isobel and Gustav with Vally Lasker's family in Thaxted (Holst Victorian House)	52
Isobel in the uniform of the Women's Reserve Ambulance (Britten Pears Arts HOL/2/15/3)	53
Gustav and Isobel at Ann Arbor, Michigan, 1923 (Holst Victorian House)	69
Isobel and Imogen with Barbara Simcoe and Dora and Lily Harvey at Paycocke's, 1923 (Britten Pears Arts HOL/2/11/2/14)	86
Isobel at Weaverhead Cottage, Thaxted (Britten Pears Arts HOL/2/11/6/43)	86
Isobel at the wheel of "Penelope" outside the music room at Brook End, c 1928	87
(Britten Pears Arts HOL/2/7/1/249)	
Isobel Holst with two dogs (Britten Pears Arts HOL/2/11/5/21)	103
Drawing of Isobel by Clare Mackail (Holst Victorian House)	115

Back cover: Portrait of Isobel by Prior Conway (James Brown) 1914
    (privately owned, image published with permission)

Chapter One
Forgotten Wives

Isobel in the music room at Monk Street, near Thaxted (Holst Victorian House)

Isobel Harrison and composer Gustavus von Holst married on 22 June 1901, exactly five months after the death of one of history's most famous wives and widows, Queen Victoria. Their marriage was to last nearly 33 years until they were separated by Gustav's death on 25 May 1934. Isobel Holst's widowhood, during which she continued to describe herself as Mrs Gustav Holst, was even longer lasting, as she died on 16 April 1969.

A year before their marriage, the *Musical Times* published an article on the "Wives of Some Great Composers". The first to be assessed was Frances Purcell, wife of one of Gustav Holst's musical heroes and about which, the article stated, little was known, including her maiden name.[1] Only a few of the wives featured in the article had received much biographical attention either before 1900 or since. Almost all became mothers as well as wives: Frances Purcell bore six children, Maria Barbara Bach seven, followed by Anna Magdalena Bach's 13, Constanze Mozart had two children during her relatively short first marriage and Cecile Mendelssohn-Bartholdy five. Finally, the author of the *Musical Times* article appeared almost

---

[1] It was Peters.

overwhelmed by Clara Schumann's virtues as a wife, mother and widow, having only briefly referred to the childless and apparently ineffective homemaker Maria Anna Haydn.[2]

Although Isobel Holst has been a particularly enigmatic figure, wives generally have received scant historical attention. In 1840 Thomas Carlyle wrote that "the history of the world is but the biography of great men." Carlyle himself was married to a characterful woman, but Jane Carlyle is chiefly remembered, if at all, as a letter-writer, rather than as a woman of letters.[3] Unless their husbands were monarchs or presidents, or they themselves were involved in scandal, most wives have received only passing attention from their husbands' biographers.[4]

Over the past three decades significant progress has been made in recording the achievements of women throughout written history. The role of women as wives has, however, been mostly taken for granted by historians and biographers. Ann Oakley has recently explored the case studies of four women married to well-known men in the early 20th century. She explores the different ways in which the achievements of wives may be either forgotten or misremembered, and emphasises the cumulative amount of domestic labour performed by wives, often with little or no recognition, and thus mostly unrecorded.

Most importantly, almost no attention is given by biographers and historians to what the famous husbands might have been able to achieve without this subterranean industry of wifely labour. The gendered assumption that this is what wives do has clouded the vision, so that wives' domestic labour, being unremarkable, is simply not there at all. This cultural neglect of domestic labour is one issue. The second issue is what she does to help his work.[5]

1934 was the year in which three of England's great composers died: Sir Edward Elgar (2 June 1857–23 February 1934), Frederick Delius (29 January 1862–10 June 1934) and Gustav Holst (21 September 1874–25 May 1934). All three composers were greatly supported by their wives throughout the vicissitudes of their subsequent careers, but the three wives devoted themselves to the task of supporting their composer husbands in different ways.

Alice, Lady Elgar, *née* Caroline Alice Roberts, is the only one of the three to have been the subject of a biography. In *Alice Elgar: Enigma of a Victorian Lady* her biographer, Percy M. Young described in 1978 how:

Alice Elgar was not what many would expect the wife of a great composer to be – in spite of her loyalty to her husband, she was very much her own woman … Alice married late in life and her temerity in marrying a poor musician aroused much hostility – her intellectual accomplishments, however, were invaluable to her husband. Lady Elgar, as she became, was no mere adjunct to her husband's life but an integral part of it.

Alice Roberts' two-volume novel Marchmont Manor was published in 1882, four years before she started piano lessons with Edward Elgar, who at the time mostly taught violin. Within a

---

[2] *The Musical Times*, 1 September 1900, 586.

[3] Rosemary Ashton, *Thomas & Jane Carlyle: Portrait of a Marriage* (Chatto and Windus, London, 2001).

[4] The same is true of hagiography. Although the most famous saint of all, Jesus' mother Mary, was married, few married women have become saints, and even fewer as a result of their lives whilst married.

[5] Ann Oakley, *Forgotten Wives: How women get written out of history* (Policy Press, Bristol, 2021), 4.

few months her poems were reflecting her growing attachment to the as yet unsuccessful composer and her faith in his future success:

> Art and music are thine own,
> And thine the soul to whom must speak
> The higher voices heard alone
> By those who long and those who seek.[6]

More poems followed, and in July 1888 Edward's setting of one of them, The Wind at Dawn, was published, having won a prize in The Magazine of Music. On 22 September 1888 Edward Elgar recorded in his diary "Engaged to dearest A.", an event which he marked at the time by giving Alice his Opus 12, Salut d'amour. The more traditional ring followed several months later, presumably when his slender means allowed, and despite being disinherited by her family on the grounds of her marrying a Roman Catholic, Alice Roberts and Edward Elgar married in a brief ceremony on 8 May 1889. Money remained tight in the early years of their marriage, and soon after the birth of their own child, Carice, on 14 August 1890, Alice was hard at work again providing the poems for Elgar's early songs. As her biographer wrote, she "was the intellectual wing of the Roberts-Elgar song combine."[7]

Alice Elgar increasingly channelled her literary skills into letter writing and diary keeping, chronicling the course of her husband's career including her own role within it. In so doing she provided deep insights into her perspective of her husband's creative genius. The fact that his creative period coincided almost completely with that of their marriage reflects her role and influence on his work.

Carice Elgar's own role as the only child of a composer meant that she was required to be unusually quiet, to the extent of being absent from many of her parents' holidays and being, like many young boys at the time, sent away to boarding school at an early age. She treasured the postcards sent by her parents, particularly her father, from their travels.[8] The impact of her unusual upbringing was profound, with Carice's headmistress describing her as having a look of "profound sadness" and "unnatural … resignation." From a more positive perspective, Alice and Edward Elgar, both of whom loved children, were providing their daughter with something they themselves had not had access to – education at a highly-regarded boarding school.[9] Carice certainly appreciated her mother's role in supporting her father and started to write about her mother, but only managed the following paragraph:

So much has been, and will be, written about my father that it seems only right that there should be an account of my mother and a record of the great devotion and self-sacrifice of her life to him – a record which may have been equalled but can hardly have been surpassed in human history. I have tried to give a picture of her early life and to show what a tremendous step she took when she decided to marry my father – comparatively unknown and coming from an entirely different sphere of life – time has shown that her intimation was right and her faith in his genius entirely justified – but the faith and love

---

[6] Percy M Young, *Alice Elgar: Enigma of a Victorian Lady* (London, Dennis Dobson, 1978), 86.
[7] Young, *Alice Elgar*, 99–112.
[8] *"Dear Carice ..."*: *Postcards from Edward Elgar to his daughter* (Elgar Birthplace Trust, 1997). Many of the postcards included a note by Alice as well as Edward.
[9] Lynn Richmond Greene, 'Elgar's Dream Children', *Elgar Society Journal*, Vol. 18(4), April 2014, 4–25.

and self-sacrifice with which she carried through her task, congenial though it was, are things which call for admiration and should be set down for all to read.[10]

On 7 April 1920 Alice Elgar died, as her husband noted in his diary, in his arms. Her reputation was reflected in the large number of obituary notices, which had been preceded by newspaper reports of concern that she was unwell. Edward Elgar played his part in setting the tone by asking the musicologist A. H. Fox Strangways, who visited him on the day of Alice's death, to write her obituary for *The Times*. This appeared the following day, under the heading "Devoted Helpmeet of Master Musician".[11] More than one subsequent notice described her as the "famous composer's devoted helper". A typical example is the *Gloucester Journal*:

Caroline Alice Roberts married, in 1889, Mr Elgar, a well-known teacher of the violin at Worcester, whose compositions had as yet met with no favour, sacrificing thereby considerable personal income. She, an amateur pianist, believed in these compositions, and set to work by every means in her power to strengthen and support the composer both by her sympathy and her practical aid. She made herself a good copyist, since an amanuensis would have been too expensive a luxury. She "laid out" his scores, copied in the voice parts, planned the barring – all this for several thousands of pages of 40-line scores. The score of "The Music Makers," for instance, alone contains 150 pages of 31 lines. She would ask overnight what size his orchestra was to be, and, hearing it was to be a small one, would say, "With a bass clarinet, I suppose?" or "Aren't you going to have a cor anglais?" And he would come down next morning to find as much of the form ready as he could fill in during the day with the orchestral parts. There is scarcely a full score of his which she has not laid out in this way.

Of the three wives of the composers who died in 1934, Alice Elgar also distinguished herself by her role in furthering her husband's social standing. To use the baby language which the Elgars often used in their correspondence to each other and their diaries, her husband was "booful" [beautiful], including on the day when he was dressed to receive his knighthood from King Edward VII following Elgar's great success in the composition of his *Coronation Ode* (Op. 44). After Alice's death, Edward Elgar received messages of condolence from the King and Queen, Queen Alexandra and Princess Louise, Duchess of Argyll. To her obituarists in 1920, her social climbing efforts were themselves meritorious:

To the languages that everybody knows she added Latin and Spanish. She accompanied Sir Edward Elgar on most foreign concert tours, and electrified the orchestra at Turin by making a speech of thanks for him to the orchestra in Italian. She translated Hoffmann's "Ritter Gluck." … But whatever she might have done in the way of literature she gave up in order to help him: and he, in return, broke his resolve to remain "Mr. Elgar" all his days, and took whatever honours came his way for her sake. The last entry in her diary is: "In one week, symphony again, and the Institut de France: Deo gratias."[12]

The Elgars' marriage was very much a love match, the "boofuls" and similar expressions reciprocated throughout. From its outset, Alice Elgar worked hard to obtain and maintain a home which kept up appearances and enabled her to entertain visitors in the style to which she considered her husband should become accustomed, as she herself had been before her marriage.[13] The results, as described in her diaries and recounted to her biographer by Carice Elgar, were far removed from the unconventional lifestyles of Frederick Delius and his wife, Jelka Rosen Delius.

---

[10] Young, *Alice Elgar*, 13.
[11] Young, *Alice Elgar*, 182.
[12] *Gloucester Journal*, Saturday 10 April 1920, 6. Several newspapers carried similar obituaries.
[13] Young, *Alice Elgar*, 108–111.

Like Alice Elgar, Hélène Sophie Emilie Rosen (30 December 1868–28 May 1935), known as Jelka, was gifted with many talents. She was the youngest of five children of an academic and multi-lingual family living in Belgrade, and both her parents had strong musical connections. Her mother was a painter, and the only daughter of the composer Ignaz Moscheles. Following the death of her father, Jelka Rosen moved with her mother to Paris and studied art from 1892 at the private Académie Colarossi in Paris. She exhibited at the Salon des Indépendants, with her paintings listed in 1894 and again in 1895. In 1894 she is described as a pupil of Gustave Courtois, exhibiting *Au bord de l'eau*; in 1895 she exhibited *De grand matin* and *En plein été*.[14]

Jelka Rosen lived at addresses in Montparnasse, where she was well-placed to meet artists and musicians, including the composers Gabriel Fauré, Maurice Ravel and Florent Schmitt and artists Auguste Rodin (with whom she subsequently exchanged a series of letters), Camille Claudel, Paul Gauguin, Edvard Munch, Henri Rousseau, as well as her fellow student Ida Gerhardi. Her favourite composer at the time was Grieg, and on 16 January 1896 one of her friends invited her to a dinner party to meet Frederick Delius, another composer and fellow Grieg enthusiast. She was later to recall:

He was there too, a tall thin man of aristocratic bearing, with dark curly hair slightly tinged with auburn, and an auburn moustache which he was perpetually twisting upwards. He wore a red tie, a memorial of earlier association with Russian revolutionaries. At that time I was full of enthusiasm for Nietzsche's Zarathustra which I was reading, and I was greatly surprised when this young Englishman said that he also knew and admired the book. It was out of my copy of it that years later he selected the text for A Mass of Life.

After dinner Jelka sang two songs by Grieg. Delius responded by offering to come to her studio to play some of his own songs, and did so a couple of days later. Jelka was smitten by Delius and his music, but was quickly consumed by "passionate anxiety":

For after a while it began to symbolize my fear that such a poet could not find enough in me to interest him seriously, that his friendship would soon come to an end and that the world then would be a blank – "und die Sonne sank" – the sun gone down for ever.[15]

Delius himself was not smitten in equal measure, and after a happy spring and summer Jelka was dismayed to learn around Christmas that he was planning a business trip to Florida:

I was miserable and a terrible fear clutched my heart that all might be over and that by the time he returned he would have forgotten our happy association. I knew that he had many women friends, French, English, Scandinavian, and some of exceeding beauty, while I was only too conscious how plain I must look with my hair tightly twisted and pulled into a figure eight on the top of my head. My clothes too, were all totally unbecoming, ordered by my dear mother from inferior dressmakers. I never had leisure to think about such things, for I worked nearly all day in my studio and in the evenings had to amuse my mother.[16]

After a wretched winter, Jelka learnt that a house and garden that she could only half afford in Grez-sur-Loing, 70 km south of Paris, were being offered for sale. Like many artists before and since, Jelka already loved Grez, and managed to persuade her mother to lend her the

---

[14] Frick Collection, blog by Stephen J. Bury, Andrew Mellon Chief Librarian. Delius Buys a Gauguin | The Frick Collection, accessed 30 July 2021.

[15] Sir Thomas Beecham, *Frederick Delius* (Hutchinson, London, 1959), 79–80.

[16] Beecham, *Frederick Delius*, 85–6.

remaining cash for the purchase. Jelka, whom the conductor Sir Thomas Beecham who became her husband's authorised biographer described as "the real heroine of the story", was beset with anxiety:

> I knew that I simply had to have my way, live in the house there, forget Paris, start again leading my own life and no longer wait for Fred who surely did not care for me at all.[17]

Quite how much he did care for her has been a matter for speculation, but when in summer 1897 Delius returned from his failed business trip he arrived at Grez with a day's notice, announcing "I suppose you can put me up." Jelka did so, Delius started churning out a succession of fresh compositions, and despite digressions elsewhere, they married in September 1903. Delius described the event to his friend and fellow composer Edvard Grieg:

> On the 25th I married my friend Jelka Rosen here in Grez. (Civilement of course) have got even further away from God and Jesus. We lived together for 6 years, but we found it really more practical to legalise our relationship – One gets everything cheaper & one receives free & without further ado a certificate of honesty and good manners.[18]

Jelka provided Delius with much more than free board and lodging for the next 21 years. Whilst, unlike Alice Elgar, she did not write poetry herself, she excelled in identifying and if necessary translating into German texts to inspire her composer husband. It was, for example, Jelka who found the works of Ernest Dowson for Delius' *Songs of Sunset*, and, less originally, those of Walt Whitman for his *Songs of Farewell*. Several of the published scores rightly credit Jelka's contribution. Delius and Jelka collaborated on the libretto of his opera, *A Village Romeo and Juliet*, which premiered in Berlin in 1907 and at Covent Garden, London, in 1910.

In the early years of their marriage Jelka continued to work hard and successfully at her painting, as well as creating a beautiful garden out of the overgrown plot in Grez. About twenty of her paintings survive, including two portraits of her husband.

Delius had been diagnosed with syphilis before he met Jelka, although in the early stages of his illness the diagnosis did not prevent his infidelity to her. He had written to her in early 1901, before their marriage: "I am not affectionate – and regret it also, but I cannot alter myself."[19] In 1910 Delius' health was already starting to decline, and he spent almost a quarter of the year in two clinics. In June he wrote to Jelka that a specialist doctor had diagnosed that his central nervous system had been affected, but the cause was not certain. Jelka wrote him over a dozen letters whilst he was in the clinic, including a couple of draft business letters for his approval and signature. At this worrying stage of her life she turned to painting, and on 27 June described to Delius how she had begun to copy their Gauguin picture, *Nevermore*.[20] By the end of the year Delius' diagnosis had worsened and he was told that his syphilis had reached the tertiary stage.[21]

Jelka Rosen Delius's contribution is recorded on several of his scores, in contrast to Isobel Holst, who is – correctly – recorded only as a dedicatee. She used her linguistic skills to the

---

[17] Beecham, *Frederick Delius*, 88.
[18] Martin Lee-Browne and Paul Guinery, *Delius and his music* (Boydell Press, 2014), 166.
[19] Lee-Browne and Guinery, *Delius and his music*, 64, 165.
[20] Rachel Lowe, *A Descriptive Catalogue with Checklists of the Letters and Related Documents in the Delius Collection of the Grainger Museum* (Delius Trust, London, 1981), 106 (Jelka to Fred) and 184 (Fred to Jelka).
[21] Lee-Browne and Guinery, *Delius and his music*, 278.

full, and there are several witnesses to her custom of silently leaving poems on the piano as potential inspiration for her husband. Their shared home at Grez became increasingly bedecked with Jelka's colourful paintings, which delighted Delius. As Delius' illness progressed, first to needing a wheelchair and thence to almost complete immobility and blindness, Jelka's painting needed to take a back seat. One writer suggested that she did not lift a paintbrush for the last 12 years of his life.[22] In 1923 Delius' first biographer, the composer Peter Warlock, described briefly how Jelka's "unfailing sympathy and devotion, allied to materially practical as well as great artistic and literary abilities, has ever proved an ideal companion and helpmate to him."[23]

Jelka's place in history is even more complex than that of Alice Elgar precisely because of the impact of Delius' almost complete incapacity during the last years of his life. After the 22-year-old Yorkshireman Eric Fenby offered to help as her husband's amanuensis in 1928 his role in bringing Delius' music to life came to the fore. It further captured the public imagination through Fenby's biography of Delius, first published in 1936, in which he vividly portrayed the household at Grez, Delius himself, who even at the time of Fenby's arrival "was such a physical wreck, and had to be watched and cared for as a baby in arms", and Fenby's own starring role in bringing Delius' music to life.[24]

In 1968 Fenby's role was further immortalised in Ken Russell's film, *Song of Summer*. When asked in 1972 whether there had been any discussion about music between Jelka and Frederick Delius, Fenby replied:

No discussion. I was the musician in the house and there was no discussion between Delius and myself. In all the time I was there I don't think we talked twenty minutes' music altogether. He wouldn't discuss music; he wouldn't explain himself.[25]

Whilst it is true that without Fenby there would have been no *Song of Summer*, his part in supporting Delius has subsequently tended to overshadow that of the ever-loyal Jelka.

Not least because of Delius' blindness and general incapacity, Jelka's role in supporting her composer husband is well-documented. She needed to write many of the later letters in his name, and long letters of her own to Delius have survived. But "much of the latter correspondence is domestic", and thus even the excellent catalogue of the Delius collection in the Grainger Museum at the University of Melbourne has adopted a policy of "recording anything of musical and biographical value and of simply indicating the range of the remaining topics."[26] Jelka Rosen Delius has not been written out of history, but rather, through her selfless devotion to her husband, she has hardly been written into it.

Much more could, and should, be written about Jelka. After her death in 1935 some of the earlier visitors to the Delius household at Grez recorded their memories. One of the fullest was by the conductor Charles Kennedy Scott:

---

[22] "Madame Delius Dead: Two days after reburial of composer: Devoted Wife Who Sacrificed Her Own Career", *Dundee Courier*, 29 May 1935.

[23] Peter Warlock (Philip Heseltine), *Frederick Delius*: reprinted with additions, annotations and comments by Hubert Foss (Bodley Head, London, 1952), 48–9.

[24] Eric Fenby, *Delius as I knew him* (Icon Books, London, 1966), 21.

[25] Transcript of interview printed in *The Delius Society Journal* Eric Fenby 85th birthday issue (Winter/Spring 1991, no 106), 15.

[26] Lowe, *A Descriptive Catalogue*, 5.

… it was all so quiet, "far from the madding crowd," just where Delius would live. His wife Jelka's laughter and the song of the birds in the garden were all that disturbed the silence. Everyone knows of Jelka's devotion.

A considerable artist by the time I knew her, she had already almost given up her painting in order to attend to Delius. But it had not soured her, the laughter was always there. Jelka was exuberant, Delius the reverse … She … usually conversed in French, but spoke English in a quaint way which often hit off a situation to perfection. Once when the publishers had printed the voice parts of *The Song of the High Hills* in a very unpractical form she said she was going to write a "thunder letter" to them about it. (Delius often suffered from this sort of presentation in print, and it made the performance of his work unnecessarily difficult.)[27]

The death of Frederick Delius in 1934 was not unexpected, although to their mutual friends, particularly Balfour Gardiner, it came as a great blow so soon after the death of Gustav Holst. Despite his infidelities, Delius and Jelka are buried together at St Peter's Church in Limpsfield, Surrey. When Edward Elgar died in 1934, he, like Frances Purcell 200 hundred years previously, shared a memorial with his wife Alice, in the Elgars' case at St Wulstan's Roman Catholic Church, Little Malvern. In contrast, Gustav Holst's mortal remains were interred beneath a simple paving stone in Chichester Cathedral, close to a memorial to the 17th-century composer and organist Thomas Weelkes. Holst's widow Isobel, who, in contrast to Jelka Rosen Delius and Alice Elgar, outlived her husband by 35 years, has no memorial, shared or solitary.

Jessie Coleridge-Taylor, widow of Gustav Holst's contemporary at the Royal College of Music Samuel Coleridge-Taylor, published her reminiscences of him in 1943, some 30 years after his tragically early death.[28] According to their somewhat embittered daughter Avril Coleridge-Taylor:

Mother not only set him on a pedestal, but climbed up, as it were, to sit close beside him as his widow.[29]

No such accusation could ever be made of Isobel Holst. Perhaps in part to compensate for her absence from her father during the last months of his life, when she was busy with her own career, it was Gustav Holst's daughter Imogen who became his most influential biographer. Starting with her longest biography of him first published in 1938, Imogen chronicled Gustav's life in music – a passion she shared with him. Imogen's focus in all her books about her father was on promoting his music and preserving his memory. The references to Gustav's wife are strikingly few, and the 1938 biography contains no photograph of her, although there is one of Gustav with Imogen and his brother Emil.[30] The author of the main scholarly biography of Gustav was Michael Short, who spent much time interviewing Imogen between 1969 and her death in 1984. The starting year of 1969 was significant, as Michael Short and Imogen met for the first time not long after Isobel's death. Despite that fact, followed by Imogen's involvement in the subsequent task of clearing out her mother's home, which would

---

[27] Warlock, *Delius*, 163.

[28] Jessie Coleridge-Taylor, *A memory sketch, or personal reminiscences of my husband, genius and musician S. Coleridge-Taylor* (John Crowther, Bognor Regis, 1943).

[29] Charles Kay, "The Marriage of Samuel Coleridge-Taylor and Jessie Walmisley", *Black Music Research Journal*, Vol. 21(2), Autumn 2001, p 174.

[30] One of Imogen's short biographies of her father, published in the Faber *Great Composers* series, includes slightly more references to Imogen than to her mother, and references to Isobel stop half-way through the book.

have stirred emotions and memories, Imogen did not talk about her mother during their protracted discussions.[31] Fellow musician and a good friend of Imogen, the conductor Chris Green, commented that although her "father predeceased his wife by many years … I only ever heard Imogen … refer infrequently to her mother who continued to live in Essex."[32]

In 1974 Imogen published a shorter biography of her father as one of her many activities commemorating the centenary of his birth. This book also contains few references to Isobel Holst. As an otherwise favourable review noted:

> … some of the photographs are appearing for the first time, and one of these, almost certainly, is that of Holst's wife, Isobel, in the music room of their Thaxted home in 1916. Looking at this I realized once again how shadowy a figure she is in Miss Holst's books. We are told precious little of Holst's married life and his presence in the home. Is this fortuitous or significant? I have felt increasingly that there is more we need to know about Holst's philosophy of 'non-attachment', its emotional and psychological origins and its consequences for his personal relationships. It could be that the two gaps, if gaps they really are, are not unrelated. … I still hope that Miss Holst will write a 'portrait' of her father in which her unique insights and experience will be directed to a discussion of every aspect of the man and the musician. There is room for such a book.[33]

In 1990 the first edition of Michael Short's *Gustav Holst: The Man and his Music* was published. It was the result of 20 years of research, including close and prolonged co-operation with Imogen Holst, who read and commented on some of the early drafts. This masterpiece, republished by Circaidy Gregory Press in 2014, was and is the leading scholarly biography of Gustav Holst. In common with Imogen Holst's writings about her father, however, references to Isobel's presence, or indeed absence, from his life are few and far between. As Holst scholar Raymond Head commented:

> Hitherto books on Holst and his music have been a family affair … This new book, however, was written under Imogen's guidance, and has many of the drawbacks of her own work. In particular, a reluctance to explain or come to any understanding of what motivated Holst's thought in music, and an unwillingness to describe with any humanity the milieu in which he worked … I have often wondered how well Imogen knew her father. Why, for instance, is there no account – anywhere – of the influence of Isobel, Gustav's wife? Without her support Holst might never have composed at all [34]

The mother-daughter relationship, and indeed the relationship between Isobel and Gustav as husband and wife, puzzled some of those close to the Holst family during Imogen's lifetime. Shortly after Imogen's death Rosamund Strode, Imogen's friend and colleague since 1948 and her successor as Benjamin Britten's music assistant, started to assemble a collection of interviews with her other friends and people who had known her family. The transcripts and notes from these interviews have been an invaluable source in illuminating the relationship between Isobel and Gustav as well as Isobel and Imogen.

Towards the end of her own life Imogen reflected on her mother's role in Gustav's career in interviews with John Morrison, in which she answered his series of often very personal

---

[31] Conversation with Michael Short, May 2014.

[32] Chris Green, "Imogen Holst – a study in commitment", *Norfolk and Suffolk Life* (February 2019).

[33] Hugh Ottaway, "Review: Holst for the Young", *The Musical Times,* vol. 115, no. 1575 (May 1974), p 392.

[34] Raymond Head, review of *Gustav Holst: The Man and His Music* by Michael Short, *Tempo* New Series, no. 176 (March 1991), pp 57–58.

questions over two days on 19–20 April 1980,[35] and with Stephen Wilkinson on 3 February 1984[36] – only a month before Imogen's own death. John Morrison's questioning about the family relationships clearly struck a sore nerve: Imogen's impassioned and lengthy response to one question in particular is reproduced on page 117 below.

If Isobel Holst ever kept a diary, it did not survive. Her husband's diaries, unlike those of the Elgars, are mostly engagement ones, typically with the briefest of notes. Only a few letters from her have been archived, and none of these are to her husband. She described herself as hating letter-writing, although like Alice Elgar and Jelka Rosen Delius she sometimes needed to write business letters on her husband's behalf. Gustav Holst only briefly had an agent, and during his repeated periods of ill-health Isobel role as an intermediary was particularly important. Gustav Holst's need to escape through walking or travelling resulted in a series of lengthy letters to Isobel: the Holst collection held in the Britten Pears Arts Archives includes 53 of these letters and postcards, starting in April 1908 when Gustav escaped from the stress of work and early parenthood to holiday in Algiers, and ending on New Year's Day 1934, when Gustav was in a nursing home.

As Hannah Eyles, formerly Holst Project Archivist, has written:

Through the Holst collection, Isobel Holst comes to the fore as a significant yet often externally undervalued and underestimated figure in the lives of two great creatives. In fact, as close as Imogen was to Gustav and despite the affinity they felt given their shared talents and passions, it was actually Isobel who brought Imogen up through her childhood, owing to the demands on Gustav to travel, and his commitment to his educational and musical campaigns.[37]

As well as preserving her husband's letters and safeguarding many of the manuscripts of his compositions, Isobel treasured her daughter's Royal College of Music examination composition from 1929, *The Unfortunate Traveller*. On discovering it when clearing out her mother's cottage shortly after her death in 1969, Imogen insisted that her friends Arthur Caton and Kate Butters should take it home with them and burn it.[38] In so doing she was curating her own, as well as her mother's, history. She kept neither her mother's books, several of which were passed down to Arthur Caton and Kate Butters, nor her LP record collection.[39]

As Imogen's mother, and Gustav's wife, Isobel Holst had no pretensions about her own musical abilities. Gustav met her when he was an impoverished young music student and she was a beautiful and independent-minded young woman. This is her story.

---

[35] Britten Pears Arts HOL/5/2/29 Transcript of Imogen Holst replying to questions by John Morrison, recorded 19–20 April 1980.

[36] Britten Pears Arts HOL/5/2/26 Partial transcript of Stephen Wilkinson talking to IH in Aldeburgh 3 February 1984.

[37] Hannah Eyles, "'Hopes, dreams and difficulties': the archives of Imogen Holst", *Brio*, vol. 54(1), Spring/Summer 2017, 16–17.

[38] Christopher Grogan ed., *Imogen Holst: A Life in Music* (Boydell Press, Woodbridge, Revised Edition 2010), 394.

[39] Isobel's record collection is now at Holst Victorian House, Cheltenham. Imogen much preferred reading musical scores to listening to gramophone records.

Chapter Two
Life before Imogen

Isobel (Holst Victorian House)

Isobel's family

Emily Isobel Harrison[40] was born at 1 Myddleton Terrace, Finsbury Road, Wood Green in North London, on 26 March 1876. Her parents were Ralph Augustus Harrison, at that time a Merchant's Clerk, and Jessie Elizabeth Harrison *née* Davis, who registered her daughter's birth some five weeks later on 2 May. The couple had not lived in the area for long, and Isobel's brother Harry Hughes Harrison had been born a year earlier in Hammersmith[41] in West London.

---

[40] The formal early records, including her birth, baptism and marriage records and her daughter Imogen's birth certificate, spell her second name as Isabel, and she is sometimes referred to as Emily rather than Isabel. As her surviving letters are signed Isobel, and in married life her name was abbreviated to Iso, I have used the spelling Isobel throughout.

[41] The Harrison family address then was 40, The Grove, Hammersmith. On the publishing contracts with Novello in 1897/8 Gustav's address is 29, The Grove, Hammersmith, where the Harrisons may have been living at the time.

In common with several other roads in the area, Finsbury Road was developed in the mid-1860s, when the new railway line carrying working men the eight miles into central London attracted several thousand new residents to a previously rural area. The 1878 electoral register records Isobel's father still living in Finsbury Road, but in 1881 the Harrison family had moved again, and were living at 87 Beaconsfield Road, Tottenham, about three miles away from Isobel's birthplace. In 1881 Isobel's father was described as a Clerk in the Music Trade, and her mother as a schoolmistress. Their frequent household moves are indicative of the fact that the properties were rented rather than owned. The household, which in 1881 included 6-year-old Harry Hughes, 5-year-old Emily Isobel and 4-month-old Ralph Willey, was modest.

Harry Hughes and Emily Isobel were both baptised at the nearby church of Holy Trinity Tottenham on 11 September 1881 – possibly to enable them to attend the associated primary school. Holy Trinity church had (and still has) an organ built by "Father" Henry Willis, the premier organ builder in Britain at that time, whose commissions included one by Queen Victoria.

The family was still living at 87 Beaconsfield Road in 1882, but by April 1883, when Ralph Willey was baptised at the same church, Isobel's father had changed jobs again and was recorded as being a photographer. Isobel's father's entry on the 1891 electoral register, drawn up in 1890, gives two further addresses – 36, River Park Road, Wood Green, a couple of miles away from Beaconsfield Road, followed by 2 Hope Villas, Finsbury Road, Wood Green, which was a few streets further north.

By 5 April 1891 (the date of the census) the Harrison family had moved once again, and were living a couple of miles away from Isobel's birthplace in Alexandra House, High Street, Tottenham. Isobel's father had changed jobs once more, to estate agent, her mother was not working at the time and 16-year-old Harry Hughes was working as a telegraph clerk. Emily Isobel and her brother Ralph were both described as scholars. Isobel's ongoing education is significant for a 15-year-old girl, as she was several years older than the compulsory school leaving age and is an indication that her family, which was not a wealthy one, must have attached some priority to her education.

Isobel's father, Ralph Augustus Harrison, had had an even less settled start to his life. The family Bible recorded details about his parents and his three siblings. George Augustus Harrison, Isobel's grandfather,[42] married Julia Maria Teresa Cordner on 2 March 1839 at St Mary's Church, Paddington. Their marriage certificate records George Augustus Harrison's father (Isobel's great grandfather) as George Harrison, Architect, and Julia's as Ralph Cordner, Gentleman. Julia was "of the Parish of Upton, Bucks." Their four children followed in quick succession. Emily Louisa was born on 15 January 1840 at Englefield Green, Surrey; George Willey was born on 10 June 1841 at Vauxhall; Julia Maria was born on 4 November 1842 at Chartreux, near Rouen, in Normandy. Finally, the Bible recorded the birth of Isobel's father Ralph Augustus, followed by the puzzling motto NE CEDE MALIS (yield not to misfortune) and the date February 1846.[43]

Ralph Augustus Harrison was born a British subject in Rouen on 4 July 1844. By 29 November 1849, when he was baptised at St Martin's in the Fields in the centre of London,

---

[42] Britten Pears Arts HOL/2/15/10 Harrison Family contains photographs of five architectural drawings with a note by Imogen Holst "Harrison drawings (my gt. gt. grandfather) from Graham & Doris Harrison. Also photograph of GH at Hammersmith Socialist Club (for Cheltenham Birthplace)".

[43] Britten Pears Arts HOL/4/5/1/2 Harrison family papers (Imogen Holst's notes).

he was living in Upper St Martin's Lane with his father George Augustus Harrison, a civil engineer, and mother Julia. At the age of 16, in 1861, he was an apprentice in Southwark, South London. In 1871 he was lodging in Enfield, North London, whilst working as a writer in a factory.

Isobel's mother, Jessie Elizabeth Davis, was born in London on 23 January 1846. Five years later she acquired a baby sister, Emily. In 1861, at the age of 15, Jessie was no longer a "scholar", unlike her sisters 11-year-old Emily and 10-year-old Eliza, and her youngest sister Isabella was also not at school. Jessie was baptised at the unusually late age of 18, on 17 September 1864. In 1871 Jessie and Eliza were both recorded as working as daily governesses.

Ralph and Jessie married at St John's Hammersmith on 23 May 1874, at which time Ralph was described as a merchant's clerk and Jessie, whose father was a solicitor's clerk at the time, had no listed profession.[44]

Having spent the first 15 years of her life living in North London, in 1891 or 1892 Isobel's family moved back to West London, where her parents had married and where rows of terraced houses were being built over previously green field sites. Other members of Isobel's extended family were already living nearby. Two aunts on her mother's side of the family were living at 57 Biscay Road, Hammersmith, in 1891. Isobel's aunt Eliza had married Robert Norbrook and they and their four children were sharing the house with her aunt Emily, who was working as a publisher's clerk (female).

Isobel and her immediate family were living at 55 Roxwell Road, Shepherd's Bush at the time of her confirmation by the Bishop of Marlborough as one of 60 candidates from St Alban's church on 31 May 1892. The church of St Alban the Martyr Fulham had itself only recently been established in a corrugated iron mission hut set up in response to the rapid population growth. The register of confirmations from 1892 to 1907 is annotated with notes of whether the candidate had subsequently moved away, into service or, in a few cases, died. There is no such note against Isobel's entry, suggesting that she maintained her church attendance there for a while after her confirmation.[45]

Isobel's younger cousin Harry Norbrook was a keen member of St Alban's congregation, and was frequently listed as an altar server in the parish magazine, winning a "reward" at the choir supper in February 1895. Five of Isobel's fellow confirmation candidates also lived in Biscay Road.

In February 1895 the Bishop of Marlborough described the congregation at a special service at St Alban's:

… it was my duty to take part in a very different service under very different conditions in the poor, crowded district of St Alban's, Fulham. There no grand church, no stately service awaited me, but a somewhat aged tent, warmed, as far as it was warmed, by open braziers of charcoal and other means – warmed by a crowded congregation of poor people, the faces of too many of them marked with lives of hunger, want, and care. They literally packed the tent. Hard by was the little iron building which now for many years has been the only place of worship for a district of between 7,000 and 8,000 poor, hard-working, respectable, uncomplaining poor. …[46]

---

[44] In 1861 he was an engineer's clerk.

[45] London Metropolitan Archives P77/ALB/011 Saint Alban, Fulham Register of confirmations 1892–1907, p 2.

[46] St. Alban's Fulham, *Parish Magazine*, vol. 1, no 3, 18 March 1895, p 2.

Isobel's family was still living at Roxwell Road in 1895,[47] when her brother Harry, who was working at the Mount Pleasant Telegraph Factory whilst a student at the Telegraphists' School of Science, was admitted as a student member of the Institution of Electrical Engineers.

A description of Harrison family life comes from Imogen Holst's idealised account of her parents' meeting and courtship, written from her father Gustav's perspective:

> His [Gustav's] Socialism was never very active, and although he admired William Morris as a man, he found that the glamour of his romantic medievalism soon wore off. But he remained in the club for the sake of the good companionship, and in 1897 he accepted an invitation to conduct the Socialist Choir.
> …
>
> One day a new soprano came to the choir practice: a Miss Isobel Harrison. She was very young, and she had bright golden hair and clear blue eyes, and she was by far the most beautiful person he had ever seen.
>
> He was twenty-two, and he had never been in love before. He was always so engrossed in music that there had been no time to give the matter a passing thought. But now he was utterly lost, and he gazed at her in despair.
>
> At first she was not much impressed by his appearance. He had grown a beard to make himself look older when applying for jobs, and he was wearing a preposterous Inverness coat that was much too big for him. But soon she got to know him, and they became engaged, with the prospect of having to wait several years before they could afford to get married.
>
> She took him in hand, and one of the first things she did was to persuade him to eat. As soon as he gave up living on dried nuts his eyes grew stronger, and his hand recovered sufficiently to use an ordinary pen. Next she commanded him to get rid of the beard. And then, very surreptitiously, she began to improve his clothes.
>
> He went to stay at her parents' house, where her father painted unsuccessful water-colours and her mother gave piano lessons. He had never known what it felt like to be able to sit over a meal in the comfortable friendliness of a home, and he basked in the warmth of an unfamiliar happiness.
>
> It was not only her beauty that gave him such joy, though his college friends had been amazed at his good fortune. It was her kindness, and her warm-hearted generosity, and her genius for bringing grace and ease and comfort into his life.
>
> He wrote her a new love-song each week, and worked harder than ever in order to make some money.[48]

Gustav's family

The warmth of the Harrison family home described here was in stark contrast to Gustav's own childhood, and it seems significant that many of the most affectionate letters which he wrote to Isobel associated her with a sense of home.

Gustavus Theodore von Holst was born in Cheltenham on 21 September 1874, two years before Isobel. His father, Adolph von Holst, was a professional piano teacher and organist who in 1871 had married one of his pupils, Clara Lediard. Clara's family disapproved of her marrying a musician, and despite Adolph's musical talent "his own family found him an uncomfortable person to live with."[49] In September 1876 Gustav's younger brother Emil was born in the same house in Cheltenham, 4 Clarence Road. Their home was not a happy one, although it hosted informal musical evenings. When Gustav was seven his mother suffered a

---

[47] Her father is shown in the electoral register at that address in 1894 and 1895, but not in the 1892 or 1893 registers, suggesting that the move around the time of Isobel's confirmation was a recent one.
[48] Imogen Holst, *Gustav Holst: A Biography* (2nd ed., OUP, 1969), 17–18.
[49] Imogen Holst, *Holst* (Faber & Faber, The Great Composers Series, 2nd ed. 1981), 14.

still birth, and died a few months later, in February 1882. Although Clara was sweet and uncomplaining:

> … before she had been married very long she began to suffer from nerves, and Adolph had to get a silent keyboard for the first few hours of his daily practice. … she could never understand why Adolph need spend quite so much time over his music. She endured for a few more years of disappointment, and then died, leaving Gustavus Theodore, aged eight,[50] and Emil Gottfried, aged six, to the tender mercies of a father who practised all the time he was at home, and whose dream of domestic happiness was to live on the top floor of a well-run hotel.
>
> The household was in a state of chaos, and Adolph's sister Nina was asked to come and look after the children. Nina was also a pianist. The happiest five minutes of her life had been spent in strewing rose petals for Liszt to walk on. She was not much use in the house, for she had no ideas about anything except music. Whenever Adolph had to go out to a rehearsal, Nina would rush to the piano and play Chopin. She helped Gustav with his practising, but she was unable to help him in any other way.
>
> He was miserable and scared and over-sensitive … he enjoyed practising the piano, and … had a passion for Grieg, but he always had to wait until his father was out of the house before venturing to play the Lyric Pieces.[51]

Gustav's first home belonged to his mother's side of the family, and a few weeks after her death Adolph and his two sons had to move out their house to a different address in Cheltenham. In 1885 Adolph married another pupil, Mary Thorley Stone. Two more sons followed, Mathias (Max), born in 1886, and Thorley, born in 1889. This second marriage brought no more jollity to the von Holst children than the first:

> Children in the von Holst household were expected to be seen and not heard, and those who offended against this or other rules would be punished in various ways, including confinement to their rooms on a diet of 'mealy-pap' … Adolph was a strict disciplinarian.[52]

Mary Thorley Stone's main preoccupation was Theosophy, rather than her family, and Gustav's early memories were scarred by sadness. School provided him with no respite, as the shy, short-sighted and asthmatic pupil was unhappy there too, despite thriving academically at Cheltenham Grammar School. Gustav's stepmother sought solace in Theosophy, his father sought it in alcohol and Gustav found it in music and walking. Whilst he was still at school Gustav had needed to help his father with the organisation of concerts as "Adolph had begun to let things slide".[53] At the age of 17 Gustav landed his first professional engagement, for the salary of £4 a year, as organist and choir master at Wyck Rissington, a small village, with a small church and a small organ, about 17 miles from his home in Cheltenham. With an additional appointment as conductor of the choral society at Bourton-on-the-Water, he usually walked from one job to the other.

In 1893, after Gustav had endured several failed attempts to gain a scholarship to study music, Gustav's father borrowed £100 (worth about £13,000 in 2021) to enable him to take up a place at the Royal College of Music (RCM) in London in May. Despite subsisting as frugally as possible, and going without meat, alcohol, train fares home to Cheltenham and even a piano, money was tight. Shortly after the borrowed £100 ran out at the end of 1894 he

---

[50] He was actually seven.

[51] I. Holst, *Gustav Holst*, 6–7.

[52] Laura Kinnear, "Theodore von Holst", *Holst Birthplace Trust Newsletter,* Issue 59 (February 2018), p 2.

[53] I. Holst, *Gustav Holst*, 9.

was awarded a scholarship to the RCM at the last possible attempt. This gave him a maintenance grant of £30 a year, which he supplemented by playing the trombone in various orchestras in seaside resorts during the holidays.[54] The RCM is located in Kensington, one of London's smartest districts, and living there would have been beyond Gustav's modest budget. Hammersmith, a mostly working-class district a few miles to the west of Kensington, was a more affordable proposition. His earliest college friend, Fritz Hart, whom he met when they sat next to each other at the entrance exam, recalled his living arrangements during their early college years:

> In those days Gustav lived in Hammersmith. He had a small, clean, but barely furnished room in a quiet little back street. ... he had no piano but managed as best he could without one, making a very sturdy virtue of necessity. ... on the whole he managed better without a piano than most of his fellow-students did with one. He had very little money and, when he did not bike, would walk long distances to save fares. In the vacations he would actually bike to Cheltenham and back, looking one of the weirdest figures imaginable, with a cap, cycling knickers, a mackintosh, a small bundle tied to his handle-bars, and his trombone slung over his shoulders. Overtaken by night as he climbed some lonely hill in the region of the Cotswolds, he would get off his machine and, after stretching his legs, unpack his trombone and proceed to blow soul-satisfying blasts on it.[55]

The Hammersmith Socialist Society and club activity

Isobel and Gustav must have met in 1896 at the latest. Imogen's later chronology of her father's life dated his joining the Hammersmith Socialist Society around 1894, and starting conducting the Hammersmith Socialist Choir and their engagement as early as 1895.[56] Isobel and Gustav's presence is recorded in the minutes of the weekly business meetings of the Hammersmith Socialist Society in 1896, when attendance was dwindling during the last year of its existence. They may well have met before then, as the Society's minute books from 1893 to 1895 are missing.[57]

The Hammersmith Socialist Society was constituted in 1890 following divisions in the Socialist League, the Hammersmith Branch of which met at William Morris's beautiful Kelmscott House on the banks of the Thames at Upper Mall Hammersmith. It too held its meetings at Kelmscott House. The conditions of membership were "a general agreement with the principles of Socialism as expressed in the Manifesto of the Society", whose object was "the spreading of the principles of Socialism, especially by lectures, street meetings and publications".[58] The Society also continued the long-running tradition of free lectures at Kelmscott House every Sunday evening at 8 pm, mostly on the subject of socialism, but with William Morris and Emery Walker's draft lecture list for June to September 1895 including such diverse themes as the Population Question on 21 July and Sir Thomas More on 28 July.[59]

---

[54] I. Holst, *Gustav Holst*, 10–15.

[55] Fritz Hart, "Early memories of GH", R.C.M. Magazine 39/2, p 49.

[56] Imogen Holst, *A Thematic Catalogue of Gustav Holst's Music* (Faber, London, 1974), xiv.

[57] Andrew Heywood, "Gustav Holst, William Morris and the Socialist Movement", *Journal of the William Morris Society,* XI(4) 39–47, Spring 1996; Chris Fletcher, "Gustav and Isobel", *Holst Birthplace Trust Newsletter, Issue 28,* May 2010.

[58] British Library (BL) Add Ms 45893, Draft Constitution and Rules of the Hammersmith Socialist Society, p3v-4.

[59] BL Add Ms 45894, f. 70, Hammersmith Socialist Society Lecture List 1895.

Several members of Isobel's family are recorded as attending meetings of the Society in 1896, with her brother Harry Hughes (Toby) Harrison being particularly active. The minutes are not always clear whether it is Harry Hughes or Ralph Augustus Harrison who was present, but the notes written by Isobel's nephew Graham Harrison in 1980 refer to several family members attending the meetings, which were unusually inclusive for the period. Graham Harrison prefaced his remarks with this disclaimer:

I really know very little about my father's family. Both his parents were dead before I was born and my father rarely spoke about them. I have a vague recollection that his father was a jack-of-all trades …

… he was, as you know, a member of the Hammersmith Socialist Society with his sister and your father. My mother was also a member, and an aunt of mine (now in her 104th year). My mother sometimes spoke of 'the Club' and it is clear that the Society had a social side as well as a political one. My mother was more interested in the social side while my father was more interested in the politics. I have the feeling that this was a happy time for him – he found stimulating companionship there and, particularly, friendship with your father.[60]

Imogen Holst also wrote in her own brief unpublished notes about the Harrison family history that Toby was a "Friend of Gustav's in Hammersmith Socialist Society [Both met their wives there!]"[61] Imogen recounted her father's enjoyment of the meetings at Kelmscott House when he was a student:

Holst became a member, and listened to lectures on Sunday evenings by Bernard Shaw and other socialists, including the sixty-year-old Morris, who then had only two more years to live. Holst set several of Morris's poems which he had discovered in the hand-printed editions of the Kelmscott Press. One of the workers in the Press was an amateur musician who made friends with him: he gave him a proof page of the famous Kelmscott Press edition of Chaucer's *The Canterbury Tales* which Holst kept all his life.

The lectures on socialism were held in a long narrow room which has been described as 'a frugal meeting-place with bare floor and matting on the white-washed walls; there were wooden chairs and forms, and a plain kitchen table on the platform'.[62]

Gustav's proof page of the Kelmscott Chaucer was indeed a treasure. Its production was one of his hero William Morris's last great works, with printing starting in August 1894 and the first two copies being finished in June 1896, a few months before Morris's untimely death on 3 October.[63]

Harry Hughes Harrison first appears in the surviving minutes of the Society when he was appointed Literature Secretary at the Annual General Meeting on 13 March 1896.[64] His role in the Society was clearly an active one and at that stage in his life he was fully committed to the socialist cause, with one of the sets of minutes which he signed referring to him as Com[rade]."[65] He was also a delegate to the May Day Demonstration Committee and his responsibilities as Literature Secretary included regular reporting on the stocks of socialist literature and the sums raised from its sale. As well as selling pamphlets by William Morris

---

[60] Britten Pears Arts HOL/4/5/1/2 Harrison family papers.
[61] Britten Pears Arts HOL/4/5/1/2 Harrison family papers Imogen Holst "The Harrison Family".
[62] Imogen Holst, *Holst* (Faber & Faber, The Great Composers Series, 2nd ed. 1981), 22–3.
[63] Helen Dore, *William Morris* (Pyramid Books, London, 1990), 123.
[64] BL Add Ms 45893, p 76.
[65] BL Add MS 45893, p 84v.

and others at the Society's meetings, they were sold in the street. Gustav's role in this endeavour was musical, and whilst his late mother had played the harmonium for services in the peaceful rural setting of Cranham parish church, Gustav

> ... on occasion would wander through Hammersmith with other disciples of William Morris. They would take a cart with them, and on this cart Holst would be seated playing a harmonium.[66]

Harry was not present on Friday 24 April 1896, when the minutes record that Mrs Watt (in the Chair) proposed:

> that Miss Emily Isabel Harrison be posted for election to the H.S.S. Vestry Election Committee. A. Watt[67] reported that the Committee had met 4 times since last Friday. The first duty was to find suitable candidates. E. Walker interviewed those who were selected, but none of them could stand. The I.L.P.[68] also determined not to officially contest the election. In consequence of this the work of the Committee had come to an end. Bullock moved and Berridge seconded that the Committee's report be adopted. Agreed.[69]

For late Victorian England, these meetings were exceptional in crossing class, gender and academic boundaries. Isobel had just turned 20, not yet an adult in contemporary terms even if she was of independent means, which she was not. The fact that the meeting was chaired by a woman was in itself unusual. Mrs Watt, whose daughter Clara Sparrow shared her given name, in 1936 noted some of her knowledge of the Hammersmith Socialists as a key to the surviving early photographs. Her husband, Andrew Watt, was "first secretary of the shop assistants union." Annie Grove (not mentioned in the 1896 minutes) "started the Socialist Choir"[70] which Gustav Holst took over in 1897. "E. Walker" was Emery Walker, the printer and engraver and close friend and neighbour of William Morris, who had been elected Secretary of the Hammersmith Socialist Society. Bullock was Samuel Bullock, who had been elected to the predecessor Hammersmith Socialist League on 23 October 1887. This may have been a small meeting, but it was a highly selective one, in which women and men from different social backgrounds attended on an equal footing.

Six members of the Society were present on May Day May 1896, when Emily Isabel Harrison was elected.[71] She and her brother Harry attended the meetings on 8 May and on 15 May, when she was appointed as delegate to the Free Maintenance Committee in place of Comrade Berridge, who had resigned. The 15 May meeting also heard a report on one of the regular Sunday lectures at Kelmscott House, where the Rev. A. L. Lilley had lectured on "the Social Mission of Christianity to a fair audience. The lecture was interesting & there was a good discussion."[72] The following week Isobel and Harry were again present at the meeting, at which Watt reported that an out-door meeting had been arranged for Sunday week at Kensal

---

[66] Harvey Grace, "Gustav Holst – Teacher", *The Musical Times* (August 1934), 690.

[67] Mrs Watt and her husband Andrew were long-standing members of the Society, and both were included in the photograph of William Morris and the Hammersmith Socialist Society taken c.1880–1881.

[68] The Independent Labour Party (I.L.P.) had been founded three years earlier, in January 1893, with Keir Hardie MP as its first chairman.

[69] BL Add Ms 45893, p 79.

[70] Martin Stott, "A garden party at Kelmscott house ... would be pleasant", *William Morris Society Magazine* (Spring 2017), pp 10–15.

[71] BL Add Ms 45893, p 79v.

[72] BL Add Ms 45893, p 80v.

Green and there was another report of Isobel's election as a delegate to the Free Maintenance Committee. The Sunday lecture had been by the Hon. Mrs Bertrand Russell on "German Social Democracy & the Woman Question", and had attracted a good audience.[73] Isobel also attended the meeting on 29 May.[74]

"Free Maintenance for all necessitous children" was one of the four main proposals included in the Manifesto of English Socialists, published on 1 May 1893. Isobel and the short-lived Committee which she joined were ahead of their time. In late 19th-century England the minority of well-meaning people who took matters into their own hands and provided free school meals to otherwise hungry children were acting illegally. In 1895, the year before Isobel was appointed to the Free Maintenance Committee, the London School Board published the report of a Special Committee on Underfed Children which questioned whether the daily provision of vegetable soup to needy children was the best approach:

Actual starvation was undoubtedly at one time the chief evil to be feared by the poor. But now that rent in London is so high and food so cheap conditions have changed.[75]

When the provision of school meals in public elementary schools in England and Wales was finally legalised by the enactment of the Education (Provision of Meals) Act 1906 Local Education Authorities were empowered – but not obliged – to provide food, either in co-operation with voluntary agencies or out of public funds, up to the limit of a half-penny rate. Living in 1890s Hammersmith, Isobel would have been well aware of the prevalence of extreme poverty. The church where she was confirmed did its bit to relieve this, and kept a register of clothes – including in some cases underwear – and loan blankets it made available to destitute parishioners.[76]

Returning to the Hammersmith Socialist Society, only nine people attended the meeting on Friday 12 June 1896. They included Harry Harrison, who signed the minutes, Isobel and "G. von Holst". This is the first record of Gustav entering Isobel's life story.

At the 12 June meeting Isobel reported that she had duly attended the last meeting of the Free Maintenance Committee, when only three delegates were present.[77] Harry chaired the next meeting, on 19 June, which Isobel also attended, and on 26 June their mother went too, with Harry seconding a proposal by Emery Walker to withdraw the Society's delegates to the Free Maintenance Committee in the light of the low attendance.[78] The same meeting also agreed that the Hammersmith Socialist Society should send two delegates, one of them Harry, to a meeting at Kelmscott House[79] about the Peace Demonstration on 26 July.[80] Harry chaired the 3 July meeting, which Isobel also attended with five other five other participants, when much of the discussion was about the Peace Demonstration. They both attended the meeting

---

[73] BL Add Ms 45893, p 81.

[74] BL Add Ms 45893, p 81v.

[75] Quoted, with several other references to evidence cited in the 1895 report, in M. E. Bulkley, *The Feeding of School Children* (London, G. Bell and Sons, 1914). The quotation above is referenced in footnote 60.

[76] London Metropolitan Archives P77/ALB/063 St Albans Relief Committee Register of clothes and loan blankets 1894–1913.

[77] BL Add Ms 45893, p 83.

[78] BL Add Ms 45893, p 84.

[79] William Morris's London home.

[80] BL Add Ms 45893, p 84.

on 10 July, when Gustav von Holst was again present. Harry reported on a fund-raising request in relation to the Peace Demonstration, and "it was agreed that the opinion of the Society anarchists should be excluded from the Congress". In signing the minutes as Chair of the meeting on 17 July Harry added a note recording that "Von Holst moved adjournment of discussion on 'Referendum' ".[81] At that meeting Harry reported further on the arrangements for the Peace Demonstration, which now included two bands which had been engaged for the local participants in the procession to march to Sloane Street, join the Chelsea and Fulham detachments there and from there move on to the Embankment. The meeting appointed Harry as the Society's delegate to the Central Peace Demonstration Committee meeting on 19 July in the Strand.

These thinly-attended meetings were held at a time which was highly charged politically in terms of both domestic and international politics. The International Peace demonstration which Isobel's brother Harry had been deputed to discuss further was co-ordinated by Eleanor Marx and held in London on Sunday 26 July 1896 before the International Congress. Although there is no record of whether Isobel or Gustav were amongst the many participants, it was a major event. Despite pouring rain, it involved a procession along the Thames Embankment with people carrying socialist red flags, 50 brass bands and, in Hyde Park itself, 12 platforms for speakers arranged in a semicircle. Disappointingly, the Society's minutes for the next weekly meeting after the demonstration do not contain a record of the event, although Isobel was again present and Harry, as "Treasurer of local committee for Peace Demonstration" reported on the total expenses for the committee, and appealed to members to contribute to addressing the deficit of seven shillings.[82]

John Bruce Glasier, a close friend of William Morris until the latter's final illness, wrote this account of the atmosphere at one of the last Sunday evening lectures:

On Sunday, August 9, 1896, I again, and for the last time, lectured at Kelmscott House. Morris was then away by his doctor's advice on a cruise to Spitzbergen with his friend John Carruthers, in the forlorn hope of regaining his health, and there was a subdued and inert air about the place. My lecture raised a brisk discussion in the meeting, but the debaters were mostly young men, newcomers into the movement. … none of the old warriors unsheathed their blades. Already the old Kelmscott regime seemed passing away. After the meeting, instead of our having supper in the house, we had supper at my sister's, and made merry till the morning hours; but the thought that he 'My Captain, O My Captain' was fading away, haunted my mirth. He returned from his cruise in no wise benefited by it[83]

In these last weeks of William Morris's life Isobel continued to be a regular attendee at the weekly meetings, and signed the minutes of the meeting on 18 September 1896 (which her brother had chaired) as Chairman of the meeting on 2 October, with Gustav von Holst again in attendance. The Kelmscott House weekly lecture on 20 September had been on the subject of "Life in the Middle Ages: Villein & Serf", and on 27 September had been on Children's Rights.[84] She and Harry were both present at the meeting on 16 October, at which deep sympathy was expressed on the death of the Society's revered founder, William Morris.[85]

---

[81] BL Add Ms 45893, pp 85–6.

[82] BL Add Ms 45893, p 87.

[83] J. Bruce Glasier, *William Morris* (Longmans, London, 1921), 140.

[84] BL Add Ms 45893, p 89v. Both topics were of interest to Isobel, the latter in relation to her previous role on the Free Maintenance Committee.

[85] BL Add Ms 45893, p 90v.

Without Morris as a driving force, the members of the Hammersmith Socialist Society were indeed bereft. Instead of the weekly lecture at Kelmscott House, Morris's "Useful Work v. Useless Toil" was read to a small audience on one occasion, in relation to the meeting on 1 November "Von Holst reported that there was no lecture but Bullock gave a reading from John Bull & a short discussion followed" and on 8 November Harry read Morris's "Monopoly". Gustav was also present at the meeting on 30 October at which a proposal was agreed "that the choir have leave to borrow the black board" – the first reference for several years to the existence of the choir. Facing dwindling attendances and the loss of Kelmscott House as a free venue for the regular meetings, a committee was appointed to consider the future of the Society, and reported to a Special General Meeting on 13 November that it should be wound up. Harry, Isobel and Gustav were all present at the special meeting, which agreed the necessary arrangements, including Harry's appointment to yet another committee.[86]

On 20 November 1896 it was Gustav's turn to chair the meeting, which Isobel and Harry also attended. George Bernard Shaw had lectured on "Repairs & Alterations in Socialism" to a large audience at Kelmscott House the previous Sunday.[87] This appears to have been Gustav's first and last time chairing a meeting of the Hammersmith Socialist Society. Harry reported to the meeting a fortnight later on the penultimate Kelmscott House lecture, at which W. G. Pearson of the SDF[88] spoke on "Socialism & the Drink Question." Harry observed:

The lecture which was a very thoughtful one treated the subject from the Socialist standpoint; showing on the one hand that drink was not necessarily the cause of poverty & on the other that poverty was not necessarily the cause of drunkenness.

Harry, Isobel and Gustav stayed loyal to the Society until the end, and all attended its final meeting on 11 December 1896. The last of the Kelmscott House lectures was on 6 December, when the artist and bookbinder T. J. Cobden-Sanderson lectured on " 'Art & Life' to a small audience of about 40 or 50 persons."[89]

Gustav was by now firm friends with Isobel as well as Harry. His college friend Fritz Hart recalled how one day in 1897 he had:

… met Gustav – who hardly ever spoke to a girl unless on a matter of purely musical business – with one of the loveliest girls I had ever seen! Gustav introduced this slight, sunny-haired girl with beautiful eyes to me as Miss Harrison, and then – just a little self-consciously, perhaps – walked off with her. Now Hurlstone[90] and I were frankly interested in girls – qua girls – and often chaffed each other in Gustav's presence about our various feminine friends. Gustav would listen, pull long faces at us in a good-humoured kind of way, and then make us talk of other matters. But one of the first things he said to me after his marriage with Isobel was: "When I used to hear you and Hurlstone talk about girls, I often chuckled to myself as I thought that, more likely than not, I'd get married before either of you!"[91]

Gustav had already turned his attention to the Hammersmith Socialist Choir. In November 1895 this had amalgamated with the local Independent Labour Party choir, and a call was

---

[86] BL Add Ms 45893, pp 91–92.

[87] BL Add Ms 45893, p 95.

[88] The Social Democratic Federation, the first Marxist political group in Britain, of which William Morris   was a member before he broke away to form the Socialist League in 1885.

[89] BL Add Ms 45893, p 95v-96.

[90] Another of Gustav's RCM contemporaries.

[91] Fritz Hart, "Early memories of GH", R.C.M. Magazine 39/2, p 52.

issued for "Musical Socialists able and willing to assist".[92] It seems likely that this was the point at which Gustav became its director. Initially under his direction the Choir continued to meet at Kelmscott House at 8 o'clock on Monday evenings. He used the pages of *The Clarion*, the weekly Socialist newspaper which included a section on Clarion Vocal Unions, to announce that "the choir is doing very well, but … they must have a few more good basses". The editor added the rallying call "Now then, basses, for the honour of Hammersmith – and Socialism."[93]

After William Morris's death the remaining stalwarts of the Hammersmith Socialist Society realised that they needed to find new premises for their meetings. It was Isobel's brother Harry Hughes Harrison who appealed "to Socialists in Hammersmith and the neighbourhood" for those who desired "to assist in the formation of a Socialist Club in Hammersmith" to contact him at the family home in Roxwell Road.[94] With considerable effort the Hammersmith Socialists rented a large house nearby at 29 The Grove Hammersmith, managing to raise £100 for the initial rent.[95] This became the new Hammersmith Socialist clubhouse, and the venue for the weekly choir rehearsals led by Gustav.

Gustav roped in his old and new friends to perform a Glee Concert and Dramatic Entertainment at The Athenaeum, Goldhawk Road, on Friday 26 March 1897 – Isobel's 21st birthday - featuring his own part-songs.[96] The second half of the evening's entertainment was a one-act "original comedy", *The Anarchist*, which Gustav had persuaded his friend Fritz Hart to write. Its theme was an anarchist plot to blow up the Albert Memorial (close to the Royal College of Music), and Gustav, Isobel and another of Gustav's college friends, Thomas Dunhill, had the three main parts. Gustav was billed as a philanthropist, Benjamin Beechcroft, and Isobel as Bunny, a lodging house keeper's daughter.[97]

Although Gustav and Isobel's amateur dramatics with the Hammersmith Socialists were intended to be humorous, under Gustav the choir, which had been founded by Annie Grove,[98] developed a more serious repertoire. It soon expanded its repertoire from the William Morris socialist chants such as "No Master", mentioned in previous business minutes of the Hammersmith Socialist Society and included in the programme which Gustav conducted on 26 March 1897. In 1895 Gustav was probably amongst the choir at the Royal College of Music who took part in the first performance of Purcell's *Dido and Aeneas* since the late 17th century. At the 1897 Glee Concert he conducted "With drooping wings" from the final scene of Dido – a far cry from the socialist chants.[99] As Gustav and the choir were developing their repertoire it is worth recording the words of Morris's "No Master":

Saith man to man, We've heard and known
That we no master need

---

[92] *The Clarion*, Saturday 23 November 1895, p 6.

[93] *The Clarion*, Saturday 12 September 1896, p 291.

[94] *Justice*, Saturday 24 July 1897, p 8.

[95] *The Clarion*, Saturday 9 July 1898, p 7.

[96] Including the first performance of *Clear and Cool*, which he conducted. Holst, *Thematic Catalogue*, 16.

[97] Heywood, "Gustav Holst, William Morris …", 42.

[98] Stott, "A garden party at Kelmscott house", 15.

[99] Imogen Holst, *The Music of Gustav Holst, third revised edition* (Oxford University Press, 1986), 136.

> To live upon this earth, our own,
> In fair and manly deed.
> The grief of slaves long passed away
> For us hath forged the chain,
> Till now each worker's patient day
> Builds up the House of Pain.
> And we, shall we too, crouch and quail,
> Ashamed, afraid of strife,
> And lest our lives untimely fail
> Embrace the Death in Life?
> Nay, cry aloud, and have no fear,
> We few against the world;
> Awake, arise! the hope we bear
> Against the curse is hurled.
> It grows and grows--are we the same,
> The feeble band, the few?
> Or what are these with eyes aflame,
> And hands to deal and do?
> This is the host that bears the word,
> No MASTER HIGH OR LOW -
> A lightning flame, a shearing sword,
> A storm to overthrow.[100]

A few months later Isobel and Gustav performed in another one-act comedy, this time written by Gustav himself, with Gustav acting the hero – "magnificently", according to his new best friend from college and fellow composer Ralph Vaughan Williams – and Isobel, by now his fiancée, conveniently cast as his wife.[101] At another concert on 5 February 1898 Isobel sang the first performance of Holst's composition for voice and piano, *Two Brown Eyes*, accompanied either by the composer or by Holst's fellow student Thomas Dunhill.[102] A further concert and performance of *The Anarchist* was to be held the following week. Both the events in February 1898 were advertised on behalf of the Hammersmith Socialist Club, which aimed "to draw together Socialists of all shades of opinion, for the purposes of mutual intercourse, and, where possible, concerted action."[103]

On 2 April 1898 Gustav conducted the Hammersmith Socialist Choir's annual concert at the Town Hall. The programme started with "The Labourers' Battle Hymn" and included "Now is the Month of Maying" (Morley), "Thus Saith my Chloris Bright" (Wilbye), "Phoebe" (Stanford), "Au Joli Bois" (old French), "Full Fathoms Five" (Wood), "Ave Maria" (Mendelssohn), and the chorus parts of Stanford's "Cavalier Songs" and Bizet's "Toreador's Song". Gustav's enthusiastic report appeared in *The Clarion*:

Owing to our members being very busy people, it was very difficult to have full practices, but enthusiasm overcame this and every other obstacle. We had the largest hall in the place, and our choir only numbers 27, but I for one could detect no thinness of tone. In fact, our greatest improvement has

---

[100] William Morris, *Chants for Socialists* (The Socialist League, London, 1892).

[101] Dr Vaughan Williams on "Gustav Holst", Extracts from a Lecture at Morley College on 20 January 1953. Michael Short, *Gustav Holst: The Man and his Music* (Oxford University Press, 1990), 31. Gustav was not Isobel's only male admirer at the time.

[102] Holst, *Thematic Catalogue*, 26.

[103] Heywood, "Gustav Holst, William Morris …", 42.

been in purity of tone and blending of voices. To sum up, we have had a real triumph, and, better still, we earned it by sheer hard work. Could not the London choirs have a meet in the summer? What says Comrade Merry? Anyway, would conductors and secretaries of choirs willing to join write to me at once? … Our practices are still going on, at 8.30 p.m. on Tuesdays, at 29, The Grove, Hammersmith.[104]

Gustav pursued his idea of "a joint Socialist choir outing for all London choirs", and in a further article in *The Clarion* asked that if anybody wanted to talk the proposal over, "will he or she please come to our practice".[105] A week later he was starting to lose heart, and thinking of abandoning the idea. He used *The Clarion* for a further appeal, to which the editor added, "Now, then, Southerners, can't we show the Northern barbarians how to sing?"[106] The multiple appeals worked. The day-long event, which took place near the Windmill on Wimbledon Common on Sunday 31 July, brought together 50 singers from the Hammersmith and London Socialist Choirs and the Clapham Independent Labour Party Choir. After several hours of sectional rehearsals the participants enjoyed a "big tea" planned by Gustav and eaten on the grass, after which "everybody adjourned to a quiet glen". The al fresco performance started with the combined choirs singing "The Labourers' Battle Hymn", and Frank Merry of the London Socialist Choir and Gustav divided the conducting of the rest of the programme between them. The anonymous reviewer wrote:

The effect of the combined choirs was very fine. In their own places, the London Socialist Choir sang with their wonted enthusiasm, while the Hammersmith choir gave their selections with careful attention to light and shade … The singing was somewhat rapturously applauded by an audience of friends who had joined the Meet, and a number of passers-by who had been attracted by the unusual phenomenon of the harmony that floated from beneath the trees. It being Sunday, the opportunity was seized by the Clapham folk to take a collection for the families of the Welsh miners, 17s. 9 1/2d. being collected. The choirs then adjourned to another place, where three orations were delivered by the respective conductors, thus proving themselves to be not only excellent musicians and successful organisers, but also dangerous rivals of our leading Socialist lecturers. Proceedings closed with "England, Arise" and the "Marseillaise."[107]

Imogen, who downplayed her father's socialism, highlighted the fact that this was his first, important, experience of conducting a choir.[108] When asked a month before her own death in 1984 what attracted Gustav to the Choir, she replied:

It certainly wasn't politics, as such; he'd no use for politics as such. It was, I think, William Morris must have been a fascinating man; the chance of conducting a Socialist Choir was lovely; he enjoyed working there, he enjoyed the encouragement of William Morris during Morris's last few years of life, and he also enjoyed meeting his youngest soprano, a local girl of seventeen who he fell in love with, who became my mother, later on when they could afford to get married.[109]

Gustav persuaded several of his college friends to perform solos in a concert at the Socialist Club in December 1897, with his choir contributing "part songs and madrigals in fine

---

[104] *The Clarion*, Saturday 4 June 1898, p 6.

[105] *The Clarion*, Saturday 2 July 1898, p 7.

[106] *The Clarion*, Saturday 9 July 1898, p 7.

[107] *The Clarion*, Saturday 3 September 1898, p 3.

[108] Bruno Lima, *Gustav Holst: A Double Life in Music*. YouTube video premiered 21 September 2021.

[109] Britten Pears Arts HOL/5/2/26 Partial transcript of Stephen Wilkinson talking to IH in Aldeburgh 3 February 1984.

style".¹¹⁰ Gustav's fellow student Ralph Vaughan Williams' recollection of their activities at the Kelmscott Club dwelt neither on music nor politics but on Isobel and Gustav's fondness for amateur dramatics in the period shortly after the death of William Morris.

About 35 years ago he [Gustav Holst] decided, like Wagner, that the only hope for an operatic libretto was for the composer to write it himself. But, unlike Wagner, that some preliminary study was necessary so by way of preliminary study he wrote two plays, – One was a serious drama on a Nordic subject (this was in the William Morris days) and the other a farce.

The serious play was, as far as I know, never performed, partly, I imagine because I was engaged to play one of the two principal parts. After two rehearsals I was "fired" and this was the beginning and end of my career on the boards. The farce was performed at least once at the Kelmscott Club. Holst himself played the hero, a Curate, and Mrs Holst took the part of the Curate's wife. There was, I think, only one other character … The plot turned on the complications that ensued on an intercepted letter – After so many years my memory of the details has rather faded, but so far as I can remember the Curate had been having a surreptitious flutter on the turf and had received from a sporting friend a letter describing the physical charms of a racehorse with considerable anatomical detail. Unfortunately the wife gets hold of the letter and takes it for granted that the "She" referred to is [a] lady of the chorus …

Those who knew Holst will realize how he must have revelled in the part of the Curate and how perfectly he caught the sanctimonious mannerisms of the State Parson – I have also a vivid recollection of Mrs Holst in the part of the self-important and suspicious wife. Her "chatelaine" with its jingling bunch of keys being much in evidence.
Altogether it was a memorable evening.¹¹¹

The music for *Two Brown Eyes* is lost, but autograph manuscripts of two of Gustav's other songs for voice and piano, *Song to the Sleeping Lady* (1897) and *Not a sound but echoing in me* (1897), both dedicated to Isobel, have survived. Gustav also dedicated two of his part-songs to Isobel – *O Spring's little children*, written and published in 1899 and his setting of William Morris's poem, *A Love Song*, written (like his much better-known *Ave Maria*, dedicated to the memory of his mother) in 1900 and published in 1902.

When Isobel and Gustav met, Gustav was eking out his hard-won scholarship at the RCM with a variety of musical jobs. In autumn 1898 he was offered an appointment with the Carl Rosa Opera Company as first trombone and répétiteur. "It seemed too good a chance to refuse, and regretfully he left the Royal College of Music."¹¹² Imogen related this decision to the fact that he was already engaged to Isobel, and saw it as a way of hastening their marriage.¹¹³ Gustav's changed circumstances and need to earn his living now his student days were well and truly over meant that his commitment to the Hammersmith Socalist Choir needed to change too, although this was reported in *The Clarion* as being only temporary:

The great director and maestro has taken leave of absence, and gone on tour. Several of the company seem to be infected with the same spirit, and … some seem possessed of a spirit of desertion. They who, from a sense of duty and earnestness of purpose, take up the position – in the absence of the

---

¹¹⁰ *Acton Gazette*, Friday 17 December 1897, p 6.
¹¹¹ Morley College archives, Letter from Ralph Vaughan Williams to Eva Hubback November 1935.
¹¹² I. Holst, *Gustav Holst*, 18–19.
¹¹³ Bruno Lima, *Gustav Holst: A Double Life in Music*. YouTube video premiered 21 September 2021.

supreme authority – of directing and keeping on the work and meetings have not a joyful or an enviable task …[114]

Two years later, when the Carl Rosa Company was facing financial difficulties, Gustav joined the Scottish Orchestra in Glasgow as second trombonist. This meant prolonged absences from his fiancée Isobel during the concert season, when the orchestra gave four concerts a week. The young couple were, however, very much dependent on finding their own way in life. Neither of their immediate families was in a position to help them financially. Gustav's father retired from his steady job as organist and choir master of All Saints Church Cheltenham in 1895, when he was only 50. His piano-playing career was already in decline and a few years later he broke his wrist, bringing it to a permanent end. He was in no position to support his young family from his second marriage, let alone help his eldest son. In 1900 Gustav's stepmother had had enough and emigrated to America, taking her two young sons with her to become boarders at the Theosophical School in San Diego, California.[115] At the time of the March 1901 census Gustav's father was lodging in two rooms in a house in Cheltenham.

When Isobel's father Ralph Augustus Harrison, described as a builder on their wedding certificate, died on 15 July 1900 at St George's Hospital he had been living at yet another London address – 193 Goldhawk Road – with yet another recorded occupation – auctioneer's clerk. This was presumably a recent move as Ralph Harrison was only recorded on the electoral register there for the year following his death, which was registered by his elder son Harry who was living at the same address. 193 Goldhawk Road may have been where Gustav stayed with the Harrison family for a time. An undated letter to Gustav from Ralph Vaughan Williams explained:

I suddenly find that I don't know what address to write to – so I am sending this to Goldhawk and asking them to forward it....[116]

Ralph Augustus Harrison's death meant that the happy family home which Isobel's husband-to-be had so enjoyed came to an end. The March 1901 census records Isobel's mother living at 57 Biscay Road in the centre of Hammersmith with her sister and brother-in-law Eliza and Robert Norbrook, who had been promoted from clerk (in 1890) to foreman at a copper plate printing works, and their family. At the age of 55 she was working as a monthly nurse, which suggests straitened circumstances. Isobel's widowed aunt Emily Louisa, whose husband Frederick Banks had been an agent for the Anti-Slavery Society, was living a mile or so away at 202 Goldhawk Road. Meanwhile Gustav was staying with Ralph and Adeline Vaughan Williams at their first married home in Barton Street Westminster.

---

[114] *The Clarion*, Saturday 3 September 1898, p 3. The Hammersmith Socialist Choir continued for several years, despite the writer's foreboding.
[115] Theodore von Holst, *Matthias Ralph Bromley von Holst (1886–1956)* typescript notes May 2015.
[116] BL Ms MUS 158 f 8.

Chapter Three
Early married life

Isobel and Gustav on honeymoon in Berlin, 1903 (Holst Victorian House)

Some five years after their first meeting, Gustav and Isobel decided not to wait any longer. Gustav wrote to Ralph and Adeline Vaughan Williams with the good news, and his friend responded:

My Dear V.
I can't tell you what pleasure it gives me that you should consider us old friends enough to confide in – also it enables me to behave like an old friend and tell you how absolutely right I feel you are – after all what's the good of waiting – I was glad when I came upon your news – characteristically sandwiched in between two operas; you've got something that's better than all the concerts in the world put together – I'm afraid I'm very disjointed but I want to express more than I can in words

    You say that you are[117] going to 'drop your laziness' – you never were lazy – but you had not a sufficient idea of the value of your time – you must really learn to be rather more churlish and not be ready to work yourself to the bone for any man who meets you in the street – not only without any pecuniary reward but with the certain knowledge that (i) the result cannot possibly be anything like commensurate with the pains expended and (ii) that the results however good will not be appreciated.

    Do remember that it's your duty to keep all your energies in reserve for the moment when they can be used to advantage (For instance don't make a new copy of 'Sita'[118] but show me the old one when

---

[117] The words "not going to let" are crossed out.

[118] Gustav's opera, which he worked on for several years.

you come back) – there I've been preaching you a sermon – but then I'm younger than you by about 3 months.[119]

At last, on 22 June 1901 Isobel and Gustav's lengthy engagement came to an end when they married at Fulham Register Office – at that time housed in the former Fulham Workhouse, which enabled Gustav to joke that they had been married in the workhouse.[120] Isobel's brother Harry Hughes Harrison, who was recorded in the 1901 census as an electrical engineer and one of five people boarding with a builder's foreman in Hammersmith, and Gustav's Aunt Nina von Holst, who had helped with his upbringing following his mother's early death, witnessed their marriage. The wedding certificate records Isobel herself as not having any profession, and her address as 18 Quain Mansions, Fulham – a few miles away from Notting Hill where Gustav had been staying and the ninth recorded address for Isobel's family during the quarter century of her pre-marital lifetime.

There was no way Isobel and Gustav could afford a honeymoon after their wedding. Gustav's salary as a trombone player in several orchestras meant they only scraped by. They moved into their first married home, which was two furnished rooms over a shop at 162 Shepherds Bush Road, near Hammersmith.[121] It seems unlikely that there would have been enough space for a piano, but shortly after their marriage Gustav dedicated one of two pieces for piano to his new wife. This dedication suggests that Isobel was a competent player, particularly as he dedicated the first piece to his pianist aunt Nina.[122] Despite their modest accommodation, the home-making skills which Isobel brought to their marriage meant being able to entertain friends in their own home. Gustav's college friend Fritz Hart was their first guest, and his account illustrates Gustav's complete preoccupation with, and dedication to, music:

On this festive occasion I caused Gustav distinct chagrin when I told him of Tom Dunhill's discovery of a pair of consecutive fifths in the newly published Ave Maria for 8-part women's choir – one of the very best of Gustav's early works. Gustav jumped up from the table, put a copy of the Ave Maria into my hands and told me to show him the worst. I did so and his jaw dropped, while his pretty young wife looked as though she feared some major disaster had taken place. Then Gustav shrugged his shoulders, damned all fifths, and returned to his half-eaten meal with unimpaired appetite.[123]

At first Isobel found Gustav's behaviour upsetting. Former Thaxted resident Barbara Simcoe recalled that Isobel:

… told my mother it used to upset her [that he needed so much time on his own] when they first met but she got used to it in the end. She used to put flowers on the table – marigolds and things like that – my mother did – make it look nice – and he used to push them away, you see, to make room for his music … She told mother that – he didn't mean to be unkind – he'd got other things on his mind.[124]

---

[119] BL Ms MUS 158, ff 30–31.
[120] Pam Croome interview with Isobel, 1968.
[121] Imogen Holst, *A Scrap-book for the Holst Birthplace Museum* (Holst Birthplace Museum Trust, 1978), 27.
[122] London, Weekes & Co (1902?).
[123] Fritz Hart, 'Early memories of GH', 52.
[124] Britten Pears Arts HOL/5/2/6 Full transcript of RS/Barbara Simcoe's taped conversations 6 November 1985.

In another version of this story it was Isobel herself who put flowers on the table only for Gustav to sweep them off to make way for his music.[125] During their first year of married life there was in fact little music. The penny notebook in which Gustav listed his compositions, using a page each year from 1896 to 1933, the year before he died, is blank for 1901 – the only year for which that is the case. Many years later Imogen attributed this to his need to support Isobel, rather than that they were enjoying their new life together:

> … my mother used to tell me of how he recognized the exact sound of the returned manuscript coming through the letterbox in the door and arriving, whoosh … What is particularly interesting to me is that in that list, he only put in the pieces of music that he was willing to acknowledge as compositions. He wrote in the early days, especially when he'd just married my mother in 1901 – she wasn't my mother then – I wasn't born until 1907, but anyhow he married her in 1901 and from then onwards, for several years, he had to write what he pathetically called 'pot-boilers' which were ghastly little pieces which were not published which came back through the letterbox with a thud, and he disowned those and didn't enter them in his list of compositions. … The very first year of his marriage, 1901, and that I'm sure is the reason because he was working hard writing these wretched little songs and piano pieces.[126]

Less than two months after their wedding Gustav and Isobel experienced yet another bereavement when Gustav's father died suddenly, of apoplexy, in Cheltenham aged 56.

The highlight of 1902 for the newly married couple must have been the premiere at the Bournemouth Winter Gardens on 24 April of Gustav's *Cotswolds Symphony*, which he had finished writing whilst on tour with his trombone in Skegness. This was the first time that Gustav had had the opportunity to hear one of his compositions performed by a professional orchestra, and he and Isobel left London at 4 am in order to arrive in time for the rehearsal. Isobel's presence was probably wise, as during the rehearsal Gustav apparently felt "too over-wrought to remember what he had meant", and needed the arrival of the ever-supportive Vaughan Williams to calm him down.[127]

The lack of space at home was alleviated by the long periods of time Gustav spent away from home with his work for the Scottish Orchestra. Gustav's correspondence between October 1902 and February 1903 with Elisina Palamidessi di Castelvecchio, who was helping him with the libretto for his opera *Youth's Choice*, illustrates his busyness and preoccupations at this time. In October and much of November he was at home in Shepherds Bush Road, but from 29 November–21 January his letters were written from three different Glasgow addresses. He described his lifestyle in a letter written to her from Glasgow in late January or early February 1903, when he had just dispatched his manuscript:

> It has gone!! My life is now a blank!! That is how I feel and I merely state it as an expression of feeling and not as actual fact for during the next fortnight I have ten concerts in various towns and a couple of railway journeys to each and after the last one on Feb 14 I return to London. …
>
> Your kindness is simply beyond praise or thanks. So instead of trying to do the impossible let me express a hope of seeing you some day. I fear we are not likely to come to Cheltenham but if you are ever in London my wife and I would so much like you to spend an afternoon with us as we should very much regret losing sight of you. (This latter phrase is slightly mixed for we can hardly lose sight of one

---

[125] See page 123 below.

[126] Britten Pears Arts HOL/5/2/26 Partial transcript of Stephen Wilkinson talking to IH in Aldeburgh 3 February 1984.

[127] I. Holst, *Gustav Holst*, 23–24.

we have not seen yet however you know what I mean). If you do come please let us know beforehand as I am away so much ... Looking forward to our meeting before long...[128]

The correspondence came to an abrupt end on 25 February, when Gustav wrote from their home in London to Signorina Castelvecchio:

> Just a hurried letter to tell you that I and my wife are going to Germany on Saturday for study and holiday combined and we are going to stop just as long as the money holds out – if possible until November. So if you come to London in September send a card to this address (which will always find me) and I will let you know when we shall be able to meet.
>
> It is a tremendous piece of luck and we are very excited over it.[129]

The "piece of luck" which enabled Isobel and Gustav's delayed honeymoon – which the correspondence suggests was a spur of the moment decision – was a small inheritance following the death of Gustav's father. They set off in March and enjoyed Berlin so much, despite snowy weather, that Gustav ended one of his long letters to Vaughan Williams: "Our time is up next Monday but my wife wants to stop on while this jolly blizzard lasts as we are more or less at home in Berlin."[130] Holst's next letter to Vaughan Williams from Berlin illustrates the importance of Isobel's advice at this early stage of his career, when he was contemplating how he could make his living in music and dreading a return to his former role as a trombonist in the White Viennese Band, playing mostly in seaside resorts and conducted by Stanislaus Würm:

> My wife has had another idea which I think I shall adopt. That is that when we return I shall not take any Worming job or go out of London until the Scottish begins. If I can get a theatre well and good, if not I will even accept your offer of lending me money rather than play two or three times a day. (You see our living in London is pretty cheap.) Then I should like to try to work systematically from August to November both at writing and studying music. ...
>
> I wonder if it would be possible to lock oneself up for so many hours every day. If so it would be far easier for me than for you as you have so many friends. I feel it would be so splendid to "go into training" as it were, in order to make one's music as beautiful as possible. And I am sure that after a few months' steady grind we should have made the beginning of our own "atmosphere" and so should not feel the need of going abroad so much ...
>
> After much deliberation we have decided not to bicycle to Dresden and probably not from there to Munich ... I think we can neither spare the money or the time. The latter is especially important as we must see the Tyrol. Also a long ride like that would mean getting into training beforehand and a lot more rest afterwards for which we have no time as I think it more important to see operas, pictures, people and cities than the country barring the Tyrol. Of course we shall have short rides ...[131]

Isobel and Gustav's German holiday was energetic as well as cultural. At the start of their married life Isobel was also trying to help her husband with music copying to raise some much-needed money. This included some work by them both for Vaughan Williams, which did not go smoothly. Gustav wrote to explain:

---

[128] BL Add Ms 61951 ff 36–37.

[129] BL Add Ms 61951 f 38.

[130] Imogen Holst and Ursula Vaughan Williams, eds. *Heirs and Rebels: Letters Written to Each Other and Occasional Writings on Music, by Ralph Vaughan Williams and Gustav Holst* (Oxford University Press, London, 1959), 14.

[131] *Heirs and Rebels*, 17–18.

I really don't know what to say about the rhapsody parts excepting that I have walked my wife off her legs day after day until she was too tired to do any copying. While lately I am sorry to say she has not been very well. Also she does not seem able to acquire a 'teshneek' but can only do it very slowly so that these few pages we send you really represent rather a lot of work. ... Please don't be very disgusted with us.[132]

History does not relate whether or not Vaughan Williams was disgusted with the results of Isobel and Gustav's copying of his *Symphonic Rhapsody*, although Gustav wrote to ask whether Isobel could finish the copying on their return from honeymoon.[133] Vaughan Williams appears to have destroyed the manuscript.[134] A subsequent letter from Gustav to Vaughan Williams written from Munich, whence they had moved on from Berlin via Dresden, announced:

We remain here until next Saturday when we bicycle away into the Tyrol for a week only and then come home to England. ... It will leave me enough money to do without a Worms job so that I can stick at home and write. Munich is lovely and so very un-English. We thought of biking to one of the lakes but not too far away though. ... We should like boating and bathing above everything else ...[135]

Another letter from Gustav to Vaughan Williams from Dresden sheds light on how Gustav regarded the escapes from the quotidien which were to become a feature of his own life for the next 30 years:

... you once said you were so ashamed of yourself because your life seemed all holiday. Now if you find that you write better for going away in the country now and then, then it is your DUTY to go and do so. Again are you able to discover what helps you in composition and what takes your thoughts entirely away from music?[136]

On their return from honeymoon Gustav followed Isobel's idea of giving up his full-time trombone playing to earn his living as a composer. Gustav and Isobel quickly discovered that the songs he composed earned him only a few pounds, and money was scarce in the von Holst household. Isobel's previously close family was in no position to help. Isobel's mother died in 1904 at the age of 58. This at last freed her elder brother Harry Hughes to marry his long-standing fiancée Clara Fraser in 1905, and they needed to set up their own home. Their younger brother Ralph, who fought in the Boer War and was a Lance Corporal in the Royal Fusiliers in 1901 and a clerk by the time of his marriage in 1920, was also trying to make his own way in life. Harry's son Graham was later to write of his Uncle Ralph, whom he liked very much, and who "had the facility of playing all the popular tunes of the day by ear on the piano", but:

He never had any money and his rare visits to us always involved the passage of hard cash to him from my father (much to my mother's annoyance). After his marriage we lost touch and the last my father

---

[132] *Heirs and Rebels*, 19.

[133] British Library Add. MS 57953, f. fragment of a letter from Gustav Holst to Ralph Vaughan Williams, Saturday, Munich.

[134] Alain Frogley and Aidan J Thompson eds., *Cambridge Companion to Vaughan Williams*, (Cambridge University Press, 2013), 85.

[135] Jon C. Mitchell, *A Comprehensive Biography of Composer Gustav Holst, with Correspondence and Diary Excerpts: Including His American Years* (Lewiston, N.Y.: E. Mellen Press, 2001), 38.

[136] British Library Add. MS 57953, Letter from Gustav Holst to Ralph Vaughan Williams.

knew was that he was a messenger in the Civil Service. ... My father never spoke to me of the early years of the three children but I do know that there was never very much money available.[137]

During their early married life Isobel therefore "made clothes for her friends and did music-copying to keep things going."[138] Isobel also initially helped maintain the scrap-books of Gustav's press cuttings.[139]

It must have soon become apparent that even with Isobel's help and thrifty housekeeping, they could not rely on Gustav's composing to pay their household bills. Performances of his work were few and far between, and he only received a few pounds for those of his compositions which did sell. This was a time when composers did not usually receive performing fees and Gustav, like his outstandingly successful college contemporary Samuel Coleridge-Taylor, lost the copyright to those of his works he managed to sell to publishers. In 1904, acting on a recommendation from Ralph Vaughan Williams who had himself briefly taught there, Gustav started teaching one long day a week at James Allen's Girls' School (JAGS) in Dulwich, south-east London, for an initial salary of £50 a year.[140] Gustav successfully completed his term's probation, and long Fridays teaching whole class singing to all the year groups became a regular feature of his life until 1920.[141]

The journey across south London to and from Dulwich was never convenient for Gustav, but the steady but modest source of income from his JAGS teaching enabled Isobel and Gustav to move south of the river Thames to Grena Road near Richmond, a greener and quieter area than the shopping district of Shepherd's Bush, and rent an end-of-terrace house, No 31, from 1904–1907, from which they moved to the presumably cheaper mid-terrace No 23 in 1908. In their early years of married life Isobel and Gustav somehow also managed to rent a two-roomed cottage as a weekend retreat on the Isle of Sheppey, an island off the Kent coast about 40 miles east of London. This was the first opportunity Isobel had to decorate a home to her own distinctive tastes. Given their financial circumstances, and the fact that "the cottage had a mud floor, and ... was overrun by the most enormous spiders"[142] It was just as well that Isobel:

> ... was excellent at making a home really comfortable. She had begun with their tiny week-end cottage in the Isle of Sheppey, furnishing it with chintz-covered packing cases and with bits of pottery she had found on a market-stall in one of the narrow back-streets of Hammersmith.[143]

In late autumn 1904 Gustav started conducting the choir and orchestra at the Passmore Edwards Settlement in Tavistock Place, Bloomsbury. The Settlement provided classes, concerts and clubs for working-class adults in the evenings and at weekends, and Gustav started with Bach's *Sleepers Wake*, persuading Isobel, who usually played 'cello or double

---

[137] Britten Pears Arts HOL/4/5/1/2 Harrison family papers Graham Harrison, Notes on the Harrison Family.

[138] I. Holst, *Gustav Holst*, 24–25.

[139] Now at Holst Victorian House Cheltenham.

[140] His salary rose to £78 in 1909.

[141] Philippa Tudor, "Gustav Holst and the Whitsun Festival in Dulwich 1920", *Dulwich Society Journal* (205, summer 2020), 29–34.

[142] I. Holst, *Gustav Holst*, 28.

[143] Imogen Holst, *Holst* (Faber & Faber, The Great Composers Series, 2nd ed. 1981), 33. A photo of the results is included in Holst, *A Scrap-book for the Holst Birthplace Museum*, 31.

bass, to learn the violin for the occasion.[144] Gustav was also involved in teaching about 60 children from the neighbouring slums. He was adept in roping in his professional friends, including Vaughan Williams as an extra viola player or singing bass in the choir, in which Isobel also sang. The amount of time he needed to devote to training his mostly unskilled amateurs was significant, however, with the Passmore Edwards December 1905 concert alone needing 15 rehearsals.[145]

In autumn 1905 Gustav added a further significant teaching commitment to his workload when he joined the formidable female staff at the recently founded St Paul's Girls' School, closer to home in Brook Green, Hammersmith. This was to become his most significant teaching role, and the only one that he retained until his death nearly 30 years later.

By late summer 1906 Isobel was pregnant. She experienced a pregnancy so uncomfortable that she thought she was expecting twins. It was a long-awaited pregnancy by early 20th-century standards: towards the end of her life Isobel commented that the birth was "after six years."[146] Although at Christmas Isobel and Gustav were staying with Ralph and Adeline Vaughan Williams in Chelsea, in early January 1907 Isobel was feeling "so tired & not at all well" whilst Gustav was away on a walking tour, having changed his earlier plan to go to Paris. It must have been a worrying time, especially when on 22 January Gustav himself "was at home ill … & unable to do any work". Isobel wrote on 31 January 1907 to one of her closest friends at the time, the singer Maja Kjöhler, "The twins are having high jinks all day, every day now & I am always in pain & misery".[147] Another affectionate letter from Isobel to Maja Kjöhler dated 25 February 1907 demonstrates just how limited Isobel and Gustav's resources were:

I wonder if you have a spare chest of drawers stored at Greenfields that you could lend me for a time? I simply have nowhere to put the small creature's things & we cant afford just now to buy a chest.…[148]

A couple of weeks later Isobel, nearing the end of her pregnancy, invited Maja to go with "Gustavchen" to a performance of Bunyan's *Pilgrim's Progress* "with music arranged by Mr Vaughan Williams". "I should so like to go but I can't leave the baby & it is so troublesome just now!!"[149]

Money was tight in the extreme. Gustav announced Isobel's pregnancy to his friend Fritz Hart by ending a letter to him with the comment: "If you should hear of a second-hand perambulator going cheaply, let me know. Nuff said!"[150] 1906 was the year that Gustav set the words of Christina Rossetti's poem "In the Bleak Midwinter" to music. Much of the poem must have resonated with him:

What can I give him, poor as I am?
If I were a shepherd, I would bring a lamb.

---

[144] I. Holst, *Gustav Holst*, 25. The Passmore Edwards Settlement appointment was comparatively short-lived, and Gustav stopped teaching there in 1908.
[145] Short, *Gustav Holst*, 53, 62–3.
[146] *Saffron Walden Weekly News*, c. early April 1968.
[147] Britten Pears Arts HOL/1/5/3/1 Letters from Isobel Holst to Maja Kjöhler (most of the 15 letters in this collection are signed using Isobel's nickname Belchen).
[148] Britten Pears Arts HOL 1/5/3/2.
[149] Britten Pears Arts HOL 1/5/3/1 Letter from Isobel Holst to Maja Kjöhler, 14 March 1907.
[150] Fritz Hart, 'Early memories of GH', 52.

If I were a wise man, I would do my part.
Yet what I can I give him, give my heart.

Gustav responded to the financial pressures of their impending parenthood by taking on another teaching commitment, at Morley College for Working Men and Women near Waterloo Station, on 8 April 1907. Writing in 1926, Gustav's first biographer, the bachelor music critic Richard Capell, commented:

Holst's marriage incited him to turn to a different means for a livelihood. He threw up his orchestral work, and for the next twenty years he was busy teaching and, in the intervals of teaching, composing, in London.[151]

To Holst the new life did not seem, as it would have done to many, a servitude. He delighted in exercising his exceptional gifts as a teacher. His friends may have lamented that too little leisure was left for composition, but Holst never resented the claims of this work until the failure of his health in 1923–24.[152]

---

[151] Richard Capell, "Gustav Holst: Notes for a Biography (I)", *The Musical Times*, 1 December 1926, 1075.

[152] Richard Capell, "Gustav Holst: Notes for a Biography (II)", *The Musical Times*, 1 January 1927, 17.

Chapter Four
Family life in Barnes and Thaxted

Portrait photograph of Imogen and Isobel by Lizzie Caswall Smith (Holst Victorian House)

On 12 April 1907, just four days after Gustav's teaching appointment at Morley College was confirmed, Isobel and Gustav's only child was born. Gustav's first suggestion for her name was Sita, the Hindu goddess of the harvest in the Rigveda and the title of his recently completed opera. Isobel pointed out that their daughter had bright blue eyes and had also inherited her own blonde hair, making Sita an inappropriate choice of name. Her comments prevailed, and their baby was named Imogen,[153] later to be shortened to Imo, and Isobel's to Iso.

Unfortunately, "the baby howled incessantly, night and day. In despair he [Gustav] used to get up long before dawn and walk over Sheen Common in the hopes of finding a little peace." Isobel's homemaking skills, combined with Gustav's need to earn a living for them all, meant that there was only "one occasion, when everyone in the house had influenza", when "he made valiant attempts to be domesticated". As he wrote to Frances Ralph Gray, the High Mistress of St Paul's Girls' School who had rapidly become a firm and sympathetic friend:

Many thanks for all your kindness. We have at last got a charwoman in, and my brief reign as cook and 'general' has come to a most welcome end.

---

[153] Grogan ed., *Imogen Holst*, 6.

Oh! The miles of unwashed crockery (N.B. Do you measure unwashed crockery by the mile or the square root?) and unswept floors I left for my successor!

I must learn cooking.

The points I most want to learn are

a) How to cook half a dozen things at once in such a manner that they don't all boil over or burn at once as you are looking for the tablecloth,

b) How to persuade potatoes to be just a little quicker,

c) How to persuade toast not to be so quick!

I am looking forward to coming tomorrow [to school] as usual.[154]

Despite the welcome arrival of the charwoman, Isobel once again appealed to her friend Maja Kjöhler for help, inviting her to stay *en famille* at the cottage in Sheppey for 10 days, explaining that Gustav couldn't get away until Saturday, when she didn't want to travel, and "the fair Imogen says she must have two attendants". Aware that this invitation must have sounded unenticing, Isobel added that Sheppey "is just lovely at Whitsun with all the little lambs, and the trees and fields covered with blossom …"[155]

On 9 June 1907 Imogen was baptised at the recently completed church of St Michael and All Angels Barnes, a couple of miles away from the new family's own home. Gustav was now juggling three part-time teaching jobs and had limited time and the peace and quiet he needed to compose. In early January 1908 he learnt that his opera *Sita*, on which he had toiled hard for seven years and which had previously been shortlisted by the judges in 1905, had been the near miss for the Ricordi opera competition, the prize for which included the cash sum of £500, 10 times his annual salary for teaching on Fridays at JAGS.[156] Winning would have ended the young family's financial insecurity, raised Gustav's profile as a still mostly unpublished composer, and meant that his struggle to complete the opera despite painful neuritis in his right arm had been worthwhile. "The failure was a bitter blow".[157]

Vaughan Williams wrote the best of best friend letters, consoling him that:

I'm sorry (a) that you haven't got £500

(b) that you are not promised a performance.

Perhaps these are rather important side issues, but they are side issues. The really important thing is that you have not been put in the awful position when "all men speak well of you".[158]

In March Gustav was still struggling with the neuritis in his right arm which dogged him for much of his life, and "was only free from pain when he was able to put his arm a few inches from an oil stove or a gas fire." That pain, combined with overwork and exhaustion, led a doctor to prescribe a rest in a warm climate.[159] Vaughan Williams came to the rescue with the offer of £50, explaining:

It is most important – to my mind – that this should be a real holiday to make up for all your past years of strain. If you compose during it all the better – but if you have an idea all the time that you must have something to show for it – then you will spoil your holiday and effectually prevent yourself from

---

[154] I. Holst, *Gustav Holst*, 29.

[155] Britten Pears Arts HOL/1/5/3/1 Letter from Isobel Holst to Maja Kjöhler "Tuesday".

[156] Roughly equivalent to £60,000 in 2021.

[157] Imogen Holst's description in I. Holst, *Gustav Holst*, 31.

[158] British Library MS Mus 158, ff. 47–48.

[159] I. Holst, *Gustav Holst*, 31.

composing. If even you only come back teaching very well it wd mean that it came easier & left you more energy for other work.

I think abroad sounds good – but I don't know why it should be a very long abroad – enough to give you a change and a filip – but we can discuss all this when I come back.[160]

The decision that Gustav should holiday alone was taken jointly with Isobel, who stayed at home with Imogen, who was teething. By Good Friday 1908 Gustav had arrived in Algiers after an eventful rough boat crossing. The four letters which Gustav wrote to Isobel between 17 and 29 April 1908 are the earliest of the 53 surviving letters he wrote to her. Thirty years later, their daughter Imogen published extracts from them, wisely omitting some of Gustav's complaints about his journey and the behaviour of some of the Arab men he encountered[161] but also leaving out references to what Isobel needed to do to keep things going back in London. The following excerpts from the manuscript letters provide an insight into their relationship at this time.

On Easter Monday 1908 Gustav wrote to Isobel from Algiers following an initial grumpy letter about the sea crossing:

I forgot in my first letter to ask you to number every letter you send me so that I shall know if anything gets lost. Also if by any chance some publisher sends some money would you get a circular note for £5 from Cook's (they don't issue less than that) and ask them to send it to me c/o of their agents at Tunis. I don't expect that I shall need it but it might enable me to buy more things to bring home. I shall probably be in Tunis in four weeks from today and you must allow at least a week for it to reach me.

All Arabs are not like those of the docks! I am quite at home here now and have visited a Mosque 3 churches a synagogue and a Casbah and a few other things of the sort.

But the chief glory of Algiers is the native quarter. The streets are really flights of steps with dirty shops or houses on either side and the "Smell of the East"!

I thought it a good plan to send all my picture postcards to you first of all. Would you forward them? You might add a line explaining. I can't write to everyone although I sometimes feel I should like to. I believe if they are posted promptly they need not be restamped. Of course I am keeping others for ourselves, besides which there are the James Allen ones.[162] …

Just had a great disappointment. No letter from you! If you have sent any to me at Algiers they will probably be returned to you. … I shall look forward to getting a letter from you when I reach Biskra. It will be nice to know how many teeth[163] there are and how many order marks there are not!

By the bye last Saturday I heard a baby in one of the dirtiest of the native streets howl exactly like Imogen! It made me feel at home immediately. … Best Love Immer Ihr G.[164]

Gustav's third letter, written when he had moved on to Michelet, Kabylie, illustrates the habitual kindness of both Gustav and Isobel:

Dear Isobel
Before I left Algiers an English woman came to my hotel. She had been living in Constantine (not far from Bishra) with her husband a Frenchman. The latter had deserted her and she was left penniless with her 20 months old baby. The British consul is seeing to her and she is being sent home to London all expenses paid. She has immense pluck and although she had been travelling all night she was quite

---

[160] British Library MS Mus 158, ff. 49–50.
[161] Britten Pears Arts HOL 1/5/1/8/1 Letter from Gustav Holst to Isobel Holst 17 April 1908.
[162] Presumably ones destined for his pupils at James Allen's Girls' School.
[163] Baby Imogen's.
[164] Britten Pears Arts HOL 1/5/1/8/2 Letter from Gustav Holst to Isobel Holst 20 April 1908.

vigorous and cheerful. Her brothers are fairly well off and she is a fully trained dressmaker. I gave her your address and also Mrs RVW's[165] but I warned her that we were not very wealthy and that probably you could not give her anything to do. So don't bother to do so unless it is necessary as her case will not be desperate when once she gets home. But perhaps you could recommend her or anyhow see her and find out how things are with her.

Great thought – won't Mabel be wanting some things?

As the Consul only paid her bare expenses I gave her 20 fr for pocket money. She said something about paying it back by making clothes. I don't want her to do so at first. But after she is settled and doing well if she cares to make some things for you Dorrie or "Im" you do as you like.

Yesterday I took THE SUPREMELY SLOW train of the world to Tizi Ouzou. It rained like the deuce all day and I thought the only thing was to go back and take the night train to Bishra and then if it rained to go to Tunis and then if it rained to go home and then if it rained to go to bed and stop there! Also there was an incapable military band practising near the hotel sometimes solo instruments sometimes they all let fly together. It ought to have been amusing but I had six hours of it – during the rain!

To make amends today has been my greatest day in Africa so far. Although the roads were awful I started early on the bike. It has been a glorious day and the roads dried quickly and never never have I seen such mountains. At first the road went up 2300 ft in about 6 miles to Fort National. From there the road has kept up on the top overlooking not only the valleys but also the smaller mountains and the scenery has finished with snow-capped peaks. I can now see the latter from my window as I write. I fear that I have seen the best of Kalylia already but that remains to be seen. The French are wonderful road makers![166]

Gustav had intended to be abroad for two months, but lost his return ticket and needed to cut his holiday short as a result. Isobel followed his instructions in forwarding on one of his Algerian postcards to Maja Kjöhler:

Gustav asks me to send this to you with his love & best wishes for the success of the concert! So sorry I cant come, but I am without a servant.[167] G. has had his ticket stolen & so will have to return on May 10th instead of June 20th!! I ought to have gone to look after him![168]

At the end of his adventurous holiday the intrepid traveller wrote gratefully to Isobel, including an account of his bazaar purchases for her:

I have bought
    A Kabyle necklace, metal and enamel
    A tray brass and enamel. The pure brass ones were either fakes or else very dear. I think you will like this one
    A beautiful brass jar. This I am really proud of. I haggled over it in grand style …

… it [the holiday] has been just the right amount of the right thing – four weeks of entire change. As for resting entirely, it is a little difficult especially when one is alone. But I feel in fine form for composition and fresh and fit for anything – excepting from 12 to 4 when the heat here is something surprising.

So far I have not had any letter from you but the English mail comes in tomorrow. I am writing this today as it is my day of rest.

    Goodbye dearest
    I do hope you are all well and happy.

---

[165] Adeline Vaughan Williams.
[166] Britten Pears Arts HOL 1/5/1/8/3 Letter from Gustav Holst to Isobel Holst 23 April 1908.
[167] Presumably with whom she might have left one-year-old Imogen.
[168] Britten Pears Arts HOL 1/5/3/1 Postcard from Isobel Holst to Maja Kjöhler 21 April 1908.

Ihr G.[169]

Once back in London Gustav resumed his heavy schedule juggling part-time teaching commitments. The Morley College Syllabus for 1908–1909 listed him as teaching five of the eight music evening classes – lectures on Bach on Mondays, sightsinging and voice production at 7.30 pm on Tuesdays followed by the Choral Society at 8.30 pm, Orchestra on Wednesdays and Harmony and Counterpoint on Thursdays.

During the summer of 1908 there was an entire change for the whole von Holst family when they moved again, to a beautiful eight roomed, three-storey house at 10 The Terrace, Barnes, overlooking the river Thames. This was next door to a small school which had been run for several years by Gustav's aunt Anna Newman (*née* Lediard) and her daughter Mary. Something of a rebel, Anna had lived as a self-sufficient schoolteacher in Barnes for around 20 years, and was living at 9 The Terrace with her daughter and adopted son at the time of the 1901 census. Sadly, Anna died at the age of 62 only a few months after the little family had moved next door, and her body was buried in Cheltenham on 23 December 1908.

Their years at 10 The Terrace were generally a happy time for the von Holsts. Isobel grew fond of the house, and Gustav enjoyed a surge of productivity there. He had his own music room on the top floor, as far away from the busy street outside as possible, and was able to work with easy access to a piano, unlike his days at the Royal College of Music when before his lessons with Stanford he would arrive at College early to try to find a piano on which to try out his compositions. The first thing Gustav composed at Barnes was his one-act chamber opera *Savitri*, and he followed this with the *Choral Hymns from the Rig Veda*, two *Suites for military band*, *Two Psalms*, and the *Beni Mora Suite* for orchestra.

In 1910, as well as Gustav revising his *Beni Mora* Oriental Suite, Gustav and Isobel worked together on the score of *The Praise of King Olaf* for a large wind band and choir. This was written for the Festival of Empire held at Crystal Palace in summer 1911 in connection with the coronation of George V. Isobel's large handwriting was not well suited to copying musical scores, but possibly to save Gustav's hand, which often gave way when writing due to his neuritis, she nobly copied out the libretto for that and the associated Raven Song.[170]

1910 also saw a performance of a revised version of *A Somerset Rhapsody* in the presence of the Queen, which Gustav later described as "my first real success". His other works included arrangements of existing material. In 1911 Holst continued to have an abundance of orchestral parts to correct. For the historic Morley College performance under Holst's direction of Purcell's *Fairy Queen* Morley students copied 1,500 pages of vocal and orchestral parts, many of which survive in the Lambeth Archives. In relation to his own works, Holst had "made a new year's resolution that he was going to get his things performed, somehow or other. The resolution had a surprising and almost immediate effect."[171] 1911 compositions included his beautiful *Invocation* for cello and orchestra (originally titled *A Song of the Evening*), which was first performed at the Queen's Hall London on 2 May.

Although Gustav's Aunt Anna had died, at the time of the 1911 census Gustav's cousin Mary Newman (aged 40 and single) had 8 female boarding pupils aged 5–19, and was still living next door with a servant and governess in the 17-roomed house at 9 The Terrace.

Imogen wrote of her early family life at 10 The Terrace Barnes:

---

[169] Britten Pears Arts HOL 1/5/1/8/4 Letter from Gustav Holst to Isobel Holst 29 April 1908.
[170] BL Add Ms 57876.
[171] Imogen Holst, *Gustav Holst: A Biography*, 37.

… they were living at Barnes, next door to Aunt Anna's school, in a beautiful bow-fronted brick house overlooking the river. He had a large music room on the top floor, and in the evenings the grey, muddy river would collect all the colours of the sky and shine with a magical light that filled his three windows. And later, in the dusk, there would be the twinkling lights on the barges.

It was an unhealthy house to live in, for at the spring tides the river overflowed into the streets, and often the floods would come in at the front door. He never felt really well there, and he was perpetually suffering from a relaxed throat. But that view of the river compensated for a great deal.[172]

Imogen's memory would have been jogged by the fact that Isobel and Gustav's friend, the artist Millicent Lisle Woodforde (1880–1923), produced at least six paintings of her friends and their home there. Five of these are now publicly owned and accessible on the ArtUK website. Woodforde's paintings were almost certainly painted as gifts in 1910 or 1911. Isobel or Imogen kept them for about 50 years, despite repeated house moves by them both. The best known is of Gustav correcting proofs in his music room on the top floor. This was usually his private refuge, removed from the distractions of his busy teaching and family life, and as Imogen later observed, "he would not have allowed her in his room if he had been composing".[173] It was not just friends, however artistic, who were not allowed into Gustav's private domain. In an interview later in her life Imogen reflected:

I first got to know my father as someone who played tunes on the piano for me to dance to. This was in an old house on the river at Barnes. He had his composing room at the top of the house, and that was a room that one didn't go into. But downstairs I got to know him as a person.[174]

Millicent Lisle Woodforde's portrait of Gustav in his music room was given to the National Portrait Gallery London by Isobel and Imogen in 1962, a year in which Isobel's health was deteriorating and Imogen moved to a new home in Aldeburgh. It is one of the most famous images of the composer, and the one which Imogen regarded as the best portrait of Gustav. Woodforde also painted at least three portraits of Isobel in her home environment, two of which are displayed at Holst Victorian House Cheltenham. One is a serenely beautiful depiction of Isobel in the drawing room of the home she had lovingly decorated. Whilst Millicent's portrait of Gustav depicts Gustav correcting orchestral parts in his top floor music room, Isobel is shown surrounded by books.[175] A further painting by Woodforde of Isobel in the same room appears to be lost. It travelled with the Holst family to their new home in Thaxted, Essex, when they moved there in 1914, and a photograph shows it on a wall there. Woodforde also painted Isobel in a very different pose, with her beautiful long hair and her shawl unpinned, gazing into the distance by the top floor window of Gustav's composing room. Unlike Imogen, Isobel must have been allowed into Gustav's top floor composing domain at least occasionally. Another of Woodforde's portraits of Isobel,[176] on display at Holst Victorian House since 2016, shows her with her hair down, gazing out of the top floor window with a crescent moon in the sky.

---

[172] I. Holst, *Gustav Holst*, 38.

[173] Holst, *A Scrap-book for the Holst Birthplace Museum*, 47.

[174] Imogen Holst, notes for a BBC Woman's Hour Talk, February 1965, quoted in Grogan ed., *Imogen Holst*, 3.

[175] Philippa Tudor, "Millicent Lisle Woodforde and her paintings of the Holsts' home at 10 The Terrace Barnes", Holst Birthplace Museum website, July 2013.

[176] This painting is reproduced on the front cover.

This is also the view captured by Woodforde in her painting *The Thames at Night from the Music Room at 10, Barnes Terrace, London*. This Whistler-esque depiction captures with shades of blue and grey the twinkling lights reflected along the river Thames from the viewpoint of the top floor of the von Holsts' home. The von Holsts lived there long before the flood defence wall was built, when Barnes was notoriously prone to flooding and the proximity to the river was a mixed blessing, but the view from, and of, the house are much the same today. A sixth painting[177] by Woodforde of the Holst's home at Barnes depicts the staircase which led between the austerity of Gustav's composing room and the cosier domestic domain downstairs, with the faint outline of a figure – presumably either Isobel or Lottie Barber, their cook housekeeper at the time of the 1911 census. Woodforde's paintings of the downstairs interior convey Isobel's distinctive decorating style, during this period with strikingly dark and rich blues and greens, in contrast to the sparsely furnished and muted colours of the top floor composing room.

These paintings by Millicent Lisle Woodforde capture an idealised image of Gustav and Isobel at home in the early years of their married life when Gustav's later fame would have been hard to predict. They also add colour not only to Imogen Holst's earliest memories of her home life, but to our 21st century perception of what this might have been like. As Gustav and Isobel's lives were anything but monochrome, the paintings bring us a bit closer to them both.

Whilst living in Barnes Isobel used her talents as a dressmaker and interest in amateur dramatics to help put on a Christmas play at St Paul's Girls' School. Gustav's multi-talented pupil Clare Mackail, granddaughter of the artist Edward Burne-Jones as well as daughter of William Morris's biographer, prepared the costume sketches for Isobel.[178] In a letter written to Isobel in 1965 which also recalled the production of "The Masque of Dame Christian" at St Paul's Girls' School, for which Gustav wrote the music, Clare recalled: "What days they were, & how well I remember my first sight of you, & of Imogen like a fairy."[179]

Isobel was also the recipient of an autographed copy of the hugely popular Christmas mystery play *Eager Heart*, written by her and Gustav's long-standing friend Alice Buckton and inscribed Christmas 1909.[180] Isobel and Gustav's friendship with Alice Buckton was an enduring one, with Gustav writing several pieces of music or arrangements for her. Buckton insisted, however, that those undertaking the roles in *Eager Heart* were not identified in the programmes, so despite a later reference to Isobel being "usually chosen as a Madonna in spiritual plays"[181] there is no documentary evidence of her acting in any of the many performances of *Eager Heart*, whether in London or whilst staying with Buckton at her later home in Glastonbury.

In the summer of 1911 Isobel and four-year-old Imogen were once again at home in Barnes whilst Gustav was walking in Switzerland, for part of the time with his Morley College

---

[177] Both paintings described in this paragraph are part of the Richmond upon Thames Borough Art Collection and rarely displayed, but images are available on the ArtUK website.

[178] Tim McGee, *Barely Clare: The little-known life of Clare Mackail* (2020), pp 23–4.

[179] Another letter from Clare Mackail to Imogen, dated 2.1.75 described "having known you from the age of three, as a dancing fairy."

[180] Britten Pears Arts HOL/2/20/1/14 'To Isobel von Holst … Eager Heart, Christmas 1909 A. M. Buckton'.

[181] See page 78 below.

colleague and fellow composer Cecil Coles.[182] His letter to Isobel emphasised her role in encouraging him to take this break:

So far, I have only had one letter. If you have written another to me here, it will be forwarded to Lucerne. (This isn't a complaint – I know how busy you are!) … I am a bit more in form than I was – bless you for making me come! I'm having the biggest rest I've ever had in my life.

I am very sorry you are alone. I have been hoping that you may have invited someone to stay with you, but I fear not as I cannot think of anyone you would like to have. You'll keep me posted with news of Imogen. … If the weather remains bad, I shall be sorely tempted to come home on Saturday and to leave the Engadine to another time. It's extraordinary how ready one is to come home! Beg pardon – it isn't extraordinary at all!!

N.B. The above is a compliment.

However, I'm having a real good time. The only drawback is that I'm not as young and vigorous as I was. I don't get over the ground as I did once and, like Hamlet, I am fat and scant of breath. However, that only means that you were wise as ever in making me come. … Best love to you both. I hope Imogen is taking good care of you and seeing that you practise the bass daily. …[183]

One of the von Holsts' frequent visitors at home was Mabel Rodwell Jones, who taught English at JAGS and was an ardent supporter of Gustav and his music. The constrained upbringing which Gustav had endured had influenced his expectations of how Imogen should behave. She "constantly told us [JAGS pupils] how Imogen Holst had been taught, even as a tiny child, to sit very still and be very quiet whenever music was played."[184]

Aside from work, family life continued to have its fun moments. 10 The Terrace Barnes has one of the best views for watching the annual Oxford and Cambridge Boat Race. A young family friend, Sebastian Brown, remembered the von Holst family moving to their new home (from Grena Road, which was closer to where his own family lived) and being invited on Boat Race Day, including on the occasion when one of the boats sank.[185]

In March 1913 Gustav went on a month's holiday to Spain and Majorca with Clifford and Arnold Bax and Balfour Gardiner,[186] as the guest of the latter, once again leaving Imogen and Isobel behind. Gustav's fellow-travellers sought to enliven their travels with "pyrotechnical discussions", during most of which Gustav retreated into audience mode. Shortly after the foursome had spent the night in the Benedictine monastery at Montserrat, their after-dinner drink of verdad led to a conversation about women's intellectual limitations and inability to think of ideas in the abstract. Gustav felt roused to comment, which must in part reflect his relationship with Isobel:

I've taught girls all my life … And I don't think there's much difference between women and men.

---

[182] At Christmas 1917 Gustav received Coles' manuscript score, splashed with bloodstains and mud, intended as part of a suite *Behind the Lines*. Cecil Coles was fatally wounded while attempting to rescue casualties from a wood near the Somme on 26 April 1918.

[183] Britten Pears Arts HOL 1/5/1/8/5 Letter from Gustav Holst to Isobel Holst [postmarked 7 August] 1911.

[184] JAGS archives, Holst file, recollections from May Moore, who left JAGS in 1924.

[185] Britten Pears Arts HOL/4/3/1/10 Correspondence re Sebastian Brown's conversation with Rosamund Strode 19 January 1994. This seems likely to have been in 1912, the year in which both Oxford and Cambridge's boats sank, and the only year when both boats have done so.

[186] Gustav's fellow composer and generous and long-standing friend and supporter.

As his host opined: "They're incomprehensible to me. I should feel more at home with an Eskimo … And such an extraordinary shape" and Arnold Bax expanded: "They can't be impersonal … They don't consider an idea that's put forward, but the person who advances it", Gustav retorted:

I can only say that my experience provides more exceptions to your rule than illustrations of it.[187]

Although the 1913 holiday was very much a men-only affair, the ever-generous Balfour Gardiner enjoyed Isobel's company. One of Imogen's early memories was of a time when he visited her parents in Barnes:

… he was very fond of my mother because he was interested in the sort of thing my mother was interested in, old buildings and gardens, and all that, and he said, 'Oh Isobel, I've brought you a little honey' – he kept bees – and he held out to her – this was in the entrance hall – he held out in each hand two pound pots of honey from his bees. And I can still hear my mother's voice say, 'Oh Balfour, how lovely; thank you' … after he'd gone, my mother went into the kitchen, which was a room rather apart, a side room, and I heard her say 'OH, OH', so I trotted after her to see what had happened, and the kitchen table was practically covered with pound pots of honey. And Balfour having arrived, you see, and having been let in, must have said to the servant – because in those days you know, people had servants, it's one of the differences – must have said, 'Hide these away, would you …' But that I've never forgotten, and it is an absolute, in a nutshell, example of Balfour's generosity.[188]

Imogen started at kindergarten school in 1912, which must have given Isobel more leisure time, and in 1913 she set off on her own solo adventure for a long weekend in the New Forest in Hampshire. By this time Gustav's fellow music teacher at St Paul's Girls' School Vally Lasker was a good friend of Isobel as well as her husband, and when 5-year-old Imogen had started music lessons with Vally Isobel told her daughter "You will like her". Vally soon "belonged as if she were part of the family."[189] It was to her rather than to Gustav that Isobel recorded the various mishaps she had endured as a "foolish seeker after happiness" in a lengthy epistle which demonstrates her quirky sense of humour:

Dearest Vally
Here begineth the first chapter of accidents according to the gospel of Isobel the first wife of Gustavus the Great in the year of our Lord 1913! Upon a certain day a foolish person named at the top of this chapter did leave her home & friends & take upon herself a certain journey into a far country whither she did expect to find that elusive thing called happiness! And behold! The first part of her journey was without trouble – she dined well in the train that bore her to Southampton W. where she arrived in good time! She looked round for a friendly face & behold none was there for her to see, so thumping herself on her left hip pocket to assure herself that her purse was there, she handed in the correct half of her Friday to Tuesday ticket & went without the station to discover how she should get to the end of her journey! … [as part of her eventful journey Isobel took a ferry crossing, and the boatman] had just pulled out from shore when a thunderstorm which had been threatening, came on with a good will & as there was a small girl with only a cotton overall[190] in the boat the foolish person of our story gave her coat to the small child in question & got very wet. Im writing this out of doors & the cows are all round me & so to get done quick I shall alter the "stile" of my narrative! Also I cant be responsible for any mistakes in the spelling because it is going to rain again presently & wet weather always upsets my spelling. Well to cut a long story short I walked 7 miles in the rain through the New Forest carrying

---

[187] Clifford Bax, *Inland Far* (London, Heinemann, 1925), 228.

[188] Britten Pears Arts HOL/5/2/29 Transcript of Imogen Holst replying to questions by John Morrison, recorded 19–20 April 1980.

[189] Alan Gibbs, *Holst Among Friends* (Thames Publishing, London, 2000), 144.

[190] Perhaps reminding Isobel of Imogen, whom she had left behind and was about 6 at the time.

my bag all the time! ... altho tired & wet as I was I could not help constantly[191] admiring its beauty ... When we arrived I knocked at the door & no one came so I turned the handle & walked in. Not a soul was in the place – I looked round for clothes likely to belong to anyone I knew & saw nothing! ... The first thing I saw was my letter to Milly[192] among a lot of other unopened letters on the mantelpiece so I then understood why I had not been met – no one knew anything about my coming. It turned out that Milly had gone into Southampton on Tuesday intending to return on Wed & so they had not sent on her letters. Joyce didnt know that Milly had invited me & so altho she saw there was a letter from me she didnt think it mattered. ... Joyce & Alice did not come in until about 8 p.m. ... & were very concerned about me etc & both went for Milly hammer & tongs. Milly is really the most casual person I know she goes of for days & never says a word to anyone. Her father who is staying at the farm opposite says she is the maddest of a mad family – He says she comes up to him one day & says "Oh father Im going to Canada tomorrow for about a year – send on my letters will you! ...

I have lots more to tell you when I return & I think you may rely on having a very pleasant & contented person to live with when I come back – even at breakfast time!!

Give my best love to my family & tell them Im longing to come back
Ever & Ever Yours
Isobel.[193]

Isobel added a postscript to her letter to Vally saying that perhaps she would "believe how strong I am now – I'm none the worse for it all!"

During the summer of 1913 the von Holsts moved the few miles from Barnes to 10 Luxemburg Gardens, Brook Green. The move took them away from the damp of the River Thames which affected Gustav's health and was conveniently just round the corner from St Paul's Girls' School (SPGS). It was there that, also in the summer of 1913, the new music wing opened, including a sound-proof room built specially for Gustav and where he subsequently frequently spent his Sundays and August holidays composing.

Whilst Isobel created and cared for their family home, SPGS, particularly in August, became Gustav's musical one. As the conductor Sir Thomas Armstrong explained many years later in Vally Lasker's funeral address:

He was a man not much inclined to take care of himself, and the school, thanks to Miss Gray's recognition of his genius, gave him a quiet room to work in, a measure of security, good opportunities for the performance of his smaller works, and what we all need – the assurance that his work was not unimportant, not unwanted. He gave them, in return, his vision, his devotion to the ideals of the school, his integrity, his sense of music's place in life.[194]

Isobel and Gustav's London homes were never very long-lasting, and in the winter of 1913–1914 they were, as so often, short of funds. Vaughan Williams lent Gustav £30, which he was able to pay back on 29 March 1914, when he and Isobel were still living at 10 Luxemburg Gardens: "It has saved the situation very effectively and I am sorry I could not return it before."[195] Isobel and Gustav were soon struggling financially again. In June 1914 Balfour Gardiner, Clifford and Arnold Bax and Vaughan Williams clubbed together to start sending

---

[191] Double underlined.

[192] Probably Millicent Lisle Woodforde.

[193] Britten Pears Arts HOL/1/5/3/2 Isobel Holst to Vally Lasker from The School House, Sunday [1913].

[194] Thomas Armstrong, *Vally Lasker*: address given at her funeral service in St. Peter's Church, Kensington Park Road, on 18 April 1978.

[195] BL Add Ms 57953 f 14.

Gustav money in quarterly instalments. Clifford Bax wrote tactfully to Gustav to state that the arrangement would be confidential, and that Vaughan Williams thought:

> … we ought to say that owing to the mutability of all things human the fund might possibly cease or at any rate diminish, although of course there is none of us who means that it should ever do either. But I mention this so that you may see the desirability of using it for extra-ordinary purposes, and not come to depend on it too much. …[196]

The von Holsts could not really afford their own home in London, and they soon had to give up 10 Luxemburg Gardens. That may explain why during the summer of 1914 Isobel stayed for a while with their former near neighbours James Brown and his wife and son Sebastian at Ashford in Middlesex. James Brown was briefly a violin teacher at Morley College who in 1912 had met and begun painting with Lucien Pissarro. In 1914 the Lucien Pissarros, like the Holsts, were under such financial pressure that after 20 years in production their private printing press closed. Brown managed to persuade Isobel to help Mrs Pissarro over the letting of the Pissarros' house to a Belgian refugee by writing to Mrs Vaughan Williams, as Vaughan Williams had "exceptional opportunities of getting into touch with the right people for that purpose".[197] Isobel's stay resulted in another serene oil portrait of her by Brown, signed with his painting pseudonym of Prior Conway and dated 1914. Brown also painted a small watercolour of Imogen and his son Sebastian Brown together at Ashford in August 1914[198] and sketched Isobel on a number of occasions, including when she was embroidering or darning in 1916.[199] These portraits capture her enduring beauty at the time, and suggest the close relationship between Isobel and the Brown family. Eighty years later Sebastian recalled that his mother and Isobel "got on very well", and remembered "the two of them playing tennis and weighing themselves every day", whilst his father and Gustav had been "friendly at first, then they fell out."[200]

The Pissarro connection was to have an even greater impact on the von Holst family. Whilst on a solitary walking holiday in Essex in the 1913 Christmas holidays Gustav had discovered the peace and quiet he craved at Thaxted in Essex. When an isolated 17th-century cottage at Monk Street, at the top of a hill two miles south of Thaxted, became available for rent from Mrs Pissarro's brother, the prolific writer S. L. Bensusan[201] in 1914, Gustav and Isobel went to see it together. Despite arriving at the cottage during a rainstorm, and the fact that water had to be drawn from an outside hand-pump, they decided straight away to rent

---

[196] Britten Pears Arts HOL/1/5/2/5 Letter from Clifford Bax to Gustav Holst, 18 June 1914.

[197] Ashmolean Museum Oxford Print Collection Letter from John Brown to Mrs Lucien Pissarro [3 October 1914]. I am most grateful to Roland Goslett for information about James Brown, including copies of his notes of his conversations with James Brown's son Sebastian in 1987.

[198] I am grateful for permission to photograph and publish the image of the portrait of Isobel, which is privately owned. I have been unable to trace the watercolour of Imogen and Sebastian, which was listed in *Three on Holiday at Rye 1913: A Group of Post Impressionists*, Catalogue with an Introduction by Malcolm Eastman, No 57.

[199] A photocopy of this sketch, "Isobel, contre jour P. C onway 1916" is at Britten Pears Arts HOL/4/3/1/10.

[200] Britten Pears Arts HOL/4/3/1/10 Correspondence re Brown HL's notes on Sebastian Brown's conversation with RS 19 January 1994.

[201] Bensusan was the ghost writer for many of the articles published by Daisy Countess of Warwick: see Sushila Anand, *Daisy: The Life and Loves of the Countess of Warwick* (Piatkus, London, 2008), 182, 209, 231, 273.

it.[202] One factor in their decision might have been that a small branch train line, the Elsenham & Thaxted Light Railway, had opened in spring 1913. Reducing their living costs by moving out of London into a modest and unmodernised cottage would have been another. The cottage also had "a wonderful view across meadows and willow trees to the church spire in the distance."[203] Thaxted and its surrounding area were to be Isobel's home for the next 50 or so years.

The move to Thaxted was a major lifestyle change for Isobel in particular, who unlike Gustav did not need to commute regularly to London and who had grown up in a succession of terraced houses in crowded Victorian London. Despite, or because of, this, Isobel embraced country life wholeheartedly. She never lost her "very slight accent" – "a little London one", which meant that "she spoke a bit carefully".[204] Her daughter Imogen, by contrast, exemplified received pronunciation. Monk Street Cottage, whilst quiet and picturesque and cheaper than living in London, was basic in the extreme, and must have been hard work for Isobel to housekeep. A description of it in 1924, when it needed substantial repairs to make it serviceable for a new and more demanding tenant, described it as:

built of Lath & Plaster with Thatch roof, lighted by means of oil lamps, and heated by ordinary coal fires. The outbuildings comprise:– Lean-to Boarded and corrugated iron coal shed, & boarded and tiled E.C.[205]

As well as lacking electricity and modern sanitary arrangements, water needed to be pumped – something which the whole family took turns at. A family photograph of their "next door neighbours but 3", retired farmer William Yeldham and his wife Ann, show them dressed in simple country clothes, with Mr Yeldham wearing a traditional smock jacket and Mrs Yeldham in her apron and shawl, sitting in front of the unmade Monk Street road.[206] In addition to the first of a succession of dogs, Chum, Isobel was persuaded to buy a goat, Capricorn, in the hope of providing a healthy supply of milk, and it alternated between bleating and escaping to eat the roses which she also tended.[207]

Whilst Isobel redoubled her domestic workload, Gustav added to his own by taking on teaching at a second school in Dulwich.[208] The von Holsts' move to Thaxted was timely as it took the family home away from what was soon to become war-time London. Fear of bombing may have been one of the reasons behind the fact that when Imogen contracted typhoid in 1915, her convalescence at Thaxted during the summer was overseen principally by Jessie and May Beames, daughters of a friend of Gustav's fellow Morley teacher James Brown from

---

[202] Short, *Gustav Holst*, 117–18.

[203] Its precise location is described by Lawrence Barker, *In Search of Mars*, Essex record office blog.co.uk, posted 23 June 2014.

[204] Britten Pears Arts HOL/5/2/23 Partial transcript of RS/Ann Burns née Crittall taped conversation 26 April 1991.

[205] E.C. is an abbreviation for earth closet. Essex Record Office (ERO) D/F 35/8/308 letter dated 22 October 1924. The substantial repairs undertaken in 1924 cost over £45.

[206] Britten Pears Arts HOL/2/11/1/15 Photograph of Mr and Mrs Yeldham with grandchild 1915–16. The Yeldham's son Ernest Herbert Yeldham, who lived in the same cottage at Monk Street, was described as a Willow Merchant after his death in 1932.

[207] Imogen Holst, *Gustav Holst at Thaxted*, First published 1966.

[208] Britten Pears Arts HOL/1/6/4 Gustav Holst engagement diary 1915.

Ashford,[209] rather than by Isobel and Gustav, who visited at weekends.[210] Jessie, the elder daughter, was only about 10 years older than her young charge, but fortunately the arrangement seems to have worked wonderfully well.

Despite the war, August for Gustav meant the freedom to compose without interruption. He wrote from St Paul's Girls' School to Vally Lasker on 22 August 1915:

I suppose a real composer always lives the life I am leading just at present. In which case he is much to be envied. It is 9 pm and I've been at school 12 hrs having a heavenly time getting all my meals and making a hell of a mess generally. How Nora would squirm if she could see my room now. Tell Isobel to let me know if my being here delays you and her coming to town and if so when you propose coming. Otherwise I'll stay on until I dry up which does not seem imminent just now. …[211]

It was also from St Paul's Girls' School that Gustav wrote a combined birthday and thankyou letter to Jessie Beames on 28 August, by which time she had left Thaxted:

Also I want to thank you very heartily and very deeply for all you have done for Imogen. Perhaps it is not so much what you do to her as what you are to her. Anyhow having had you as a friend is one of the best things that could have happened to her and although she knows it now she will realize it more deeply when she gets older.

And I hope that many little children will be as happy in their friends as she has been.[212]

In a newspaper interview towards the end of her life Isobel explained Imogen's childcare arrangements at this time:

… when they needed country air and a place out of London for their young daughter, it seemed natural that they should come to live near Thaxted. They bought a little cottage at Monk Street, now demolished and where the rather delicate child was cared for by a wonderful and devoted country woman while her mother did war work in London.[213]

In 1916 Gustav organised the first of what became a series of Whitsun music festivals at Thaxted, bringing together some of his pupils from Morley College and St Paul's Girls' School. Once again Isobel was in a demanding supportive role. Gustav's penny notebook recorded, as usual, his detailed planning, including asking Isobel about clothes for the musicians – a potentially delicate matter given the differing financial circumstances of Gustav's different groups of pupils, which included factory workers from Thaxted. The solution, possibly suggested by Isobel herself, was that the older girls should wear coloured veils, which Isobel would make in the colour chosen by the wearer for a shilling each, with Vally Lasker taking the money and a few spares being kept in reserve at the vicarage.[214] Contemporary photos show the veils being worn during the weekend, and as the Morley Magazine reported:

---

[209] Several male members of the Beames family also made their living as musicians.
[210] Grogan ed., *Imogen Holst*, 6.
[211] Britten Pears Arts HOL/1/5/1/14.
[212] Private collection. I am grateful to Michael Goatcher for a photocopy of this letter.
[213] Pam Croome interview with Isobel, 1968.
[214] Britten Pears Arts HOL/1/7 Gustav Holst notebook (1916).

On both afternoons, too, Mrs. von Holst entertained the musicians in their hundreds at Monk Street Cottage for tea; driven indoors by the rain they resorted at once to music – Elizabethan love songs, rounds and part-songs accompanied by violins, penny whistles, piano, and even mouth organ![215]

Gustav's Whitsun festivals – a long weekend of music-making and jollity – were one of the highlights of his life, and became an annual event. Thaxted was the venue for the first three years. They brought together several strands of his life, including, through the sustained involvement of his pupil Clare Mackail and her father and William Morris's biographer Professor J. W. Mackail, his early days with the Hammersmith Socialist Society.[216] This could only have been possible with Isobel's practical and hospitable support. Gustav's 1916 part-song *Bring Us In Good Ale* used to remind Imogen of how Isobel came to the rescue for one of Conrad Noel's supposedly bring-and-share Sunday meals at Thaxted vicarage:

I can remember one occasion when a breathless tenor arrived at our home:- would my mother please lend them a loaf and some butter because no-one had brought anything except beer! I always think of it when this carol gets to the verse: "Bring us in good ale and bring us *nothing else*".[217]

The Morley College records are extensive, and show that Isobel supported the music-making there on a number of occasions. In the programme for the concert conducted by her husband on 29 January 1916, for example, when the ranks of Morley's musicians were already depleted by the vicissitudes of war, Isobel is listed both as a second soprano and as one of only two Double Bassists.[218] Her support for Gustav's work at this pioneering college for working men and women was appreciated by a Morleyite, who recorded that:

In June 1916 the Music students turned the tables on Gustav Holst and entertained him and Mrs. Holst to a tea, presented him with a gift of books and Mrs. Holst with a bouquet, following these by a unique and charming selection of songs, choruses, and old orchestral music. The Magazine notes this gathering as a "red letter day" in the history of Morley College.[219]

Vally Lasker was presented with a pair of vases on the same occasion, and the gifts "gave these two ladies pleasant shocks of surprise, and evoked from them graceful words of thanks".[220] Isobel's assistance with the nascent orchestra at St Paul's Girls' School may have been less successful. Nancy Gotch, a pupil there from 1913–1917, recalling her time on the viola desk with Vally Lasker, said of Gustav as their conductor:

We could have played anything if he had willed it so. His fair-haired wife played the double bass and she sometimes argued with him; we listened in silent awe when it happened. It never lasted long.[221]

Nancy's daughter Rosamund Strode later elaborated:

---

[215] *Morley College Magazine* February 1916, pp 10–11.

[216] Both Mackails feature in photographs taken at Thaxted, several of which Clare passed on to Imogen, complete with notes identifying some of the participants. For the 1922 Whitsun Festival, which was held at All Saints' church, Blackheath, Professor Mackail lectured on Greek drama before the bank holiday performance of Holst's *Alcestis choruses*.

[217] Short, *Gustav Holst*, 142.

[218] James Brown, who painted Isobel's portrait in 1914 and who taught violin and orchestral classes at Morley from 1915–16, was the Leader.

[219] I am most grateful to Elaine Andrews, Learning Resources Centre Manager at Morley College, for this reference in addition to her extensive help in accessing the Morley College archives.

[220] *Morley College Magazine* June 1916.

[221] Quoted in Short, *Gustav Holst*, 107.

… my mother told me that they got very embarrassed because she used to argue across at Gustav – and he'd say 'you're behind' – in the double bass – and she'd say 'I'm not' And that was very embarrassing for the girls, so she can't have been terribly good – but prepared to have a go.[222]

For the Morley concert on 1 June 1918, which Gustav conducted, Isobel was the principal double bass. By that stage in WWI male orchestral players were in short supply, but other members of the orchestra roped in by Gustav included the outstanding French horn player of his generation Adolf Borsdorf. Aside from supporting her husband in music-making at Morley and St Paul's Girls' School, did Isobel mind her often rather solitary existence? One of her few surviving letters to Vally Lasker, written in 1916 from the Monk Street cottage, gives insights into her attitude to socialising as well as to her relationship with Vally.

Dear Vally.
    Lo, your time of peace & quietness draweth to a close!
    For behold, before another week passeth thy house shall be invaded by thine enemy etc. etc. Don't mind me, I've just come back from Church!
    I suppose you've heard from Gustav that we are returning on Thursday[223] by the 11 something. Ive already got the keys in my purse so that is all right but as it is early closing day in London would you be so kind as to get some bread for us. Not a modest 2d loaf but two fat Christian loaves of a good size! We will bring butter & eggs with us & in the afternoon I can go to Kensington & get something for supper. Whitwell[224] wont have Chum[225] again as he wont let people come in the shop, which is not exactly good for trade! We are bringing him up to town & May wants to mind him until the Spring. … Did you hear or see anything of the raid last night? A zepp. was brought down in flames 6 miles from Chelmsford & everybody has been by today to see the remains.[226]
    I must confess these raids are getting on my nerves a bit. Somehow I felt there was going to be a raid last night. We three were all out in the garden taking turns at the pump about 10.p.m. & it was such a perfect raid night, so still & cloudy, I thought it would be strange if we did not have one. After laying awake half the night it is a great comfort to wake up in the morning & realize that one is still alive! But perhaps this does not appeal to you? In the words of the Irishman I suppose you'd like to wake up & find yourself dead!!
    However this is a digression. I suppose you've heard from Gustav that Balfour[227] was so "fetched" by my "delightful" letter that he altered his plans for leave & asked if he could come here for the 30th! I promptly wrote back & told I'd see him further first! Those may not have been my exact words, but anyhow he isn't coming.
    He wants Gustav to go to Ashampstead[228] instead & he is trying to get Arnold[229] & Fred as well. I wrote to Mrs Simmons & told her that I dont play the piano or the cello, neither do I make music in

---

[222] Britten Pears Arts HOL/5/2/15 Full transcript of RS/Barbara Simcoe's taped conversation 16 July 1988.

[223] The letter is dated "Sunday night".

[224] The Thaxted grocer.

[225] Their dog.

[226] See Paul Rusiecki, *The Impact of Catastrophe: The people of Essex and the First World War (1914–1920)* (Essex Record Office, Chelmsford, 2008), 148–9.

[227] Balfour Gardiner, who according to Gustav's diary had already been due to visit Thaxted on 31 October 1915.

[228] Balfour Gardiner's country home.

[229] The composer Arnold Bax, who was also an excellent pianist.

any way whatsoever, & I told her the sweep was coming[230] & I asked her not to come & see me & in spite of all this she sent over a pressing invitation for me to come over in the afternoon today & stay to dinner & meet her husband! I didnt go, but I wrote a polite little note full of lies & gave it & four pieces of cake to the four children who brought the note & then I had some tea & went to church. I am now dutifully writing you the last of the long series of long letters that I write you when I am absent from your presence & which will naturally cease when I dwell under your roof! I am very tired owing to my zepp. night & Im sure all the words are wrongly spelt but never mind. Thank you for the green silk which was a beautiful match but you only put a 1d stamp on & as one only gets 1 oz for a penny now, one cant send parcels with a P stamp!

Imogen got a little cold driving to Dunmow the other day but she is better now. There is no more news. Life for the next few days will be an awful rush. I'm making Xmas pudding & mincemeat tomorrow, & Ive already started packing. I suppose you are all "makeyousicking" at Chatsworth road[231] tonight? No offense!

I mustn't say 'yours ever' to you I suppose, so I will only put
Isobel Holst[232]

Isobel's signature on this letter is noteworthy as the "von" in her marital surname is missing. Gustav was to drop it formally by deed poll on 18 September 1918 as its Germanic connotations were thought to be a hindrance to his proposed war-related work with the YMCA Education Department. Her reluctance to entertain Gustav's wealthy friend and patron Balfour Gardiner at Thaxted at that time may have been in part due to consciousness of the contrast between his homes and her own humble living conditions, as well as to her withdrawal from active music-making as her husband's fame grew. Despite this, Balfour Gardiner visited the Holsts' various homes in Thaxted over the years, and Isobel in turn dined with Balfour, on one occasion giving him advice about alterations and decorations to his cottage.[233]

During 1917 the air raids over London and the South East intensified. Gustav's diary entries mentioned several occasions when his Morley classes were disrupted or even cancelled.[234] After Easter 1917 10-year-old Imogen started boarding school at Eothen, near Caterham in Surrey. On 13 July she wrote from school to her father after another air raid:

We did not hear much of the raid, but what worried me was that mother could not come. But she is coming on Sunday to make up for it. Jane, the now Miss Joseph, said that she was coming to Thaxted, and Jessie wrote and told me that she was coming to stay with us for a fortnight if she could. … I am inclosing a letter to Vally, will you give it to her please.[235]

Imogen's letter shows the extent to which the family's home and musical life were intertwined. Gustav's former pupil Jane Joseph was now a teacher at Imogen's school, where Imogen would have had to address her as "Miss Joseph" whilst knowing that she was a welcome visitor at home, as was Vally Lasker. It also provides evidence of the enduring presence in her young life of Jessie Beames, whose elder brother had been killed in action in

---

[230] The reference to the sweep should have been true, as an earlier part of the letter refers to trying to get the sweep to come to Monk Street from Thaxted town.
[231] Vally Lasker's address at that time was 77 Chatsworth Road, Brondesbury, north west London.
[232] Britten Pears Arts HOL/1/5/3/2.
[233] Stephen Lloyd, *H. Balfour Gardiner* (Cambridge University Press, 1984), 121, 123, 157, 158, 188.
[234] Gustav Holst diary entries for 24 September, 25 September (no class) and 1 October 1917 "harmony class no choir".
[235] Britten Pears Arts HOL/1/5/2/23/1 Letter from Imogen Holst to Gustav Holst 13 July 1917.

France in February 1917. 1917 was a year of change for the von Holst family too, as a pay increase for Gustav's teaching at St Paul's Girls' School[236] meant they were able to move from the remote Monk Street Cottage to "The Steps" in the centre of Thaxted, which was to be their home until 1925.

---

[236] Britten Pears Arts HOL/1/5/2/20 Letter from F. R Gray to Gustav Holst. His fee for the orchestra increased to 15 guineas and his fee for each of the seven singing divisions to seven guineas a term.

Isobel and Nora Day outside the music room of Monk Street Cottage
(Britten Pears Arts HOL/2/11/14/3)

Isobel and Gustav with Vally Lasker's family in Thaxted (Holst Victorian House)

Chapter Five
War Work and the Planets Suite

Isobel in the uniform of the Women's Reserve Ambulance (Britten Pears Arts HOL/2/15/3)

Isobel swung into action from the start of the Great War, at a time when, as the High Mistress of St Paul's Girls' School, Frances Gray, was later to write, "the first thought in every mind was, What can I do to help?". For Isobel, as the cash-strapped mother of a seven-year-old child, the answer was in using her dress-making skills to cut countless Red Cross shirts to the authorised pattern for volunteer pupils to sew up during their school summer holidays. Frances Gray's account of the early years of her school is unusual in paying tribute to both Gustav – on the teaching staff and a good friend – and Isobel Holst:

On 13th August [1914] several members of the Staff met and discussed plans. Owing to the admirable organisation at St James's Palace we were already provided with patterns and directions, and a large quantity of work was prepared. Next day, in response to a circular-letter, about seventy girls appeared: I believe all who were in London at the time … We were all anxious to do our best, but I think no one would think it unfair if I mentioned the labours of Miss Noakes who, from the first, undertook to send prepared work to girls at a distance if they asked for it, of Miss Lynch who created our Red Cross Organisation, and of Mrs Holst whose perfect art of cutting out shirts must have ministered to the comfort of many a nurse as well as of many a patient. I find in an early Paulina mention of some of our results. As time went on we ceased to chronicle numbers and amounts: it seemed the natural thing to do all we could and quite unnecessary to record our doings.[237]

As time went on Isobel, whose brief time in the Hammersmith Socialist Society had given her experience of participation on an equal footing to men, was keen to volunteer for a more active

---

[237] Saint Paul's Girls' School Book (Published by St. Paul's Girls' School, London, 1925), 14.

role. The use of motorised ambulances in WWI, and of women to drive them, were both novelties, and the latter was controversial. The bravery of the volunteers on duty with the Women's Reserve Ambulance in responding to London's first zeppelin attack in September 1915 helped the cause of those women who were keen to participate by deeds not words, although criticisms of women either taking away work from men, or of enjoying themselves (or both) endured. The American suffragist journalist Mabel Potter Daggett catalogued some of the volunteers' duties:

Stick-at-nothings, the London newspapers have nicknamed the women's Reserve Ambulance Corps of 400 women who wear a khaki uniform with a green cross armlet. … They are making beds and waiting on table, these young women, who, many of them, in stately English homes have all their lives been served by butlers and footmen. I saw a Green Cross girl at the military headquarters of the corps in Piccadilly making to Commandant Mabel Beatty her report of another phase of war work. She was such a young thing, I should say perhaps eighteen, and delicately bred. I know I noticed the slender aristocratic hand that she lifted to her hat in salute to her superior officer: "I have," she said, "this morning burned three amputated arms, two legs and a section of a jaw bone. And I have carried my end of five heavy coffins to the dead wagon." That's all in her day's work. She's a hospital orderly. And it's one of the things an orderly is for, to dispose of the byproducts of a great war hospital.

See also, these ambulances that bring the wounded from Charing Cross. They are "manned" by a woman outside as well as the nurse within. There is a girl at the wheel in the driver's seat. The Motor Transport Section of the Green Cross Society accomplishes an average weekly mileage of 2,000 miles transporting wounded and munitions. Like this they respond for any service to which the exigencies of war may call. There was the time of the first serious Zeppelin raid on London, when amid the crash of falling bombs and the horror of fire flaming suddenly in the darkness, the shrieks of the maimed and dying filled the night with terror and the populace seemed to stand frozen to inaction at the scene about them. Right up to the centre of the worst carnage rolled a Green Cross ambulance, from which leaped out eight khaki-clad women. They were, mind you, women of the carefully sheltered class, who sit in dinner-gowns under soft candlelight in beautifully appointed English houses. And they never before in all their lives had witnessed an evil sight. But they set to work promptly by the side of the police to pick up the dead and the dying, putting the highway to order as calmly as they might have gone about adjusting the curtains and the pillows to set a drawing-room to rights. "Thanks," said the police, when some time later an ambulance arrived from the nearest headquarters, "the ladies have done this job." Since then the Women's Reserve Ambulance Corps is officially attached to the "D" Division of the Metropolitan Police for air-raid relief.[238]

It was probably in 1917, with Imogen safely away from London at boarding school, that Isobel was able to join these independent-spirited women and work for the Green Cross as a part-time driver in the Women's Reserve Ambulance. Although the Green Cross included aristocratic and wealthy volunteers, Isobel joined as a Private – the lowest rank in British army hierarchy – with her service number 592 in the B company. Gustav's diaries for 1917 and 1918 include a Mayfair telephone number for her which Imogen assumed was the Green Cross office.[239]

Whilst Isobel was fully occupied in the war effort, to his great disappointment, Gustav felt he was failing to play his part. Imogen described this time in their lives:

The war was in its third year, and he could do nothing about it except encourage Morleyites to sing parodies of grand opera in the underground stations during the worst of the air raids. Again and again

---

[238] Mabel Potter Daggett, *Women Wanted: the story written in blood red letters on the horizon of the Great World War* (George H. Doran, New York, 1918).

[239] Note by Imogen on GH's 1917 diary.

he had applied for [war] work, but he was always rejected. His uselessness filled him with despair when he thought of his brother Emil who had left the New York stage to join the army, and of his wife who was driving lorry-loads of wounded soldiers to hospital, and of Vaughan Williams who was fighting in France, and of Cecil Coles and Edward Mason and George Butterworth and the others who had died.[240]

In September 1917 the music teacher and artist James Brown and his family moved to Dunstable House, Sheen Road, Richmond. The house was a large one, with space for musical soirées and art exhibitions as well as lodgers, who included Isobel as well as some of James's music pupils. James Brown's son Sebastian many years later recalled Isobel making and selling things such as candlesticks and ashtrays, and painting plain pottery,[241] and staying there whilst Gustav was in Salonika.[242] It would have been convenient, if Isobel's Green Cross ambulance duties involved delivering patients to the newly-opened Royal Star and Garter Home in Richmond as well as the Richmond Red Cross hospital on Richmond Green.

Given Isobel's early involvement in the Hammersmith Socialist Society it also seems particularly important to note here that on 6 February 1918 the Representation of the People Act was passed. Although there is no evidence that Isobel maintained active participation in party political activity, as a woman over 30 this Act granted her the right to vote in general elections.[243] Isobel, alongside her husband, registered to do so at the first opportunity.[244]

Living at "The Steps" in the centre of Thaxted and close to the church enabled the Holsts to participate in community activities more easily. Barbara Simcoe, daughter of Isobel's great friend Ethel Simcoe, recalled that when living at The Steps "they always had the carol singers in after midnight Mass, and of course some people, country people, rather stayed too long." Gustav's technique of encouraging them to leave was "saying very quietly 'Before you go I do wish you'd sign our Visitors' Book'."[245] Isobel played the cello – the photograph of the music room at The Steps shows it propped in a corner. According to Barbara Simcoe:

She was very good at upholstery and needlework – and gardens. And of course when they were at The Steps I remember they had Adams, the houseman, he would drive as well, and he was a good cook, and he used to do the table and all that sort of thing.[246]

The programme for Gustav's Morley students' summer concert on 1 June 1918 listed Isobel as "Isabel von Holst". This is the last recorded occasion on which she used the "von" before Gustav changed his German-sounding name to improve his acceptability for his own war service by deed poll dated 18 September 1918. It was not until the summer of 1918 that Gustav was accepted for war service, apart from "in Holland and some other countries". In two letters Percy Scholes, editor of *The Music Student* and Organising Secretary of the YMCA Universities Committee Music Section, paid tribute not only to Gustav's willingness to serve under difficult conditions, but also to Isobel's willingness to support him in going:

---

[240] I. Holst, *Gustav Holst*, 51–52.

[241] Britten Pears Arts HOL/4/3/1/10 Note of information from Sebastian Brown.

[242] Information from Roland Goslett.

[243] Although the Act greatly expanded the right of women to vote there was still a property qualification. By contrast, Isobel's brother Harry was enrolled on electoral registers as early as 1912.

[244] ERO C/E 2/81 1918 Electoral Register for Saffron Walden (Parish of Thaxted).

[245] Britten Pears Arts HOL/5/2/6 Full transcript of RS/Barbara Simcoe's taped conversations 6 November 1985.

[246] Britten Pears Arts HOL/5/2/6 Full transcript of RS/Barbara Simcoe's taped conversations 6 November 1985.

As you know I am most anxious to have your help in the big Musical task we have undertaken. Will you, therefore, let me know whether you would be prepared to go to one of the fields of war if required?

I think it quite possible that I could find you a splendid sphere of work in Salonica or in Mesopotamia. I know it is a big thing to suggest to a man with a wife and child, but there is no harm in asking your views. I have had a man here to-day from Salonica and the need there is very great. I have also had a suggestion this week that I should go to Mesopotamia myself, which is, unfortunately, impossible. Please think this over and let me know your mind.

In closing this letter I just want to say how much I appreciate the fact that your wife is evidently willing to make the sacrifice of letting you take up work of this character.

Percy Scholes ended a further letter five days later with his "kindest regards, and again admiration for the way in which your wife and yourself look at this opportunity of service."[247]

Before Gustav left for his tour of duty, Balfour Gardiner gave him the exceptionally generous gift of a private performance of *The Planets Suite* at The Queen's Hall in London, which at the time was one of London's largest concert halls, with a seating capacity of 2,500. The concert was conducted by the young Adrian Boult and took place on Sunday 29 September, and the first orchestral performance of Gustav's hugely innovative composition was an outstanding success. Isobel, accompanied by 11-year-old Imogen, was of course present, and it was with them that Gustav, who at this stage of his career was not used to ovations and always detested gush, escaped from his enthusiastic admirers after the performance to meet up with the vicar of Thaxted, Conrad Noel, in a basement tea-shop nearby.[248]

Most of Gustav's long letters to his wife were written during his mission with the YMCA at the end of WWI. As none of Isobel's letters to him appear to have survived, this correspondence provides one-sided insights into their relationship. It starts at the very beginning of his mission with a postcard dated 1 November [1918] whilst *en route* in France:

Your packing was absolutely perfect – I keep on discovering fresh treasures each time I look into my haversack – bless you for it and all else …[249]

Writing home was not easy for much of his mission. The first postcard mentions that it was written "on my knee in the streets of a certain port", adding "All I can tell you about the latter is that the ladies' heels are from 6 to 12 inches high". Nevertheless, Gustav wrote to Isobel frequently at the various stopping points on his journey, with further surviving postcards dated 6 and 10 November. He started his first very long letter to his wife in a tiny port in Italy on the evening of Armistice Day, 11 November 1918, completing it the following day. At the end of the letter he explains the context in which most of his remaining war service letters should be read:

Boult suggested that, if you approve, I should write long letters to you the first sheet of which should be private and the rest you should send round to friends. There is nothing private in this letter but owing to interruptions it is a bit scattered.[250]

Gustav's next letter to Isobel two days later dealt mostly with business, starting with an abrupt request to "Get Adrian Boult's address and give him this letter. You will see how important

---

[247] Mitchell, *Comprehensive Biography*, 159–61.
[248] Short, *Gustav Holst*, 162.
[249] Britten Pears Arts HOL 1/5/1/8/6 Postcard from Gustav to Isobel Holst 1 November 1918.
[250] Britten Pears Arts HOL 1/5/1/8/9 Letter from Gustav to Isobel Holst 10–12 November 1918.

it is."²⁵¹ His next letter was much longer and chattier, written over two days on 19 and 20 November and describing his difficult voyage from Italy which had started the day after he last wrote. Gustav was conscious of being out of touch with accurate and up-to-date news of the momentous events taking place at the end of the war, and the last page of his letter includes a typical plea:

And I am pining for home news. I do hope I shall get piles of letters from you and others when I reach Piccadilly Circus. My last letter was one to you enclosing a long one to Adrian Boult. This one is not meant to be private. Probably I'll write the latter sort before I leave here. Also I must write 'shop' to Vally and Terry.²⁵² I wrote 'shop' to Nora²⁵³ about a fortnight ago.

I suppose the flue is better in London. About here it is a thousand times worse – it is really a plague. Tell Muriel I gave her jacket – along with most of your chocolate and three tins of condensed milk – to a starving Serbian family in Galipoli.²⁵⁴

One of Isobel's tasks at this time was in sharing information about Gustav's activities whilst overseas to his friends and colleagues at home. As he explained in a letter to Vally Lasker on 21 November 1918:

If any unexpected thing happens – say with regard to any MSS being wanted for performance – try and arrange details without waiting to hear from me. We are on the borders of civilisation and it is only by luck that letters get through … I am a little anxious for you and Isobel with regard to last Monday's Full Moon … I have sent a complete chronicle of my doings to Isobel so you will not need to have them told over again.²⁵⁵

Gustav's communications with Isobel could on occasion be "shoppy" themselves, perhaps due to a combination of the arduous circumstances of his travels combined with the difficulties which he often experienced with his handwriting as a result of his neuritis. To a postcard of Corfu sent the following week "an hour or so" before his boat was due to leave he appended the message:

Have you sold the piano?
"   "   " bicycle?
Hurry up about the piano.²⁵⁶

Gustav wrote two private letters to Isobel the following week, having arrived safely at the YMCA in Salonica. The first, dated 4 December, was marked private and headed Letter 1, with the injunction "From henceforth let us number our letters to each other":

Dearest Isobel
We arrived here last Sunday morning Dec 1 and had a rather depressing welcome or rather absence of welcome which was due to circumstances and was no one's fault in particular. But we had not had our clothes off for four days and nights and therefore felt rather bewildered. As this is not a 'public' letter I will leave out all description of the journey and here – that shall come later.

---

²⁵¹Britten Pears Arts HOL 1/5/1/8/10 Letter from Gustav to Isobel Holst 14 November 1918.

²⁵² Dr Richard Terry, choir director at Westminster Cathedral, who was deputising for Gustav at Morley College.

²⁵³ Nora Day, who with Vally Lasker and Jane Joseph was one of Gustav's most important "scribes".

²⁵⁴ Britten Pears Arts HOL 1/5/1/8/11 Letter from Gustav to Isobel Holst 19–20 November 1918.

²⁵⁵ Britten Pears Arts HOL/1/5/1/14/7 Letter from Gustav Holst to Vally Lasker 21 November 1918.

²⁵⁶ Britten Pears Arts HOL 1/5/1/8 Postcard dated Nov 27 [1918].

Another blow on Sunday was that there was no letter from you. There were two nice long ones from Mabel Jones[257] and Vally and three nice short ones from Ruthven, Melita and Betty Simon but of course that was not the same thing.

However yesterday I got your splendid long letter and it did do me good. It was a case of a long hunger being satisfied completely with a right good feast and bless you a thousand times for it! You ask me what I want. The chief things I want are a multitude of long letters from you. The next thing I want is ditto from everyone else.

I've got the soldier's intense eagerness for news from home badly! After that there is a big drop in wants. Food is excellent – the good ordinary YM sort. I've got a big pair of officers' boots today – my present boots will take a week to dry.

Dulcie's[258] leather stockings have simply saved me.

Want no III – I can do with another pair.

The mud here is beyond belief. After today we abandon cleaning our boots and shall oil them until the spring.

I feel inclined to ask you to send out one of my pairs of boots, first putting on rubber soles. We'll call this Want no IV[259] send them at once. Letter writing will be difficult for the next fortnight. Will you ask all to forgive me if I delay? The work promises well but to start it thoroughly will take up all my time.

Vera Woolcombe owes you 25/-. Would you get it from her?

I think I wrote to you about finance from Italy.

Pay Nina[260] £10 or £15 on Feb 1 and on Aug 1 if you can – not otherwise.

So glad about Pauls.

The next point in your letter is wants. I've already given four.

Want V is warm socks. I'm warm at night in bed. Otherwise one is warm when walking except when you step in a deep hole in the road at night and fall into 4 inches of mud!

I've really got enough socks but probably by Jan I could do with more.

Want no VI is music – see separate list. Perhaps Nora or Vally would see to it. Tell them I will write when I can.

For the rest of your letter I can only bless and thank you. Perhaps I shall be able to answer it later. Meanwhile write some more! BL DD G[261]

He wrote again the next day, for the first time writing on the YMCA headed paper "On Active Service with the British Expeditionary Force."

Dear Isobel

In my letter yesterday I never thought of Xmas. And today is the last day for mails.

So a very very happy and peaceful one to both my fair Eyes[262] with many blessings on them and may they enable me to continue to look on the world through them with all the joy they have brought me in the past which is rather a selfish way of putting it but there are times when one does feel for oneself as it occurred to me the other night when our troop train ran into a Greek one and none of us were injured so we got breakfast then and there while the man responsible for the event was placed under arrest and I'll tell you all about it some day but just now I almost think it is time to add a full

---

[257] Mabel Rodwell Jones, one of Gustav's fellow teachers at James Allen's Girls' School (JAGS) who played in the Morley orchestra.

[258] Dulcie Nutting, one of Gustav's former pupils at JAGS and subsequently a Morleyite.

[259] "but if it's a bother don't send them. But if you do" words crossed out.

[260] Gustav's aunt, who he arranged to take over music classes at Morley College on a number of occasions.

[261] Britten Pears Arts HOL 1/5/1/8/13 Letter from Gustav to Isobel Holst 4 December 1918.

[262] ie Isobel and Imogen.

stop because I've lost my way in this sentence almost as completely as I did in the rain on Monday night when I fell down between GH2 and home three times and have not got my coat clean yet but it doesn't matter because I've borrowed one and anyhow my new boots are splendid and the sun is shining and peace is coming and also a happy New Year to all and so all I says is why worry because we are all coming home some day and until then Best Love and now for a

.

     BL

          G[263]

On Christmas day itself Isobel and 11-year-old Imogen were in Thaxted Church as usual, together with their friend Jessie Beames. Gustav wrote to Imogen: "I am thinking of you and Mother … and thinking of you like this makes me almost as happy as if I were with you."[264]

    A letter from Gustav to Isobel from Salonica on 29 December 1918 illustrates her role in dealing with music publishers during his time abroad:

I have just heard from Vally of your illness. It's good to know you are on the mend but do be extra careful until next April. I'll let you know when you can sleep in a damp bed without risk but it won't be yet! I do hope you were able to have a good Thaxted Xmas with good health and lots of fun.
Augener's wish to publish the 'Dancing Day' and have sent this cheque of £5.5. It can only be paid into our account at Hammersmith … Let Augeners (18 Grt Marlborough St) know if it is not in this letter.

    I cannot agree to certain conditions they have laid down and so I have altered the agreement form they sent me and have returned it. If they don't like the alterations they will send you the form in which case send them the cheque. Keep it a week after it arrives in order to see what they do.

    … if the money holds out well I have a great scheme – on my return I would like to have so many months at home writing Parsifal[265] as I wrote Savitri[266] after Algeria. This is only a dream at present.

    About going back to the old work, or getting 'something better' I am sceptical about the latter. You see, my old work was very jolly. There was a fearful lot of it, but it was the real thing – real people to teach and real music to give them and no 'palaver'. Now the only 'better' thing I can conceive is something to do with committees, education schemes, co-ordination. In other words, talking about a thing instead of doing it. It may be necessary – I fear it is – but I don't feel it is my job whereas teaching a kindergarten or Thaxted choir is. I believe you thought I was going to get away from teaching atmosphere. I've been in it worse than ever from the day we left! My only consolation is dear old Bagnall who has been a slum school headmaster for 30 years and who therefore knows that the moment one ceases to think of human beings and dwells mentally amid schemes and systems one is just damned as a teacher.

    This is a bit mixed but I cannot take you behind the scenes until I get home.

    All I mean is that I'm not so keen on a big education job and I don't see that I should be offered any other sort of 'something better'. However we'll 'wait and see' …

He wrote a further page on New Year's Eve.

Just read yrs of Dec 16th. I'm so sorry to hear of all yr trouble – poor old dear you have been in the soup this time. And the eye trouble is really very serious because the ill effects last so long. Keep me well posted up with news about you and get Imogen and Vally to do the same.

    Don't worry about getting any work – just concentrate on getting Well and don't imagine you are really so just because you feel all right for a day or two.

---

[263] Britten Pears Arts HOL 1/5/1/8/14 Letter from Gustav to Isobel Holst 5 December 1918.
[264] Britten Pears Arts HOL 2/8/2/104/1.
[265] Gustav Holst's *The Perfect Fool* is based on Parsifal.
[266] Gustav's one act chamber opera.

The news about Imogen is splendid. Bless Her she is a joy for ever as well as a thing of beauty. Of course we don't want her forced into a prodigy but under people like Miss Pye and Miss Shuttleworth I should be quite willing for her to specialize in music even at her present age. So if you care to discuss it do so. I feel that like everything else it is a question of people entirely. She is under the right people and if they think she could be excused certain schoolwork it would be certain to be successful. Mind you settle about the violin. And could she have private theory lessons from Jane?[267] I mean something that would stimulate and guide her creative powers. Jane would do this better than anyone else I know.[268]

A fortnight later Isobel's Christmas parcel to her husband had finally arrived, after nearly two months in transit. Gustav wrote to her on 13 January 1919:

I was very glad to get a photo of Imogen although it really is not very good – it lacks simplicity. One feels this very strongly when it is alongside of the snapshot of you in uniform – the best one you've ever had done. …

I've had lots of letters – Jane Vally Mabel Conrad Jean Alice Hedwig Mrs Wood. I hope next mail will bring one from you.

Sorry this letter is so scrappy. There has not been much I can tell you in a letter. For instance I cannot go into details over my private opinion of the army scheme of education or of a fierce row I am having with a Colonel …[269]

Gustav also wrote a less "scrappy" letter to Vally Lasker on the same day, reflecting on his views on the role of an artist:

Thanks very much for the socks but please don't spend money on me until your oppositions are over!

The Directorship of the RCM is an excellent example of the sort of big job that kills an artist. Parry sacrificed himself to save an awkward situation but I still feel that the sacrifice was too great. I don't mind Allen taking it on but I dread RVW being offered something of the sort. I suppose he would decline. But he would accept if the question of self sacrifice and duty came in as it did with Parry.

The whole matter is too complicated for a letter but I have very definite ideas on it and someday I'll inflict them on you. Briefly, an artist should do creative work and anything that brings him in contact with people's characters and souls – such as teaching. And he should avoid all routine, organisation or questions of mechanical efficiency.

Thank you very much indeed for what you said about the Planets and for what you did NOT say.
…

Finally I've found a really good piano in a camp at which I lectured this afternoon. …[270]

Two days later Gustav wrote in response to a delayed Boxing Day letter from Isobel:

How good it is to get letters! I believe I have said so before! Your packing was a triumph and all the lovely goodies were intact. They are mostly consumed already. Yr Xmas news was splendid especially about the three organists and the Dulwich programme.[271] … You did quite right about the Dulwich

---

[267] Jane Joseph.

[268] Britten Pears Arts HOL 1/5/1/8/17 Letter from Gustav to Isobel Holst 29–31 December 1918. Quoted in part in Imogen Holst, *Gustav Holst 1874–1934: a guide to his centenary* (Cambridge Music Shop, 1974), 19.

[269] Britten Pears Arts HOL 1/5/1/8/19 Letter from Gustav to Isobel Holst 13 January 1919.

[270] Britten Pears Arts HOL 1/5/1/14/10 Letter from Gustav Holst to Vally Lasker 13 January 1919.

[271] On 19 December 1918 the prize-giving programme at James Allen's Girls' School in Dulwich included a carol by Imogen.

cheque. By the bye have you enough money? I have far too much! … It's good to know your eyes are better. Don't get a job – let the house! It will pay you much better … BL old thing G[272]

On 27 January a second Christmas parcel from Isobel arrived. Gustav wrote in thanks having had an initial celebratory session with his YMCA roommate accompanied by tea, biscuits and candlelight:

The first parcel was good but this is superb! I think what made the difference was that the 2nd was all homemade. We've left enough for a second 'do' because I want Bagnall and Smith to sample it[273]

The frequent requests for Isobel to write clearly hit home. On 9 February 1919 Gustav wrote her a private letter:

Don't be always apologising for not writing or not sending interesting news.[274] Your letters are not as numerous as Jane's[275] – nobody else's could be – but you and Imogen are both bricks at writing when you have so little time and you yourself write such long letters which in itself is a joy. When I see your fist I settle down to a good long read and you never disappoint me. And I don't want interesting news – I want just what you always send me. Ordinary details of home life become quite thrilling out here!
    So 'carry on'!
    I ought to have explained more clearly to Vally about letters. I'm glad she sent the Augener[276] letter to you. Apparently she was nearly sending it to me! It is all my fault.
    I've had a very kind and wise letter from Jane about Imogen. I hope you quite understand that I only suggested Imogen specialising if Miss Pye and Miss Shuttleworth really recommend it. I expect it is all right. Little points can be so easily confused when one is 2000 miles away! Still I thought I would mention it. Personally I am delighted that she is learning the violin instead of geometry but I do hope that you and Miss Pye are equally delighted because I should be very sorry if I had unconsciously[277] persuaded you against your judgement.
    I wonder if Imogen will be as big a duffer at languages as her father! Anyhow she must have a good struggle. Each time I go abroad I realise that English and French will take you over Europe if you know them well enough but you must know both.
    I've just re-read your letter and I see that it's all right and that you and Miss Pye are doing what you feel to be right. I won't tear this up but you can ignore all this part. (Jane's letter was a really nice unpretentious one – in fact, Jane at her very best).
    Terry has written a very sweet letter but reading between the lines I wonder whether the Morleyites really do their best to back him up in his difficult position. I suppose 'some does and some doesn't' and one ought not to expect more but I do feel a little disappointed. Of course he does not mention anything beyond that the students remain very loyal to me and perhaps again I am making a fuss about nothing so I'll shut up about it.
    I am sending a parcel containing 3 pairs of socks (notice the remains of Macedonian Mending)[278] the old leather things and a Greek book Jane told the publishers to send me a translation and they sent this! (Parcel will be sent off later by next mail)

---

[272] Britten Pears Arts HOL 1/5/1/8/19 Letter from Gustav to Isobel Holst 15 January [1919].

[273] Britten Pears Arts HOL 1/5/1/8/21 Letter from Gustav to Isobel Holst 27–28 January 1919.

[274] Despite this, a pencil addition at the top of the letter reads "Keep on letting me know how you are."

[275] Jane Joseph.

[276] The music publishers.

[277] The words "forced you" are crossed out here.

[278] Gustav struggled to darn his socks himself in Macedonia, particularly in the absence of wool.

> The rest of the letter will not be quite so private so I'll start again.[279]

A probably incomplete letter from Gustav from Constantinople on 18 February 1919 thanked Isobel for sending him cocoa but added "please don't – I can go into any YMCA in the world and demand any amount. (You and your daughter may send homemade things whenever you like.)" There were yet more references to money and to Isobel not feeling obliged to work – "Nora is a real dear … I do hope she's not overworking. But I feel we may accept the money – Nora is quite well off. I hope you won't take any job."[280]

A long letter a week later referred to another food present which Isobel had sent:

Amongst the first Xmas parcel was a tin marked camphor. I realised what a thoughtful wife I had who could think about summer problems in winter and I kept it (the illusion) up until it (the honey) began to get sticky round the edges! I'm so glad I didn't discover what was inside before because if I had I should not be eating honey now …[281]

On 27 February 1919 the first public performance of five movements of *The Planets* took place at The Queen's Hall in London. Adrian Boult was again the conductor, and sent Gustav a congratulatory telegram whilst Isobel sent a bundle of some of the many press cuttings, neither of which reached him for another four weeks.[282] In March 1919 Isobel had to celebrate her 43rd birthday in Gustav's absence. He wrote a private letter to her on Sunday 2nd:

I have sent off a biscuit tin containing a rug, a thing women wear as an apron (it looks like a small rug) a sheep bell and a heap of picture postcards. Could you spare some of the latter for Miss Clark's girl guides at Dulwich[283] – those I sent them were lost in the post.

The rest of the parcel is 'for loo mummah'[284] with many many happy, peaceful, influenzaless, returns of the DAY with heaps of real love and imaginary kisses from your old man.

I hope these things are your sort. I partly chose them because they all – barring the postcards – were made in Macedonia. All the time I have been wondering whether you could have got them cheaper in London. I gave about £3.10 for the lot. I did the business with great care and preparation. …

I enclose Imogen's letter. I have had three from her – all splendid. The last one ends
PS I simply love the violin.
PSS Monsieur Mangot is topping.
PPSS Theory with Jane is ripping.
Cheerish!
(I wonder which is the greater compliment, topping or ripping.) Jane has told me about the theory lessons which seem a great success. I thought they would be. … I hope Jane will never give her homework. I have suggested to Jane that Imogen should be played to. She doesn't hear much music as I never play. Otherwise I've left it to them both to do as they please. …

I'm writing to Scholes to get his ideas as to the date of my return. … I have suggested finishing here by the end of May. It would be jolly to celebrate June 22[285] together. I've put this as pure

---

[279] Britten Pears Arts HOL/1/5/1/8/22 Letter from Gustav to Isobel Holst 9 February 1919. A further letter was appended, including the postscript "I'm afraid I haven't the time, opportunity or inclination for composition. I discovered that the two essentials for me to write are silence and solitude neither of which I get here. But I want to get something done on my return."
[280] Britten Pears Arts HOL/1/5/1/8/24 Letter from Gustav to Isobel Holst 18 February 1919.
[281] Britten Pears Arts HOL/1/5/1/8/25 Letter from Gustav to Isobel Holst 25–26 February 1919.
[282] Mitchell, *Comprehensive Biography*, 180–181.
[283] Previous letters had referred to postcards which he had sent for the girls at JAGS.
[284] Imogen's baby talk for "For you Mummy".
[285] Their wedding anniversary.

suggestion to Scholes and I wish you would go and see him and make him realise that I am anxious to do all he wants as far as I can – he has been very good to me and I don't want to let him down in any way.

If I got home by June 22 I should have 10 weeks for loafing and composing – ten weeks of earthly paradise.

I had meant to have suggested that you should meet me in Paris and have a week's holiday there in spite of the expense – or else at Rouen.

But I hear that we shall be sent home by military train and that probably you would not be able to go to France unless you had a specific reason. So we'll leave it open. It may be possible.

I wish you'd tell me what sort of work you want me to do when I return. I know I'm groovy[286] but grooviness has one great advantage – at the end of a week's work I can shut myself up and forget everything but composing. Here where the work is not nearly so hard I cannot. But apart from this I really would like to know any ideas you have on the matter.

De Morada the dancer wants to do the Sneezing Charm at the Palladium and Terry wants to do it at Morley.[287] I've asked her if she could wait until I return – she will probably write to you to know when that will be.

Don't take on a job especially a motoring one. Take things easily while you can.

I'm proudanappy[288] to hear Morley is doing me. Ask Terry if Twistleton[289] may sing the solo in the Dancing Day.[290]

And Best Love and, again, many glorious returns of the anniversary of the arrival of the source of much joy to the world in general and to me in particular and won't we have a time on June 22nd I don't think xxxxx Gustav"[291]

Another private letter (opened by the censor) from Gustav (temporarily in Athens) to Isobel dated 12 March 1919 discussed plans for their home life on his return to England as well as telling Isobel his preference for the next big concert of his work:

Yr letter of Feb 18 came just as I was leaving for Athens. I am very sorry you've had a return of the flue[292] and wish you had not to take that car to Reading. The leather case is delightful – thanks very much. But did it cost twopence three farthings or twenty eight shillings and fourpence? …

About 'home' and the 'Steps'.[293] I've no clear idea at all and would far rather leave everything to you.

I long for the feeling of a home!

Also I dream of Thaxted, Ashampstead, SPGS in August[294] (not before!) bicycling to Eothen[295] and some sort of home with you in London. We really ought to have the latter in the autumn. This is the only point I feel clear about. But we need not settle this until later.

---

[286] ie stuck in a groove, or rut.

[287] Gustav wrote the incidental music for a play called *The Sneezing Charm* by Clifford Bax in 1918, but despite the hope expressed in this letter, it was not performed as a ballet.

[288] Intended as a Cockney version of "proud and happy".

[289] Lilian Twiselton, one of Gustav's first and talented students at Morley.

[290] Gustav's part song "This have I done for my true love", which he regarded as his finest. It was written in 1916 for the first Whitsun Festival at Thaxted.

[291] Britten Pears Arts HOL/1/5/1/8/26 Letter from Gustav to Isobel Holst 2 March 1919.

[292] The flu pandemic of 1918–20 resulted in c. 250,000 deaths in the UK alone.

[293] The Holsts' home in Thaxted.

[294] St Paul's Girls' School. The reference to August may mean that GH was particularly looking forward to returning to his sound-proofed composing room there during the school summer holiday.

[295] Imogen's boarding school.

I don't want you to refuse a good 'let' for my sake because it will be so nice to feel the absence of money troubles. And – apart from writing – I can always wrangle a couple of weekends at the vicarage[296] … And as for writing the trouble is that I don't know what place suits it best except SPGS in August.

It may be that Balfour will have to stick in the army for the summer in which case I shall ask him if you and I could spend a fortnight at Ashampstead in July.

I'm afraid all this is not very helpful, so I'll sum up

Let the Steps if you can. If you can't, I should love to go there.

I'd like a strong dose of home life with you anywhere when I get home.

In the autumn, we ought to have something somewhere in London even if it's only a couple of rooms. And the something ought to be independent of friends.

For writing I want silence and solitude. I hope to begin writing after I've had a fortnight seeing people and gallivanting about and settling down.

Thanks so much for Imogen's letters. The valentine just came at the right moment. I had just realised with horror that I was a fond weak parent who could see no wrong in his daughter. And now I know to my relief that she writes valentines in geography lessons! I will return the letters when I write to you about Athens which I will do on my return to Salonica. It is the biggest experience I've had since Bishra![297]

I'm here with Inglis the late YMCA hut leader at GH2 Salonica. He is on his way home and may call on you. Give him your nicest tea in your room if he does. He was very good to me when I arrived in Salonica.

I hope to be in Constantinople by this time next week and shall then know how the Planets went.

…

By the bye Athens has reminded me of Hecuba's Lament (the Trojan Women). If there is any talk of doing a new thing of mine at a big concert do suggest this. Balfour, CKS, etc don't care for it I believe.[298]

An Easter Day appendix to a more descriptive letter of 16 March, designed for wider reading, refers to the fact that Gustav had briefly contemplated prolonging his work in Salonica:

A week ago I was wondering whether it would be possible to stop out here another year in order to get some real work done before I leave. I feel it would be too unfair on Terry[299] and all the other good people who are doing my work. All the same I've not accomplished much yet.

Gustav had now seen the reviews of *The Planets* performance and Isobel was clearly not yet fully recovered. His letter ended:

I'm returning press cuttings etc. Will you ask Mabel to put them in the book? It's all quite nice except that people seem to dislike Saturn which is my favourite.

Oh my dear, DO get well![300]

26 March 1919 was Isobel's 43rd birthday. Gustav wrote to her again:

Many happy returns of the day! I've mentioned this before but it is none the worse for that. I tried to celebrate the event by getting a letter from you but have not succeeded up till now (4.30 PM). This is

---

[296] In Thaxted.
[297] During Gustav's Algerian holiday in 1908.
[298] Britten Pears Arts HOL/1/5/1/8/27 Letter from Gustav to Isobel Holst 12 March 1919. In fact CKS (Charles Kennedy Scott) conducted both the first London performance in 1923 and the first performance with Gustav in attendance, in March 1929.
[299] Richard Terry, deputising at Morley.
[300] Britten Pears Arts HOL/1/5/1/8/28 Letter from Gustav to Isobel Holst March 1919.

not meant as a reflection on you. Neither on the postal authorities – I have no reflections on them that are fit for ladies' society. ... I fear my letter from Athens was a very muddled unsatisfactory one ... I have asked Scholes whether I can leave here about June 1 and should like to be back home by June 22 – naturally![301]

But travelling is so uncertain nowadays – delays in getting permits, delays through absence of ships or blocks on the line etc. By the bye it was a ridiculous idea to suggest your meeting me at Paris. I didn't realise then that ordinary civilian travelling is not allowed – at least I believe it isn't. One lives here in an atmosphere of rumours. ...

I ought to be back by the middle of July at the very latest and then I want to feel at home – to be at home rather.

So it all looks like settling in Thaxted for the summer. In fact I cannot conceive of anything nicer. I shall want to see people in town a good deal – Ralph, Adrian, Balfour etc[302] and must try and wangle a bicycle somehow. Perhaps I shall be allowed[303] to invite them for weekends in Thaxted! Also perhaps people would put me up for a night in town occasionally. As for what we do in the autumn my mind is quite a blank especially after your news of the house famine.[304] It looks as if the 'Steps' will be a white elephant to us. However I'll leave all that to you and time – two aids in the problems of life that do not usually let me down!

If the news of Imogen is the nicest thing I get the news of you is the worst. And the absence of news makes me fidgety. I wish you could have a little of the sunshine here – it is glorious and there is a gentle breeze from the sea that just makes it right.

Poor old dear you've had one thing after another. I'm trying to resist platitudes like 'DO take care of yourself'! But, seriously, can't you really coddle yourself a bit? ... Keep the Bensusans' cheque ...

Oh my dear, I just dread settling down to really hard work in the autumn after all this! I'm supposed to be a hard worker out here but men here either don't know or have forgotten what work means ...[305]

Correspondence was still going astray. On 3 April 1919 Gustav thanked Isobel for her letter of 3 March and for a cable which had got stuck at the Poste Restante. His reply refers to the further restraints of post-war correspondence:

… you tell me of a letter from you I never received – it contained news of the divorce between M and E. It is a horrid business – don't send details as letters are still opened by the censor occasionally.

On a happier note:

Yr news of Imogen – barring the earache – is splendid. In fact the news of her has been the nicest of the many nice things I've had out here. Mangeot[306] must be very good. I also get delightful accounts from Jane who is doing just what I wanted – enlarging her horizon in music without filling her head with 'facts'.[307]

Despite his attachment to Isobel and Imogen, and Isobel's understandable concerns about the family's income whilst Gustav was not being paid for his regular teaching jobs, in early May Gustav wrote from Constantinople to the High Mistress of St Paul's Girls' School to explain

---

[301] ie for their wedding anniversary.
[302] Ralph Vaughan Williams, Adrian Boult and Balfour Gardiner.
[303] By Isobel.
[304] 5,133 acres of the Easton Lodge Estate, including large numbers of properties in Dunmow, Easton and Thaxted, were offered for sale at auction by the Countess of Warwick on 1 July 1919. See the sale catalogue, *The Outlying Portions of the Easton Lodge Estate Essex* (London, 1919).
[305] Britten Pears Arts HOL 1/5/1/8/29 Letter from Gustav to Isobel Holst 26 March 1919.
[306] Imogen's violin teacher.
[307] Britten Pears Arts HOL 1/5/1/8/30 Letter from Gustav to Isobel Holst 3 April 1919.

that the YMCA might ask him to stay on until either Christmas 1919 or spring 1920, which would have meant another year apart from his family. Although he felt that his work at home was more important, his work for the YMCA was pioneering:

> … and it might be that at the end of a year I might lay the foundations for someone else to carry on with. So I have decided to stay on if asked on condition that you are satisfied that the music will not suffer at school. Otherwise I shall come back as soon as possible after next month. I have asked my wife to speak or write to you about it.[308]

Isobel was indeed deputed by Gustav to discuss a possible extension with his employers, including at Morley College.[309] By 31 May 1919, however, GH felt able to write Isobel what he called "a fairy story" – his outline plans for his homecoming. At that stage they were as follows:

Chapter I
I arrive at Southampton at about 3 AM on a Friday morning – the reason being that this is a fairy story. I despatch telegrams to Dunstable House[310] Thaxted and St Paul's (of course the telegraph office being a fairy one is never shut) so as to be sure of your getting one at least.
Chap II
Arrive Waterloo about 8 A.M. and FIND YOU.
Nuf Ced.
Chap III
Breakfast at the Ritz, 103 Talgarth Rd,[311] Dancocks or any similarly convenient spot.
9. AM St Pauls: Play for prayers and upset the school routine as far as possible.
10. AM Leave for Dulwich
11. Arrive at J.A.G.S and upset them.
Chap IV
11.30 Bus to Caterham
12.30 IMOGEN Alarums and Excursions.
1 PM Lunch with My Family – picnic if possible.
2 PM Elope with the abovementioned Family
3 PM Arrive at Oxford Circus
3.5 PM Buy Buns
3.45 Arrive at Bloomsbury Square
3.46 Upset the office
4 Demand tea
4.5 Tea for self and family is provided
4.5 Eat Buns, Drink Tea and Talk Hard.
Chap V
5. to 5.30 Not completed. Probably repitition or developement of 4.-5.
5.30 Take family and luggage to Liverpool Str. (I mean, they will take me).
6.30 Train for Thaxted
Chap VI
8.30 Arrive at Thaxted

---

[308] Mitchell, *Comprehensive Biography*, 187.

[309] Short, *Gustav Holst,* 172–173.

[310] The Browns' house in Richmond, where Isobel had been staying when in London whilst Gustav was away.

[311] Vally Lasker's home in Hammersmith close to St Paul's Girls' School, which she had moved to from north London and where Gustav and Isobel frequently stayed.

8.45 " " The Steps – Mrs Palmer awaits us with resplendent repast
11 or 11.30 or 1 AM or any convenient time
Bed with sheets on it.
Chap VII
7.30 AM to 11. PM Spoilt by my family
Chap VIII
Sunday
7.30 AM to 11. PM Ditto plus a little organ playing and visits
Chap IX
Monday Return My Daughter to Miss Pye with many thanks for the loan.
Disturb the Music Section of the YMCA for the rest of the day.
Tuesday and the 14 following days.
Waste all the spare time and most of the non-spare of all the friends I have.
Then retire to the Steps to get over it all.[312]

Whilst Gustav's plans for his future teaching both in London and for the YMCA remained uncertain he deputed Isobel as an intermediary with three of his employers.[313] Isobel was making her own plans, and Gustav responded to them in a private letter:

I've got yr letter of May 4th telling me about your idea of dressmaking and craftwork at Thaxted. It sounds very promising. Good luck to you and it! I think you are quite right not to have a shop. You will get quite enough work to do without that bother.

    Bless you, I didn't want a place in London because of schoolmarms. I wanted it for Me. I wanted an 'Ome! Somewhere where my missus cooks me a meal and where I can bring in a pal and where I can put my boots on the best droringroom sofa and so on. …

    I'm coming back on leave and going back in Sep if everything can be arranged. I need a rest badly and am longing to be home. …"

He signed off excitedly "Ich brauche Sie mein Honig!! By the bye what's your address? … S.Y.L. no – SYS Lawks – just think of it – S not L".[314]

    Gustav's next surviving letter in the series, dated 13 June, refers to another possible venture by Isobel. It confirmed his initial homecoming arrangements, followed by uncertainty as to where Isobel would be on his arrival:

I got yours of May 21 telling me about your PGs.[315] It's quite a good plan and I hope I shant be in the way! … On arriving in England I'll send wires to you at Richmond Thaxted and St Paul's. On getting to my station … I'll wait 20 minutes after which if nobody appears I'll go to St Pauls. If you are at Thaxted would you leave word at St Pauls as to where I am to go. You see, I don't know whether you are still keeping your Richmond room[316] or not.

    I must have a room to sleep in in London sometimes – RVW, Vally, Jane, Miss Gray[317] etc if Dunstable House is impossible. But I want – oh how I want! – to feel at home with homemade bread with butter on it and so on. …[318]

---

[312] Britten Pears Arts HOL 1/5/1/8/34 Letter from Gustav to Isobel Holst 31 May 1919.

[313] Britten Pears Arts HOL 1/5/1/8/32 Letter from Gustav to Isobel Holst 5 May 1919.

[314] Britten Pears Arts HOL 1/5/1/8/35 Letter from Gustav to Isobel Holst 1 June 1919.

[315] Paying Guests.

[316] At Dunstable House with James Brown and his family.

[317] ie staying with Ralph Vaughan Williams, Vally Lasker, Jane Joseph or Frances Gray, the High Mistress of St Paul's Girls' School.

[318] Britten Pears Arts HOL 1/5/1/8/36 Letter from Gustav to Isobel Holst 13 June 1919.

Despite the strongly affectionate tone of some of these letters to Isobel from abroad, being at home for Gustav did not mean being home *en famille* for long. In a brief note to Isobel written at Constantinople on 16 June Gustav announced that he was sailing for home the next day. "J'ai besoin a vous mon meille!!!" A postscript written on board ship, having discovered that he had neglected to post this note, added that his friend, the composer and teacher W. G. Whittaker, was coming to London in August. As usual he asked Isobel's permission to have a friend to stay: "please may I bring him to Thaxted? And I want to take him a cycling tour if my wife will kindly wangle me a bike." [319] On board ship on 20 June Gustav was still uncertain as to whether or not Isobel was staying in Richmond, so planned to head for St Paul's Girls' School (which as he noted was conveniently on the telephone) if she was not at the station when he arrived:

I wish you could stay the weekend in town however I'll leave all details to you … I'm in terrific form and full of thoughts of you Imogen MS paper and other pleasant things.

"SYS" had become "almost SYN", and he added a teasing postscript "If you don't arrange that I see my daughter within 24 hours of my arrival there will be trouble!!!!"[320]

Gustav's hoped-for wedding day reunion with his wife was not to be. He wrote her one of his most charming personal letters from Italy on 22 June 1919 instead:

Dear Isobel
I got up long before sunrise this morning[321] and have been thinking of you and this day all the time. Many many happy returns of the day my dearest and many many thanks for all you have done for me and for all you have been to me.
It seems quite ridiculous to think that we have been married eighteen years. Also it is quite nice. And it is also nice that it is so ridiculous!
My train starts in a few hours and although I have few hopes of arriving on Saturday it is not impossible. And it ought to be Sunday or Monday at the latest.
Best Love and Best Blessings
Gustav.[322]

Having shopped at the Co-op stores for some embroidery for Isobel before boarding the ship from Constantinople,[323] Gustav finally arrived in London on 28 June, reaching Victoria at 10.30 pm and Vally Lasker's flat at 103 Talgarth Road half an hour later. The next day, a Sunday, he saw his Aunt Nina and half-brother Max in the morning, and Imogen at Caterham in the afternoon. On Monday 30 June he played for morning prayers at St Paul's Girls' School and visited the Royal College of Music and the YMCA. It was not until Monday afternoon that Isobel and Gustav were reunited at Thaxted.[324] A photograph of the Thaxted Peace Day celebrations on 19 July shows tables and chairs set up outside the Holsts' home, amongst others, suggesting that Isobel was one of those helping with the children's tea party.[325]

---

[319] Britten Pears Arts HOL 1/5/1/8/37 Letter from Gustav to Isobel Holst 16 June 1919.
[320] Britten Pears Arts HOL 1/5/1/8/38 Letter from Gustav to Isobel Holst 20 June 1919.
[321] Gustav's diary entry for that day notes "up at 4.20. Walk and bathe and write to Isobel."
[322] Britten Pears Arts HOL 1/5/1/8/39 Letter from Gustav to Isobel Holst 22 June 1919.
[323] Mitchell, *Comprehensive Biography*, 189.
[324] Britten Pears Arts Gustav Holst's diary for 1919.
[325] Photograph and information from Michael Goatcher.

Chapter Six
Fame and its Aftermath

Gustav and Isobel at Ann Arbor, Michigan, 1923 (Holst Victorian House)

On his return from war service in 1919 the regular pattern of Gustav's week was to spend Monday to Wednesday in London and the rest of the week in Thaxted, catching the early train to Liverpool Street Station on Monday mornings to fit in with his teaching commitments.[326] In late 1920 Gustav conducted three public performances of the Jupiter, Venus and Mercury movements from his *Planets Suite*, and invited his and Isobel's long-standing friend Maja Kjöhler to accompany her to one of these performances.[327]

Isobel herself was mostly based in Thaxted and the surrounding area from 1919 until near the end of her life almost 50 years later. Although she repeatedly had ideas for new ventures of her own, unlike her husband's these were typically practical rather than musical. After the early years of their marriage there is no evidence that she tried to help Gustav with scores, and Gustav had no shortage of willing helpers in his fellow teachers and former pupils. We have seen that Isobel was not a natural copyist and enlisting the help of friends meant that Gustav was able to avoid the difficulties of working together as husband and wife. As he wrote to Isobel during his service with the YMCA explaining why, "after severe and continuous cogitation", he had asked his former pupil Jane Joseph to undertake the more

---

[326] *Gustav Holst: Letters to W. G. Whittaker*, ed. Michael Short (Glasgow, 1974), pp 48–49.
[327] Britten Pears Arts HOL 1/5/1/13/10 Letter from Gustav Holst to Maja Kjöhler.

unusual task of writing the libretto for one of his operas, "being my old pupil she won't take offence if I tell her that it won't do."[328]

Gustav's new London base was slow to materialise, whilst his desire for solitude was undiminished. In January 1920 he wrote from Thaxted to the High Mistress of St Paul's Girls' School:

If you have not found a male caretaker for your house who will stay for the whole of the holidays would you accept one who would greatly appreciate the privilege of spending half each week there? Meaning Me.[329]

Despite Gustav's peripatetic lifestyle, which meant that he and Isobel were frequently apart, in an essay published in 1920 Vaughan Williams, perhaps Gustav's closest male friend, felt able to write:

So many artists are conquered by life and its realities. Money-making, marriage, family cares, all the practical things of life are too much for them, and as artists they succumb and the creative impulse shrivels and dies. But to Holst the interests, responsibilities, and realities of life are not a hindrance but a stimulus – they are the very stuff out of which he has knit his art, the soil on which it flourishes. To a foolish friend who once said to him: 'I suppose you did not marry to help your composition', he answered: 'That is exactly what I did do.'[330]

In 1921 Thaxted's notoriety as a hotbed of Christian socialism, led by the Revd Conrad Noel, was at its height, when he displayed the Sein Féin and communist red flags in church. Imogen recalled nearly 60 years later:

In 1921, which was a time of what … the press called … the Battle of the Flags, he had the Sein Fein flag one side and the Russian Red Flag the other side, up on … the chancel … Thaxted was in the news, and … it happened to coincide … with a real heatwave summer … all the wells dried up in Thaxted … It was appalling, the water shortage. We had a sweet factory … And the Thaxted people were employed making sweets … one day Conrad came into our house … and he came in, walked through the door, because he was very friendly with my mother and father – and he said to my father 'Gustav, what do you think? Even the bees are getting converted to Socialism'. My father said 'Really?' And Conrad said 'Yes, look at this' and drew out from under his cassock … a jar of bright red honey. And my mother, I can remember, thought 'this is awful', and sort of shuddered.[331]

In 1921 Gustav's contemporary fame was approaching its height, with frequent requests for performances of his works, including with him conducting. In 1919 *The Hymn of Jesus* became one of Gustav's first major compositions to be published. Its first public performance at The Queen's Hall in March 1920 was an outstanding success, and the first edition soon sold out. After years of struggle Gustav's fame arrived almost overnight. Invitations to conduct, publishers' contracts and some of the earliest gramophone recording contracts followed one after another between 1920 and 1923. Whilst this eased the family's financial fortunes it was

---

[328] Britten Pears Arts HOL/1/5/1/8/18 Fragment of a letter from Gustav to Isobel Holst.
[329] Britten Pears Arts HOL/1/5/1/7/3 Letter from Gustav Holst to Frances R. Gray 26 January.
[330] Ralph Vaughan Williams, 'Gustav Holst: An Essay and a note', in *National Music and other essays*, 2nd ed. (Oxford, 1987), 133.
[331] Britten Pears Arts HOL/5/2/29 Transcript of Imogen Holst replying to questions by John Morrison, recorded 19–20 April 1980. The explanation for the socialist red honey was that because of the water shortage the bees had flown in the sweet factory and taken the sugar from the boiling sweets.

an uncomfortable time for Gustav. Isobel had a busy role trying to make her unphotogenic husband look his best for his many public appearances:

> Whenever he had to conduct one of his works his wife would be careful to see that all was well with his dress suit, which he would insist on calling his 'crepe de chine'. And she would continually remind him to have his hair cut. At the last minute he would rush to a barber's shop in the Hammersmith Broadway, and ask them to take off a fair amount so that he needn't be bothered to come back again for some time. He would then appear on the platform at the Queen's Hall looking like a newly released convict.[332]

Most of the letters written during Gustav's YMCA mission were addressed between Isobel and Gustav, with the latter sometimes signing himself simply as "G". In September 1921, however, when 14-year-old Imogen, having left boarding school at Caversham at Christmas 1920, started in the 5th form of St Paul's Girls' School, she announced to a fellow pupil that she called her father – who was still a teacher there – "Gussie", adding "and I call my mother Iso". Isobel and Gustav still had no London home, which inevitably impacted on family life. Whilst Gustav was busy with his music, Isobel apparently gave her daughter "the impression of being simply disinterested, reinforcing a temperamental barrier between mother and daughter that was to prevent them from ever becoming close."[333]

Imogen was rapidly growing up and the family's lifestyle was changing again. In an undated joint letter from Isobel and Gustav to Vally Lasker written in the early 1920s Isobel wrote:

> Imogen has had a great time & has behaved beautifully all the time & made many conquests. As soon as I get back I must turn my attention to house hunting & will bear in mind your requirements as to spare room, & distance! … I have danced both my pairs of beautiful black stockings into sad holes! … Heaps of love from us all Yours ever & ever I.[334]

Near the start of Imogen's second term at St Paul's Girls' School its long-awaited boarding house, Bute House, opened in February 1922.[335] Imogen was one of its first boarding pupils. The timing was ideal in terms of solving the problem of her childcare whilst the only family home was in Thaxted, but as a teenager Imogen was miserable there. She did not have the usual respite of spending the Easter holidays at home in Thaxted, as she was dispatched to stay with a school friend instead. Activities she otherwise enjoyed at Thaxted were climbing trees, paddling, going on walks and playing tennis.[336] In mid-July 1922 the Holst family at last moved into a London home of their own at 32 Gunterstone Road, Barons Court, a couple of roads away from Vally Lasker's flat in Talgarth Road and similarly convenient for St Paul's Girls' School and thus for both Gustav's teaching and composing and for Imogen as a pupil for her final school years. The Gunterstone Road house was large, and Barbara Simcoe from Thaxted, who stayed there, recalled it having a basement. Lily Harvey, another young girl from Thaxted who had a lovely soprano voice, went with them as their housekeeper.[337] Isobel

---

[332] I. Holst, *Gustav Holst*, 82–83.

[333] Grogan, *Imogen Holst*, 16–18.

[334] Britten Pears Arts HOL/1/5/1/14 Letter from Imogen and Gustav Holst to Vally Lasker.

[335] Howard Bailes, *Once a Paulina* (James & James, London, 2000), 56.

[336] Grogan, *Imogen Holst*, 18, 20.

[337] Britten Pears Arts HOL/5/2/6 Full transcript of RS/Barbara Simcoe's taped conversations 6 November 1985.

had her own ideas for Gunterstone, which apparently included planning to decorate the music room green and gold and the kitchen vermillion – the vivid "Thaxted colours" she favoured.[338] For the next three years, until Imogen left school in 1925, the family had the London home that Gustav had longed for when abroad. Yet as Imogen – who at the time was excited about the decorating plans – wrote in 1972:

> His wife enjoyed having a town house and a country house for the two or three years of their comparative prosperity, but he himself never minded where he lived.[339]

Gustav was once again entering the downward trajectory of his pattern of overwork followed by exhaustion. In autumn 1922 he received two offers from the University of Michigan School of Music – to conduct at its prestigious Annual May Festival in 1923 and, separately, of a professorial position there. The memory of the couple's prolonged separation during Gustav's war service may in part have been what led Gustav to insist on Isobel accompanying him as the condition of his accepting the conducting offer, but he was also conscious that he was once again feeling under pressure. He wrote to his prospective hosts on 7 December 1922:

> I should be delighted to come and conduct the Hymn of Jesus next May if it could be arranged that I and my wife got a good holiday. We have both been overworking for some years and I have been looking for a chance to get a term off."[340]

Isobel, Gustav and Imogen spent a family Christmas together at Thaxted, with Gustav relaxing after his busy term. His post-Christmas thank you letter to his friend Whittaker described how much they were all enjoying the books he had given them, and described the holiday:

> I'm having quite a good time. I'm not even pretending to walk or cycle and am eating and drinking hugely …
>   Last night I was acting in charades – a curate holding a dancing class in a teetotal night club. Conrad Noel was a performing lion.
>   Such is life – in Thaxted at Xmas.[341]

Although Gustav had been offered $1,000 for conducting at the University of Michigan, he wrote politely but bluntly on 11 January 1923 to say that this was not enough:

> I have been told unofficially that when I reach Ann Arbor I may be offered the Professorship to which I have replied that I cannot even consider the offer unless my wife is present with me in Ann Arbor and of course I cannot afford to bring her for the fee you offer. Therefore Dr. Maclean is cabling to suggest that if she is to go I should have another 600 dollars[342] for her expenses. Please excuse me mentioning this matter.[343]

Four subsequent letters from the Holsts' American hosts took pains to refer repeatedly to their delight to be welcoming husband and wife. The fourth letter announced a further increase of the payment, to a total of $2000, and the wish "that you and Mrs. Holst will have the happiest sort of trip to America."[344]

---

[338] Grogan, *Imogen Holst*, 18.

[339] Imogen Holst, *Holst* (Novello short biographies, 1972), 11.

[340] Mitchell, *Comprehensive Biography*, 246.

[341] *Gustav Holst: Letters to W. G. Whittaker*, p 77.

[342] Close to US$10,000 in 2021.

[343] Mitchell, *Comprehensive Biography*, 248.

[344] Mitchell, *Comprehensive Biography*, 249–254.

It was just as well that Gustav had insisted on being accompanied to America by his wife. On 11 February 1923 he fell whilst rehearsing for a concert at University College Reading. At the time the harm seemed slight, and the concert went ahead with him conducting. It quickly became apparent that the repercussions were more serious, and initially Gustav was advised by his doctor to spend a week in bed. In fact he was unable to work for a month, during which Ralph Vaughan Williams and Balfour Gardiner helped by deputising for his teaching, and his diary is blank for the rest of the year.

It had already been Isobel who had responded to a request by their hosts for photos of Gustav (the latter had replied unhelpfully in January "I am sorry I have no spare photos of myself. I will try and send you some later"). It now fell to Isobel to take over making the arrangements for their visit. She wrote from 32 Gunterstone Road to the Acting Head of the Department of Music at Ann Arbor on 26 February:

Unfortunately my husband is ill & so I have to attend to his correspondence. About a fortnight ago he fell backwards off the concert platform at Reading University where he was conducting, & got slight concussion of the brain. He was in bed about a week & then his doctor allowed him to go back to work but said he must look upon himself as an invalid. This, I am afraid he did not do & now he has had a nervous breakdown & the doctor has sent him away into the country for a complete rest cure of at least three weeks! He is not to have any letters or attend to any business. He is just to vegetate, as it is the only chance of his recovery. Before he went away he gave me brief instructions about his business matters. He says he does not wish to say anything about the music. It must speak for itself!

I sent you 6 photos about 2 weeks ago & am surprised you have not received them. I will send you some more as soon as possible. Also I am sending some books with articles about my husband, which you may like to take extracts from.

We are looking forward to our visit to America with much pleasure & I am doing everything in my power to get my husband well for it.

Three days later Isobel wrote from London to Charles Sink, the Secretary and Business Manager of University of Michigan School of Music, who had been making the detailed arrangements for their visit:

I am attending to my husband's correspondence because he is ill. About a fortnight ago he fell backwards off the concert platform at Reading University, where he was conducting[,] on the back of his head.

He was in bed for a week with slight concussion & then he went back to work too soon & now he has had to see a specialist who says there is no permanent injury but he must have complete rest, away from here for at least three weeks. He is not to have any letters or think of any business arrangement at all, & so I shall not be able to send your letter on to him for another week.

Will this do?

It is most kind of you to allow us such a generous amount for expenses & we appreciate it greatly, & look forward with much pleasure to meeting you in America.

I will ascertain about the orchestral works as soon as possible & let you know.[345]

After much planning, including Isobel lending Barbara Simcoe her sewing machine whilst she was away,[346] Gustav was well enough to travel and he and Isobel duly left Southampton

---

[345] Mitchell, *Comprehensive Biography*, 255–7.

[346] In another typical example of Isobel's kindness, Barbara Simcoe recalled that "I looked after it so well she gave it to me when she came back. I sold it later for £5 and I wish I hadn't now." Britten Pears Arts HOL/5/2/15 Full transcript of RS/Barbara Simcoe's taped conversation 16 July 1988.

for New York on 21 April 1923. Fortunately, when the Holsts arrived in Ann Arbor they enjoyed themselves greatly. As Gustav wrote to his friend W. G. Whittaker:

> A week or so in Ann Arbor is worth a month rushing about. The people are not only kind but intelligently kind and without fussing you in the least they will give you one of the happiest times of your life.[347]

Photographs of Isobel and Gustav relaxing at Ann Arbor show them looking happy and relaxed, with Gustav uncharacteristically smiling.[348] In thanksgiving, Gustav presented the University with the manuscript score of his latest composition, his Fugal Concerto for Flute and Oboe, "as a token of gratitude for all the kindness shown to my wife and myself during our visit to Ann Arbor."[349]

In a long letter written on 21 and 27 May 1923 to Vally Lasker, Isobel described how she, as well as Gustav, was having the time of her life:

> At last I have a moment to write & tell you about the Festival. I have enclosed the press cuttings to Mabel & she will pass them on to you. The Critics don't write as well as ours but they were all very much impressed & talked a lot after the concerts about it being "grand stuff" and what America wants & has been waiting for etc, & "Its been just dandy having you right here with us Mr Holst". The extraordinary thing about Americans is that their taste in music is appalling & yet when they get anything like the HofJ,[350] they go right over at once & just worship it. Poor Gustav nearly gave up in despair over the Amen Chorus but in the end they sang it beautifully & the performance was the finest I have heard. Stocks orchestra is splendid – with the exception of the double basses who play with the old "grunter" bow & are consequently rather rough & a bit heavy – but the woodwind & brass are perfect. Gustav finished his concerto here – The Librarian gave him a private room in the Library to work in – & he has presented the original score to the University Library. They are fearfully proud of it & have put it in a glass case in the entrance hall with the outside cover with its dedication open & the first pages open also. Several players of Stocks orchestra played it twice beautifully at a Reception at President Burtons house last Thursday.
>
> May 27th at Beryl Clarks house 760 Webb Avenue Detroit.
>
> You wouldn't believe how difficult it is to get letters written here! The telephone goes all day and someone wants you to go out or they want to come & see you & there you are – just in the middle of this letter someone rang up & offered to take me [on] a 40 mile drive & of course I went which was bad for the letter.
>
> We are spending the weekend with the Clarks & then at 5 pm on Sunday we take the boat from Detroit to Buffalo & thence on to Niagara Falls – we are 14 hours on the boat & it ought to be a very jolly journey. We shall be two or three days at Niagara Falls. The conductor there gave a Holst concert not long ago & he came over to Ann Arbor for the Hymn & asked us to come to Niagara. Then we go on to Toronto in Ontario State & then through Washington to Ashville North Carolina. After that Gustav wants to get home as soon as possible for the P.F.[351] so we shall try for the first boat from Montreal. We have had a lovely invitation to go to Keene Valley in the Adirondacks for the whole summer, or as long or as short a time as we like, but alas the P.F. will prevent it!. – why do things always happen that way. Gustav wants me to stay behind and accept it & they are most pressing but I feel it is my duty to come back even if we are too late for a performance of the P.F. Of course if it should happen that we cant get a boat we shall go to the Adirondacks for a short time while we wait.

---

[347] Mitchell, *Comprehensive Biography*, 268.
[348] Short, *Gustav Holst*, plate 22.
[349] Mitchell, *Comprehensive Biography*, 272.
[350] Gustav Holst's *The Hymn of Jesus*.
[351] A forthcoming performance of Gustav's opera, *The Perfect Fool*.

These people own 4000 acres there all forest land & a lake & two motor cars & of course we should have a lovely time.

The letters & notices of the P.F. have just arrived – its good that it went so well & I'm longing to see it.

… Beryl Clarke has two charming daughters – Josephine aged 3½ & Magdeline 20 months. He[r] husband is delightful & bath's the children & paints the outside of the house & is much more like the "Mother" than she is. … They pay their worthless maid of all work £4.0.0 a week – not dollars – & she have every evening out & every Sunday afternoon & evening & one day a week which is from 10 Am to 10 p.m. She does not clean windows or do washing. They have everything electric including washing & ironing machines & they pay a woman £1.0.0. a day to do the washing!!! Builders labourers earn about £4.0.0 to £5.0.0. a day![352] They all have cars & spend their time off at the movies. Detroit is the great place for making cars & the streets are full of them …

We are trying to get home by the first week in July & I expect we shall soon fix on a boat & then we will let you know. More news later. Much love Isobel.[353]

Their exciting time in America provided Isobel with many stories of their adventures to recount with gusto on her return. She had her hair permed whilst there – a novelty in England at the time[354] – and relished the generous hospitality of their hosts, especially Austin Lidbury, who came to stay with the family at Thaxted on a return visit. Years later Imogen related her mother's account:

… when they were staying in America with Austin Lidbury – both she and my father – they'd all been to a rehearsal of one of my father's works, and they drove back and Lid, as we all called him, was wildly excited with the music and everything and he said "Oh, come in, we must have a drink to celebrate this", and dashed to his cellar door and opened it wide without having put the police warning switch down. And before he came up from the cellar, saying "I think this is the right bottle", hammering on the door, police sirens, the police were there. My mother was also a very good actress … And she used to tell that story very dramatically.[355]

Whilst in America Isobel and Gustav visited Chicago in June, meeting up with Gustav's stepbrother Thorley and other relatives.[356] Their two-month long adventure together had been a great success.

On their return to England the rest of 1923 was also exceptionally busy. Gustav and Isobel returned in time to attend the performance of a dual bill of his earlier opera *Savitri* with his new composition, *The Perfect Fool* at Covent Garden on 28 June. It did not go well. Gustav's usually loyal music critic friend Richard Capell described it as a "performance so ill-considered that no-one without previous acquaintance could have seen its bearings".[357]

As usual however, Gustav brushed off the criticism, and his popularity remained high. The year saw a succession of performances of his work, in part fuelled by his completion of the first recording of *The Planets*. Back home in Thaxted, Isobel's activities included running the "shilling fund" at church, which the rector Conrad Noel suggested would be the only way

---

[352] Triple underlined.

[353] Britten Pears Arts HOL/1/5/3/2 Letter from Isobel Holst to Vally Lasker, 21 and 27 May 1923.

[354] Information from Sylvia Heath, née Putterill.

[355] Britten Pears Arts HOL/5/2/29 Transcript of Imogen Holst replying to questions by John Morrison, recorded 19–20 April 1980.

[356] Short, *Gustav Holst*, 210.

[357] Philippa Tudor, "The composer and the critic: Gustav Holst and Edwin Evans", *Musical Times* (vol. 117, no. 1937, Winter 2016, p 78.

of paying the flamboyant Marquis d'Oisy for some of the decorative work he was proposing.[358] The ballerina Lydia Lopokova met both Gustav and Isobel in autumn 1923 and described Isobel in a letter to her husband, the economist John Maynard Keynes, as "a handsome woman with a good country complexion; she is usually chosen as a Madonna in spiritual plays" – a reference to her lasting beauty as well as her long-standing enthusiasm for acting.[359]

The father and daughter musical bond was growing ever stronger as Imogen's musical talents developed, and Gustav was increasingly able to ask his daughter for her views on points of detail in his compositions.[360] At this time, however, Imogen was still very much interested in dancing as well as music. This was part of her teenage daughter's life which Isobel did feel fitted to support, at least as chaperone, and she was also an enthusiastic dancer herself before her arthritis started to set in a few years later. In 1923 Isobel and Imogen (but not Gustav) joined the English Folk Dance Society (EFDS), which had been founded by Cecil Sharp in 1911.[361] At Thaxted the garden at The Steps is unusually large for a house in the centre of town, and big enough for dancing: Imogen was photographed dancing there. She particularly enjoyed dancing with Arthur Caton, on whom the beautiful bookplate in Imogen's books is based. Very slim, good looking and a beautiful dancer, Barbara Simcoe agreed that she "liked him" too. According to Barbara, "They were very fond of each other, Arthur and Imogen, but I think Isobel sort of broke it up". Rosamund Strode had gathered a similar impression when speaking to Arthur Caton himself, and thought that the reason the Holsts went to Paycocke's for a rare family holiday in the summer of 1923 "was to get her away from him". Barbara Simcoe agreed that that was quite likely.[362] Fortunately the Holsts relished staying *en famille* at Paycocke's, a beautiful Tudor merchant's house in Essex owned by Lord Noel-Buxton, cousin of Conrad Noel, the vicar of Thaxted.[363]

In the autumn term of 1923 Gustav continued with his hectic schedule of teaching commitments, with "a lot of teaching at the RCM and huge classes here [St Paul's Girls' School], Dulwich, and Morley". There were also five further performances of his work at the Queen's Hall. The schedule for recording *The Planets* with the London Symphony Orchestra, with Gustav conducting without the benefit of electric technology, was particularly punishing, taking place over four days in 1923 (23–24 August, 30 October and 6 November). Fifty years later Imogen recalled the toll this took on her father:

I was never actually in the recording studio with him, but I do remember an occasion after making his 1923 pre-electric recording of *The Planets* he came home so tired that he was unable to walk up the stairs to bed. I recall his description of the terrible recording conditions in those days. Everyone was crowded into a tiny room, and even Aubrey Brain, that wonderful horn player, broke down 13 times at

---

[358] J.W.S. Litten, *The Marquis d'Oisy – Aesthete, Exotic and Enigma* (Anglo-Catholic History Society, 2014), 10–11. The painted vestment cupboard which Noel considered to be the priority is still in use in Thaxted church. I am grateful to Michael Goatcher for this reference.

[359] Mitchell, *Comprehensive Biography*, 298–9.

[360] For example, Holst, *Thematic Catalogue*, p 149.

[361] Gibbs, *Holst among friends*, 140 (n 9).

[362] Britten Pears Arts HOL/5/2/6 Full transcript of RS/Barbara Simcoe's taped conversations 6 November 1985.

[363] Grogan, *Imogen Holst*, 22. Imogen wrote to a schoolfriend "it is a dream. And it is great fun living in a dream … We are tremendously proud of it, and as it isn't our own we can swank about it to our heart's content."

the beginning of *Venus*, just because of the physical discomfort. In that way, recording was much more arduous in the early days.

Conditions were already better for the 1926 electric performance. But there was still the difficulty in those days that you simply had to go on recording – there was no sticking together of bits of tape. A whole side had to be done at a time … and there was no stopping for a second chance.[364]

By Christmas Gustav was exhausted. An exceptionally generous gift of £1500 from a director at Rolls Royce had enabled him to cut down his teaching commitments significantly, and in January 1924 he was able to spend most of his time at home in Thaxted, going to London only one day a week. By the end of January he was finding even that too much, as he explained to his close friend Whittaker:

… it hasn't been an entire success. I have a longing to be by myself or with not more than one or two people at a time and I dread parties or business meetings etc. And I have a fear lest people shall imagine that success has spoilt me and that old acquaintances and old surroundings are not good enough for me. (Please note that I mean people and not friends.)[365]

In February 1924, however, Gustav realised that his nerves were in such a bad state that he needed to withdraw completely. He wrote again to Whittaker from 32 Gunterstone Road, still the Holsts' London home:

This is a horrible blow. My head got queer on Monday and worse on Tuesday … I sent a deputy to the RCM yesterday and spend most of the day dozing by the fire and lying in bed. But it was of no use … I should be fit for nothing for the following week at least … I'm going to indulge in Silence, Solitude and Heat (not mere warmth)[366]

It soon became clear that the shared fun and excitement of 1923 were over. Gustav was experiencing a nervous breakdown, and his doctor prescribed complete rest until the end of the calendar year. This must have been a difficult time for Isobel, who became a visitor at her own home in Thaxted and needed to spend more time than usual in London with Imogen. As for Imogen, who had her 17th birthday in April 1924, she was still a pupil at St Paul's Girls' School and thus acutely conscious of the disruption caused by Gustav being unable to fulfil his teaching commitments there. Isobel's reactions to the situation are not recorded, but Imogen, nearly 17, described her own in a series of letters to her school friend Helen Asquith:

Vally and Nora[367] have been to see me. Poor dears, they will have an awful time of it now that Gussie isn't coming back. I do hope the form will be kind to them, especially Nora … THE most thrilling prospect. We may be going to Bruges in the hols, just Iso and I!! Isn't it too exciting for words. …

Imogen wrote again on 25 March:

Gussie's illness is really a very great trial to his family; we get hundreds of letters every day from adoring females (strangers, of course) asking how he is and sympathizing and hoping it won't affect his genius in any way. Poor Gussie, if he saw half his correspondence it would affect his genius in a great many ways![368]

---

[364] Imogen Holst interview with Alan Blyth for *Gramophone* September 1974, reprinted by James McCarthy, *Gramophone*, 12 April 2013.
[365] *Gustav Holst: Letters to W. G. Whittaker*, pp 80–81.
[366] *Gustav Holst: Letters to W. G. Whittaker*, p 140.
[367] Vally Lasker and Nora Day, fellow music teachers at SPGS.
[368] Mitchell, *Comprehensive Biography*, 304.

> Gussie ... has developed a sudden passion for Thaxted scenery, before he treated it with a mild indifference. That is all very well, but it leaves him in complete possession of the place, and he has to be absolutely alone, his family is/are banished. Hence the visit to Bruges

A further blow was in store. The Bruges holiday had to be cancelled after a gramophone company failure led to the Holsts losing much needed royalties from the recording of *The Planets Suite* which had contributed to Gustav's exhaustion. Imogen wrote again to Helen Asquith on 6 April:

> I don't know what we are going to do in the hols:- the Bruges expedition is off, worse luck. You see Gussie's gramophone people have gone bankrupt, which means that we have lost over £100 in royalties on the "Planets" during the last year. This is rather a blow, of course, as we had rather been counting on it.
>
> Gussie won't let us come anywhere near him at Thaxted, so I expect we shall spend the hols in London. We might go down to Oxford for a few days, to stay with some friends there

Fortunately Helen Asquith's mother responded by inviting Imogen to stay for the holidays, which meant that in Easter 1924 Isobel was alone once more.[369]

The teenage Imogen might have been even more confused had she known that although her father needed his family to stay away from Thaxted, he felt able to see his composer friends, although only one at a time. Gustav noted in one of his notebooks under 1924 that he was "Alone in Thaxted March to Dec". That, however, was not the whole story. For example, in early April, "RVW and I ... had a lovely, easy going, middle aged, weekend together",[370] and after his friend Whittaker had received a Carnegie award in April 1924 Gustav wrote to him from Thaxted:

> I suppose you won't spend a night with me here when you come south? If you do I'll teach you to be lazy – it will be a new experience for you and will probably give you a shock. I've forgotten what work feels like! ... if you find that you can come send me a wire at the last moment.[371]

Whilst recuperating from his nervous breakdown Gustav was able to live what he considered to be the life of a real composer. As he explained in one of 10 surviving letters he wrote to Vally Lasker in 1924:

> I feel there is no alternative but to obey the doctors now and not in the next autumn as I have been hoping to do all this time.
>
> As I understand it, the trouble is sheer nerves. Whenever I have anything to look forward to ... I get queer ... And therefore the only thing left is to go the whole hog and cut off every sort of work except composition indefinitely.[372]

Gustav himself remained in no fit state for writing business-type letters, and it was to Isobel that Vaughan Williams directed Vally Lasker for making arrangements about the copyright of *The Planets*.[373] It was Isobel too who had the task of writing to Edwin Evans, one of the two music critics whom Gustav regarded as a friend, in a letter clearly intended to maintain Gustav's profile during his convalescence at Thaxted:

---

[369] Grogan, *Imogen Holst*, 24–6.

[370] Britten Pears Arts HOL/1/5/1/14/23 Letter from Gustav Holst to Vally Lasker Thaxted 7 April 1924.

[371] *Gustav Holst: Letters to W. G. Whittaker*, p 83.

[372] Britten Pears Arts HOL/1/5/1/14/22 Letter from Gustav Holst to Vally Lasker March 1924.

[373] British Library MS Mus. 1714/1/6, f. 85 Vaughan Williams letter to Vally Lasker April 1924.

Has your Musical Journal appeared yet? And if so, is my article in it? I am out of things here & have lost touch with so much but I am getting much better than I was and am half thinking of going to the Salzburg Festival in August if I can stand so much new music … Excuse dictated letter – hand rather bad.[374]

The 1924 Whit Monday celebrations were held at Bute House, the boarding house for St Paul's Girls' School, with Isobel and Imogen, but not Gustav, present.[375] It was just as well that the Holsts still had their Gunterstone Road house. Helen Asquith never visited the family at Thaxted, but occasionally did so in London, and found Imogen's relationship with her mother puzzling. In 1988 she commented on the Holsts at this time:

I got the impression, somehow, that they were very detached, and I think one wondered, even in those days, whether it was a happy marriage. … I got the impression all the time I knew her [Imogen], she was absolutely devoted to Gustav. She talked about him, but she didn't talk about Iso, much. … She was a very shadowy figure, all the time I knew Imo.[376]

By 1 June 1924 Gustav's semi-solitary life at Thaxted was reaping dividends for him at least. As a result of his continuing struggle with ill-health, he had resolved to give up all his teaching commitments except for St Paul's Girls' School. By 1 June 1924 he had decided to relinquish teaching even at his beloved Morley, and his former students initiated a leaving collection for him. Gustav commented: "… if it is to be something for me there is really nothing I feel I need. Isobel suggested a silent portable typewriter which is a good idea. In fact the only good idea."

Reflecting in the same letter to Vally Lasker, he wrote:

As for me the last six weeks have been probably the most wonderful in my life. It seems incredible that one could dare to look forward to more and yet there is no great reason why I should not find myself wrapped up in something else in a week or two. To sit all day in the garden and to watch the symphony grow up alongside of the flowers and vegetables and then to find that it is done! …

I am coming up [to London] on Wed to go with Isobel to Balfour's for a few days. I hope to be back at 32 on Saturday and to go to Toc H on Sunday morning and then return here the same afternoon leaving the symphony behind. Will you then go through it and make more remarks? Amy is to finish the Finale and Mabel correct the words.[377]

The reference to Toc H in Gustav's letter was as the venue for the annual Whitsun Festival which Gustav had initiated at Thaxted in 1916. The church where its headquarters were based was All Hallows by the Tower in central London. It had been assumed that Gustav would be in Thaxted and unable to attend, and it was therefore a delightful surprise when he took his place in the congregation.[378] Predictably after this exciting time, 10 days later Gustav felt he was "in a worse muddle than ever".[379]

Although Isobel visited Gustav during his recuperation in Thaxted, it was a manservant, Hubert Adams, who attended to his daily needs. Gustav was appreciative of the efforts Adams

---

[374] Westminster City Archives CML/212, letter to Edwin Evans from Gustav Holst 28 April 1924.

[375] Gibbs, *Holst Among Friends*, 97.

[376] Britten Pears Arts HOL/5/2/17 Transcript of RS/Lady Helen Asquith's taped conversation 31 August 1988.

[377] Britten Pears Arts HOL/1/5/1/14/28 Letter from Gustav Holst to Vally Lasker 1 June 1924.

[378] Gibbs, *Holst Among Friends*, 94.

[379] Britten Pears Arts HOL/1/5/1/14/29 Letter from Gustav Holst to Vally Lasker 10 June 1924.

took on his behalf, although these meant that during 1924 Isobel's own homemaking role in Thaxted was displaced. Hubert Adams:

… had served in an officers' mess during the war, and … combined, with incredible efficiency, the role of cook, valet, and guardian. He was an artist to his finger-tips. Visitors were turned away with tact and firmness. He would wait until Holst was at the far end of the garden before he pumped the water, remembering that the least sound would disturb him. And he took great pains to devise new and exciting dishes to lay before him, dishes so succulent that Holst declared they would rival the masterpieces of any Parisian chef.[380]

Despite their period of living mostly apart, when in autumn 1924 the British National Opera Company offered to produce Gustav's latest opera, *At the Boar's Head*, before he had finished scoring it, it was with Isobel that he discussed how to finish it in time for the first rehearsals, and once again turned to his devoted friends and colleagues Vally Lasker, Nora Day and Jane Joseph to help him complete the scoring.[381] Perhaps Isobel felt that Gustav had reached the stage in his recovery when a return to a more structured schedule would help him focus. In writing excitedly to Vally Lasker to ask for her help, Gustav explained:

It's been a big problem but now, as Isobel agrees, I have decided to try and finish it in time. Can you give me all your next six weekends – Saturdays, Sundays and perhaps Monday mornings? I'm also asking Nora and Jane and fear there is not much hope in getting Nora. I'm thinking of asking Mabel once or twice to see to the words. The idea is to work at full and pf scores and then send each bit when done to Novello who will copy but not publish until after the production. I shall attend all rehearsals – and learn much thereby – and go to Rome as soon as the thing is produced. I am not sure yet whether we can do it in time. It depends chiefly on how much help I can get. Will you let me know about weekends and also about ½ term? All this is in flat contradiction to all my late ideas but I expect you realise the reasons … It lends itself to dictation as most of it is lightly scored. I'll send some scoring paper tomorrow. Would you and Nora rule bars and bring it to 32 Gun on Sat next at 9.30?

I'm tremendously excited and hope you are Much pleased.

My normal working hours are 10–1 2.15–3.15 5–7.30 but I'm agreeable to anything barring 3.30–4.30.[382]

Reflecting over 60 years later on the exceptional help which Gustav had received from his amanuenses, including Vally Lasker, whom she "adored" as one of her teachers at St Paul's Girls' School, Helen Asquith (HA) commented to Rosamund Strode (RS):

HA: … He did have all these adoring women.
RS: Did he appear to take them all for granted?
HA: Yes, I think so. I mean I was too young to know, but I don't think there was any kind of sentimental …
RS: No, I'm sure there wasn't.
HA: No, they were just his slaves, I think.
RS: I think that's right – and I daresay like anyone else, if they were there, he might as well use them.
HA: Yes.
RS: But he actually needed them because of his neuritis. …[383]

---

[380] I. Holst, *Gustav Holst*, 103.
[381] Short, *Gustav Holst*, 229.
[382] Britten Pears Arts HOL/1/5/1/14/30 Letter from GH to Vally Lasker 26 October 1924.
[383] HOL/5/2/17 Transcript of RS/Lady Helen Asquith's taped conversation 31 August 1988.

Gustav was still not fully recovered, and, perhaps predictably given his pattern of periods of overwork followed by exhaustion, he was not up even to having even "a meal alone" in London with his friend Whittaker at the end of November 1924. As he explained to him apologetically:

My head has been bad for the last four days and I'm only fit for solitary walking, reading by the fire or bed. I hope to be fit again in a week but until then I must be here [in Thaxted] and alone.[384]

As usual, "alone" did not quite mean that. Gustav's manservant remained in loyal attendance, and instead of seeing Whittaker in London Gustav enjoyed a "nice visit from Isobel".[385]

Although Gustav was well enough to come back to London at the beginning of 1925, as his daughter later wrote:

it was several months before he could bear the noise of traffic or a crowd of people talking. His hair had turned white, and he had grown heavier: he no longer walked with a quick, agile step.[386]

Curtailing his teaching commitments removed the struggle to pay for a London home. In early 1925 Gustav and Isobel moved four miles from the centre of Thaxted to Brook End, Easton Park, a rented Tudor farmhouse which remained their home until 1929. At around the same time they gave up their London home at 32 Gunterstone Road, and Isobel became permanently based in Essex, with Imogen boarding at Bute House in school term-time.[387] Brook End was one of the many properties in the area owned by Frances, Countess of Warwick, whose intimate friends had included the Prince of Wales, the future King Edward VII, and her chosen neighbours reflected her combined interests in socialism and the arts. As she wrote:

My neighbours have been a constant delight and inspiration. My mind flies, above all, to my tenants at the Glebe, to H.G. Wells and his wife and all their interesting entourage. In my "Laundry" live Philip Guedalla and his beautiful wife … at my Home Farm, Gustav and Isobel Holst have made a cottage into an abode of delight with an old barn for their music-room. Here their only child, Imogen, sends out the wonderful music that has gained her scholarships, at an early age, that men might envy. No more than a stone's throw from the Lodge the Horrabins[388] rest from their editing of Plebs and their political canvassing of Peterborough. Near by the tall Marquis d'Oisy, image of a remote ancestor, the great Cardinal Richelieu, paints and decorates his furniture and composes pageants.[389] In the old Easton

---

[384] *Gustav Holst: Letters to W. G. Whittaker*, 86–87.

[385] Britten Pears Arts HOL/1/5/1/14/31 Letter from GH to Vally Lasker 24 November 1924.

[386] I. Holst, *Holst* (1972), 14.

[387] Grogan, *Imogen Holst*, 36.

[388] James Francis Horrabin (1884–1962), Labour MP for Peterborough 1929–31 and editor of The Plebs, journal of the workers' education campaign group the Plebs' League. In 1924 he co-wrote Working Class Education with his wife Winifred.

[389] *The Chelmsford Chronicle* 20 July 1928 reported on two performances of a pastoral play in the Marquis d'Oisy's garden at Pledgdon Green, Henham, to large audiences, preceded by another play in which he acted. Less happily, on 15 February 1924 *The Chelmsford Chronicle* had reported on a builder suing for nearly £60 of materials and work done at the Marquis's request. The reporter understood that the Marquis was an undischarged bankrupt. On 6 November 1926 *The Essex Newsman* quoted a letter from the Marquis read out at Westminster County Court in response to a summons taken out by the Soho decorating company Thornton Smith: "I am entirely dependent on what I earn as a painter, have no independent means whatsoever, and have been out of employment for the last six months".

Manor, where Edward IV and Elizabeth Woodville spent their protracted honeymoon, my youngest daughter Mercy, the wife of Basil Dean, entertains the stars of the theatrical profession at week-ends[390]

Gustav and Isobel were amongst the handful of guests invited to Mercy's 21st birthday party at Easter 1925.[391] At the time, the Countess of Warwick was still harbouring grand plans to turn her large house at Easton Lodge into a Labour College:

At Easton there will not only be sports and athletics for physical development, but there will also be music and painting to meet artistic needs; while in the schools the study of economics will be fully catered for. I feel sure that the result will make for a great forward movement in the whole Labour world ... Drama will centre around the Barn Theatre; music will be inspired with Gustav Holst as our resident neighbour; while literature will claim encouragement from H. G. Wells and Philip Guedalla, and painting be neighboured by G. Clausen, R.A., and a number of lesser lights. I see a future when a university will develop, and additional buildings grow up around the College[392]

The Countess of Warwick hoped to live in the annexe built on the side of the wing of Easton Lodge which was destroyed by fire in 1918. Under her plans, she would have continued to manage the garden, the home farm – where the Holsts were living – and the deer park.[393] She herself was, however, increasingly short of money. It was their ever-generous friend Balfour Gardiner rather than their landlady who helped fund a number of improvements arranged by Isobel for their new home at Brook End. As well as some essential renovations, these included converting a barn into the detached music room referred to by the Countess of Warwick, which Isobel must have imagined would give her husband the peace, warmth and quiet which he needed to be able to compose at home, as well as at St Paul's Girls' School.[394] According to Arthur Caton, who may have had good reason to be critical of Isobel's tastes, Isobel "spent an awful lot of money on houses – moving frequently and doing them up", and "spent thousands on Brook End".[395]

Isobel might as well not have bothered. According to their daughter, Gustav:

... was still 'oriental' enough to have no desire for a fixed home ... now, when he had the most beautiful home he was ever to live in, he preferred to be on the move the whole time. ... It was full of old oak beams that had never been stained but had worn to a soft grey. There were large open fires, and the glow from the logs was reflected in the shining pewter and the rich colours of the hangings. There was a barn that his wife had converted into a perfect music-room, with golden thatch on the roof and lead-lights in the windows, and electricity and central heating and all that one could desire.

But Holst only came down for occasional week-ends. He had no use for property of any sort. His room need only be warm and silent, with a large enough writing-table in it. His luggage could always be packed between the full scores in his music bag...

This homeless existence may have seemed ideal to him, but the great disadvantage was that he had nowhere to lose his temper when the occasion rose ... there was no respite from the courtesy and the kindliness and the over-anxious consideration that he always showed for other people. It was an aspect

---

[390] Frances, Countess of Warwick, *Life's Ebb and Flow* (London, Hutchinson, 1929), 274–5.

[391] Anand, *Daisy*, 258.

[392] *Life's Ebb and Flow*, 269.

[393] *Life's Ebb and Flow*, 266.

[394] Lloyd, *Balfour Gardiner*, 171.

[395] Britten Pears Arts HOL/5/2/4 Notes on RS's taped conversation with Arthur Caton 28 August 1985.

that never occurred to him. He did not realize that he was tying his brain into knots with a network of tiny, unimportant details.[396]

As a result, just as Gustav had had their Thaxted mostly to himself in 1924, the tables were turned in 1925, when Isobel was mostly alone in their large home at Great Easton. Fortunately Isobel's decorating flair was appreciated by others in Thaxted. Conrad Noel's successor as vicar, Jack Putterill, described her arrangements for a costumed Tudor Concert held in the 15th-century Thaxted Guild Hall:

The Guild Hall was specially decorated for the occasion by Mrs. Isobel Holst. She arranged flowers everywhere, lit it all with candles, and put lovely carpets on the floors. Refreshments were set out on the first floor and the concert was given in the room above. It was the perfect setting.[397]

A letter from Gustav to Isobel, this time addressed from St Paul's Girls' School, corroborates both his rootless existence and Isobel's Essex-based one, which meant that Gustav had attended their daughter's piano recital – a significant event in any young musician's life – without her:

I won't come on Sunday unless it is urgent. It would upset Mabel[398] a little and the artist who is drawing me wants me all Sunday afternoon and I want to finish with him PDQ. I hope you'll like his work better than I like him.

Imogen's meal and piano recital last night was a brilliant success. She plays beautifully. I've decided not to seek for fresh work next term. Being middle-aged, fat and lazy I believe I shall enjoy four months without work enormously. If I don't go abroad before Xmas do you think I could be of any use with the Xmas music either at Thaxted or Easton or both? I rather feel I should be in the way so don't suggest it to anyone else yet. I don't want to remain in[399] London or BE[400] with nothing to do. I'll either go off at once or go walking if I can't be useful.

People are asking me about Xmas presents for you and Imogen and I'm quite stumped.

I hope you won't be kept in this worrying suspense much longer

BL

G.[401]

Family holidays when all the Holst family were together were now unusual, but Isobel continued to support Imogen's enthusiasm for folk dancing, if not her adolescent relationship with Arthur Caton. Vaughan Williams had expected to see Isobel and Imogen at the EFDS on 30 December 1924,[402] and in August 1926 Gustav's diary notes Imogen spending three weeks at the EFDS in Cambridge, with Isobel attending for the second week. Imogen had inherited her parents' enthusiasm for pageants, and in July 1926 she arranged and conducted the music for one of the Marquis D'Oisy's pageants held at Pledgdon Green (where he lived) by the Essex Folk Dance Society. A fortnight after the pageant two of the participants – one the

---

[396] I. Holst, *Gustav Holst*, 118–19. It was, however, in the Brook End music room that Gustav completed *Egdon Heath*, which he considered his best composition from the time of its writing until his death.

[397] J. Putterill, *Thaxted Quest for Social Justice* (Precision Press, Marlow, 1977), 38. I am grateful to Michael Goatcher for this reference.

[398] Mabel Rodwell Jones was one of several friends with whom Gustav stayed when in London.

[399] "England" has been crossed out here.

[400] Brook End.

[401] Britten Pears Arts HOL/1/5/1/8/42 Letter from Gustav to Isobel Holst "Thursday".

[402] BL Ms MUS 158 ff 72–3, letter from RVW to GH dated Dec 31 [1924].

brother of Imogen's long-standing school friend Jane Schofield – were married and Isobel and Imogen attended the wedding together, with Gustav playing the organ.[403] Closer to home, the 1927 Thaxted Folk Dance Society accounts show a payment to Mrs Holst for five shillings for refreshments.[404]

Imogen's main biography of her father emphasises her own closeness to him around this time, attending two or three large receptions with her in tow, and Imogen's occasionally joining her father for his usually solitary Sundays in his sound-proof room at St Paul's Girls' School, companionably sharing orange juice, stilton cheese, pints of very strong coffee and the Sunday papers. The absence of any mention of Isobel is striking, despite the fact that, like Imogen, she too occasionally attended concerts and receptions with Gustav.[405] Still more strikingly, on the next page Imogen found it appropriate to reflect:

This life of sheltered solitude he found entirely satisfying. But his closest friends were worried about him. And a few of them wished that he could develop the symptoms of a grand passion. It might clear the air. And it might mean that 'cerebration' would no longer 'tame and bridle inspiration'. But it was no good. For he was not made that way.[406]

Despite enjoying their time in America together greatly, once he had recovered from his breakdown Gustav reverted to travelling without his wife. The cost of travelling together is likely to have been one factor. Despite the generous financial arrangements for his first American visit, Gustav received a $100 loan from the University of Michigan before leaving there – presumably because he needed it.[407] Another consideration was that Gustav revelled in walking, often all day and regardless of weather conditions, as well as energetic sight-seeing. Whilst he was perfectly content to travel alone, on other occasions he enjoyed meeting up with friends for part of his explorations, and in later years Isobel was not among his travel companions, who included Frances Gray and her sister, Vally Lasker and Nora Day as well as Imogen. During this period of her life, whilst Imogen flourished with her musical studies, Isobel was often literally left behind.

In a letter simply dated "Tuesday"[408] sent to Isobel from Freiburg in Germany Gustav describes the holiday he was having with Vally Lasker and her family after he had completed his summer speaking engagement in Switzerland. The letter illustrates his dependence on friends to make his domestic arrangements, although as previously he sought Isobel's agreement for this:

I used to think that Vally's rhapsodies about the pine forests were a little overdone but I know better now. The Black Forest is a new and a great event in my life. The average height of each tree must be at least 100 feet and they grow absolutely straight. There is little or no undergrowth. Even on the hottest

---

[403] Grogan, *Imogen Holst*, 38–9. Britten Pears Arts HOL/2/6/1/28.

[404] I am grateful to Michael Goatcher for this reference.

[405] Imogen noted on the mostly Bach promenade concert programme for 21 September 1927: "Went to this concert with Gussie and Iso etc. and saw Jelly, Adila and Dorothy in the Green Room". Britten Pears Arts HOL/2/7/1/167.

[406] I. Holst, *Gustav Holst*, 119–21. The first edition of Imogen's main biography of her father was published in 1938, only four years after his death. The author's note thanks Vaughan Williams and her mother for their advice and criticism.

[407] Mitchell, *Comprehensive Biography*, 283. Holst repaid the loan immediately on his return to England.

[408] Michael Short suggests 1925.

day there is a cool breeze in the thickest part. And the majesty of the trees is beyond words. Vally shows me her favourite spots during the day and in the evening I wander about alone in the woods and dream.

The Rebhaus consists of three or four houses in a lovely estate on the side of a hill. They have given me a magnificent room in the highest house, far better than anything I had in Switzerland. Hot and cold water laid on and a big balcony with a couch for sleeping out. Fraulein Clara Lasker who runs the place is a really fine woman. Also she was born in London and speaks English.

The only drawback is that each change of altitude has upset me in one way or another. Of course it is only temporary but it is a waste of time – also a sign of old age coming on I suppose.

I leave on Sunday and arrive in London on Monday afternoon. I propose to drive straight to Mabel's[409] with my trunk and unless you tell me not to I will ask her to see to my enormous amount of laundry. Will you send me a line at 45 St Dunstans[410] about this if you want me to do anything else with it – it is all the same to me of course. I was advised not to send any laundry at Maloja[411] as there was some doubt as to whether it would be done before I left. And as the bundle is in my trunk at Victoria I cannot have it done here. I thought of coming to Brook End[412] on Wed morning so as to spend Tuesday answering letters etc. I believe I told you that I would like to come back to London on Thursday for the Prom. Love to Imogen

Yr G

I shall sleep at 32[413] unless you tell me not to in which case I can start at 45.[414]

---

[409] Mabel Rodwell Jones.

[410] In Hammersmith, close to St. Paul's Girls' School.

[411] A luxury hotel in the Engadine, where GH had been delivering talks to guests.

[412] ie home to Brook End, Great Easton.

[413] The Holsts' London home at the time at 32 Gunterstone Road.

[414] Britten Pears Arts HOL/1/5/1/8/41 Letter from Gustav to Isobel Holst.

Isobel and Imogen with Barbara Simcoe and Dora and Lily Harvey at Paycocke's, 1923 (Britten Pears Arts HOL/2/11/2/14)

Isobel at Weaverhead Cottage, Thaxted (Britten Pears Arts HOL/2/11/6/43)

Chapter Seven
Gustav and Isobel in their Fifties

Isobel at the wheel of "Penelope" outside the music room at Brook End, c 1928
(Britten Pears Arts HOL/2/7/1/249)

On 22 March 1927 Gustav, Isobel and Imogen all attended the Gustav Holst Festival held in his honour at Cheltenham Town Hall. Gustav later described this as the most overwhelming event of his life and it was a colossal success. The group photograph, which included all three of them together with the Mayor and Corporation of Cheltenham and an array of distinguished visitors and Festival sponsors, was coincidentally published in the Cheltenham Chronicle and Gloucestershire Graphic on Isobel's birthday, 26 March.

Despite the triumph of the Cheltenham concerts, Gustav's brief period of contemporary popularity had waned. He usually shrugged off the comments of the music critics, whether good or bad. One from his former friend and colleague Richard Terry was gratuitously unkind, although it took its place with the others in his scrapbooks of press cuttings:

Holst, who soared upwards to "the Planets," has managed to weave his own winding sheet with "the Boar's Head," and to dig his own grave with his "Choral Symphony."[415]

---

[415] Sir Richard Terry, *On Music's Borders* (T. Fisher Unwin, London, 1927), 28.

The decline in performances of Gustav's work meant that family finances were once more becoming tight. The ever-generous Balfour Gardiner had made bi-monthly payments of £200 to Gustav from September 1926 to May 1927 – a total of £1000,[416] which had significant purchasing value – but Gustav's diary for August 1927 records that their Brook End home was "let for 4 weeks", whilst Gustav was away on another walking holiday. He walked the 60 or so miles to Dorchester from Bristol over a long weekend, arriving in Dorchester on Monday and:

on Tuesday … had an unforgettable lunch and motor trip with Thomas Hardy himself, who showed me Melstock, Rainbarrow and Egdon.

Gustav had walked over Egdon Heath in Dorset during Easter 1926, and that experience, combined with his reading of Thomas Hardy's novel *The Return of the Native* (entirely set on a fictitious Egdon Heath) inspired him to write a tone poem of that name in response to a commission from the New York Symphony Orchestra. This was an exciting time for Gustav, as Imogen was later to write:

Egdon Heath had given him a new lease of life. As each fresh composition was written, he felt that he was beginning all over again, with a renewed strength and vigour.[417]

He spent much of August 1927 staying in Vally Lasker's flat, whilst she was away, and reported to her on his progress or otherwise in writing *Egdon Heath*. By the end of August he felt that he had spent the past week doing little new, although he had made a fair copy of the *Egdon Heath* manuscript. He was thinking of going "for another walk" in the middle of September, but couldn't "decide until Sep 1 when Isobel comes to town."[418] Another letter from Gustav sent to Vally Lasker from her flat on 1 September 1927 refers to his plans for the middle of the month, again referencing his need to consult Isobel:

I've copied the full score of EH and finished the 2 piano version and begun my lectures.
    I am almost certain to be here on the night of Sep 16 because I want to see a Bristol man about my lectures and he may be coming to London on the 16th. I may have to take him out to lunch on the 17th which would be a) a pity: b) unavoidable. But I cannot fix anything until I hear from him and from Isobel.[419]

Having finished writing *Egdon Heath*, Gustav rewarded himself with a month-long holiday to Germany, Austria and Czechoslovakia over Christmas 1927. Meanwhile Isobel and Imogen (then aged 20) spent Christmas together at home in Brook End, where they were snowed in for three days.[420]

    1928 was an important year for the Holst family, not least because Imogen, who was in her second year at the Royal College of Music, started renting her first home of her own nearer to college. As she noted with typical simplicity: "I moved house, and went to live at 42 Craven Road".[421] It was also the year of the premieres of Gustav's *Egdon Heath*, "the biggest composition he had written for some years", and thus eagerly awaited by his fans. After

---

[416] Lloyd, *Balfour Gardiner*, 171.

[417] Imogen Holst, *Gustav Holst*, 126–127.

[418] Britten Pears Arts HOL/1/5/1/14/40 Letter from Gustav Holst to Vally Lasker 28 August 1927.

[419] Britten Pears Arts HOL/1/5/1/14/41 Letter from Gustav Holst to Vally Lasker 2 September 1927.

[420] Grogan, *Imogen Holst*, 48.

[421] Britten Pears Arts HOL/2/7/1/228 Imogen Holst scrapbook May 1926-Aug 1928.

Thomas Hardy died on 11 January 1928, aged 87, Gustav dedicated this – his personal favourite of all his compositions to the time of his own death – to him. The first European performance was conducted by Gustav himself, to a sympathetic audience at Cheltenham Town Hall. On 23 February Isobel, Gustav and Imogen all attended the first London performance of *Egdon Heath*, at the Queen's Hall – the venue for the spectacular early performances of his *Planets Suite* – and, unusually, attended the reception together afterwards.[422] This turned out to be an excruciating experience for both Isobel and Imogen.

Egdon Heath is the only one of Gustav's compositions for which the contemporary responses of all three immediate family members are recorded. Like her mother, Imogen was not one to mince her words. She described the first London performance as "disastrous":

The concert organizers had put Egdon Heath as the second item on the programme, after the overture, and the foreign conductor was not used to Queen's Hall audiences. He made the fatal mistake of starting the orchestra before some of the late arrivals in the stalls had got into their places. The quiet, mysterious opening for muted double basses was inaudible: one could see the players' bowing arms moving slowly to and fro, but nothing could be heard through the buzz of conversation and the shuffle of feet. Those members of the audience who were already in their places glared at the late-comers and said 'ssshhh' which added to the confusion. The guilty late-comers glared back, furious with the conductor for having started too soon, and even more furious with the composer for having written such a quiet opening. After this, the music had little chance of making an impression on those who had not yet seen the score. Most listeners found the work uncomfortably austere, and critics complained of its monotony.[423]

Isobel, for whom the composition had involved long periods of ensuring Gustav had the quiet and freedom that he needed, was also unimpressed. Her reported comment to the Director of the Royal College of Music, Sir Hugh Allen, was:

Oh dear, Sir Hugh, how I wish you could stop Gustav writing music like this, and get him back to his old style.[424]

As for Gustav, "Holst, as usual, was unmoved by the opinions of his listeners".[425]

Far from putting Gustav's career back on an upward trajectory, the London premiere of *Egdon Heath* suggested to some, including some of his close friends, that he had lost his way.

By the Spring Gustav was suffering from one of his frequent spells of ill-health, and, faced with his doctor's orders to be out of London as much as possible, he practically invited himself to stay with his friends George and Henrietta Bell, the former being at the time Dean of Canterbury and for whom Gustav was collaborating with John Masefield on *The Coming of*

---

[422] Britten Pears Arts HOL/2/7/1/226 Royal Philharmonic Society concert programme at Queen's Hall, note by Imogen Holst "Went to reception after this concert, with Gussie and Iso. Met Talich".
[423] Imogen Holst, *Gustav Holst (The Great Composers series)*, 72–73.
[424] Short, Gustav Holst, 264.
[425] Imogen Holst, *Gustav Holst*, 130–131.

Christ.[426] This new work received its first performance on 28 May as part of the Whitsun weekend, during which Isobel and Imogen stayed in the cathedral close together.[427]

Isobel was never a great walker, and in any case Gustav undertook almost all of his multi-day walks in the 1920s on his own, enjoying the solitude. It was probably around this time that she acquired her first car, "Penelope", a Baby Austin, in which she enjoyed giving lifts to her friends. Barbara Simcoe, whose memories of the Holsts at Thaxted date from the 1920s, described Isobel during her middle age:

… she was a beautiful woman – big, and autocratic – she was lovely – lovely complexion – very big …

she did things at home, I think. Of course in the early days she used to do a lot of music – writing music for Gustav and they, again – like my mother, us – they had poor beginnings: she used to have orange boxes and decorate them with cretonne; … she had a mother who was a strict vegetarian, and brought her up on sandals, this sort of thing, bare legs and fruit. And of course she had a hankering for all the lovely things in life – cream cakes – and I remember her taking us in the Baby Austin to Cambridge and going to Matthews and having these real cream cakes – she loved them – … yet when she had rheumatic troubles, in later life, we were very amused because she used to go to Champneys – diets – and come back and tell us these hilarious tales – about lots of people, business men … and some of the relations and friends being very naughty taking in puddings … she was marvellous when she had her operation – she was about 70 … She was unconscious for a very long time.[428]

In the summer of 1928 Gustav's diary notes their separate movements, with Isobel going to France on 13 June, due to return on 7 July (she sent Imogen a postcard from Provence, saying that they were swimming and sitting on the beach),[429] and Imogen, now an adult, going to Germany on 23 June, returning a couple of days after her mother. Despite their often arms-length approach to their daughter's education during her schooldays, Imogen's parents were clearly not quite ready to loosen the reins entirely. In October Gustav wrote to Imogen's eminent piano teacher at the Royal College of Music, Kathleen Long, to say that:

Mrs Holst and I have discussed Imogen and the piano and we feel that she really ought not to practise any more. Thanks to you, neuritis has never been more than lurking, but this autumn she has had one or two nasty little attacks. I know from bitter experience that when it once gets hold of you there is an end to all piano playing, so hope you will not mind if we keep her timetable as it is.[430]

Imogen invited her mother to accompany her as her guest to a country dancing themed "At Home" party in Cambridge on 3 November 1928. On the basis of her surviving letters, Isobel had a tendency to be forthright to the point of bluntness. When someone watching Imogen

---

[426] Lambeth Palace Library Bishop Bell Papers 153, f 138, letter dated 8 May 1928 from GH to Mrs Bell. Vally Lasker wrote on 7 March 1929 about these performances to Dr Bell: "Making music is at all times the best thing on earth, & making it in the service of God in such a glorious atmosphere as last year has been unforgettable." Dr Bell responded: "… I appreciate more than I can tell you what you say about making music in the service of God …" (Lambeth Palace Library Bishop Bell Papers 154, ff 147, 162.).

[427] Britten Pears Arts HOL/2/6/1/291 Postcard of Mercury Lane, Canterbury with note by Imogen Holst.

[428] Britten Pears Arts HOL/5/2/4 Notes on RS's taped conversation with Arthur Caton 28 August 1985.

[429] Britten Pears Arts HOL/2/6/1/304 Postcard from Isobel Holst to Imogen from Provence 15 June 1928.

[430] Britten Pears Arts HOL/1/5/1/16 Letter from Gustav Holst to Kathleen Long 16 October 1928.

dancing during the evening commented to Isobel that her daughter would soon be married, she replied "Oh, Imogen will never marry – she doesn't realise that you have to get a man interested first."[431]

Gustav suffered from ill health on and off for much of 1928 and he and Isobel also spent Christmas 1928 and New Year's Day 1929 apart. Imogen was away too, on holiday with friends in Switzerland, and she wrote to her mother, c/o Mrs Noel at Thaxted vicarage, that they had:

… parted from Gussie at half past six this morning: he was in high spirits & very happy at the prospect of a carriage to himself & a large breakfast.[432]

Gustav had embarked on a three-month solo grand tour of Italy and Sicily, and wrote to Isobel from Rome on Christmas Day, having "had midday dinner with Miss Gray[433] and her sister and spent part of the afternoon eating nougat in their bedroom." He ended the letter saying that he hoped "to hear that you're having a really good time in London when I get to Naples."[434] His diary records a hugely energetic combination of sightseeing and walking, undaunted by snow and mud, punctuated by the inevitable consequences for his health. By 23 January he had reached Syracuse via Naples. Isobel was once again in Great Easton, and Gustav's postcard to her refers to another of her ailments.[435]

Isobel was still recovering by "banting on bed, milk and rum. Gosh!" when Gustav wrote to her from Pisa on 22 February 1929. His letter included proposals for his return in March, when he was hoping to spend the days surrounding her birthday on 26 March together, and provides insight into how he juggled his professional and personal life at this time:

Kennedy Scott is doing my 'Hecuba's Lament' in March and I think I ought to go. Could you go to R's opera with me[436] on the 25th? If so and if you go to Vally's would you ask her whether I may come too? Fix up with her as soon as you can because she likes to know in good time. There'll be a ticket for you for Hecuba. My present plan is to arrive on the 23d, go to bed in the afternoon and take Mabel to the RCM in the evening if she'll come and if I can get tickets. I must see Vally and Nora alone on Sunday to settle various things so I'm inviting myself to breakfast at Vally's and asking Nora if we can lunch or dine somewhere together. Whichever she does not choose I shall hope to spend with Imogen if she is in town – or you if you are ditto. Monday morning and afternoon I shall be at school, Tuesday[437] will, I hope, be free. On Wed, I want to take the train somewhere north so as to start walking in the Lake district towards Keswick on Thursday …

He had a new plan for encouraging Isobel to write:

… As you decline to get the postcard habit, next time I have a long holiday abroad I'm going to give you 100 postcards with various interesting items of news already printed on them. All you will have to do is to cross out those that don't apply to you at the moment. Thus –
I am very ill   I have flue
" " "   well   " "   excoriation of the cuticle
" "   just so so   " "   a legacy

---

[431] Grogan, *Imogen Holst*, 56.
[432] Britten Pears Arts HOL/2/8/1/9/2 Postcard from Imogen Holst to Isobel 21 December 1928.
[433] The former High Mistress of St Paul's Girls' School, who had retired in 1927.
[434] Britten Pears Arts HOL/1/5/1/8/43 Letter from Gustav to Isobel Holst 25 December 1928.
[435] Britten Pears Arts HOL/1/5/1/8/45 Postcard from Gustav to Isobel Holst 23 January 1929.
[436] *Sir John in Love*.
[437] Isobel's birthday.

" "	in bed	" "		no money	
" "	in a hell of a temper	" "		twins[438]	

Gustav's home visit was destined to be unexpectedly brief. The day after he wrote to Isobel from Pisa he received a cable inviting him to attend the 25th anniversary of the Academy of Arts New York in April. Although the fee offered was much less than that for his previous American commitment, after his long holiday he needed to earn some money. He expected to be able to save half of the £200 expenses offered and to be able to combine it with delivering a long-overdue lecture at Yale, and it seemed too good an offer to refuse.[439] His finances were particularly tight at the time and he was contemplating the need to "overdraw a little" at the bank.

So their reunion was compressed to two days together in March, with Isobel planning to stay with Vally Lasker, as she often did. Gustav's letter to Isobel from Venice on 12 March was a jumbled mixture of his likely agenda when in London, domestic details of things he needed for America – including new pants and pyjamas, as Isobel was in charge of his packing – and, in a postscript written on the day of his departure from Venice, 14 March, his two-sentence reaction to the death of his good friend and amanuensis Jane Joseph, about which he had heard from Vally Lasker and Nora Day, rather than from Isobel. He also added that he did not think "there will be time to come to Grt Easton before the end of the month so I hope to see plenty of you in London."[440]

Gustav's second visit to America, unaccompanied by Isobel, was much less glamorous than his first. His letter to Isobel of 12 April 1929, written on Imogen's birthday when he was en route by sea to lecture at Yale, suggests his continuing appreciation of home life:

Many Happy Returns of the Day and Many Congratulations on it. I don't see why you shouldn't have some of the honour and glory. And now is the time to have some when she is having one success after another.

You once said you'd like a long voyage in a one-class boat. My advice is Don't.

If I ever cross the Atlantic again I want a most exclusive cabin in a very fast boat and my Missus to keep undesirable people away.

But what I really want is to keep off the sea altogether. I've not been sea sick but I'm very sick of the sea, the ship (which is a very good one) and the passengers (who are, on the whole, harmless) and above all, the noise – engines, waves, wind, gramophones, chattering. …

I hope all the SW gales we've had have brought you lots of rain in Essex.[441] This has been the one cheering thought about the weather. And presumably you are not as cold as we are – we are near Newfoundland and its icebergs which are excellent things in books.

There is too much grousing about this letter. But the truth is that I've had too much gadding about – four months on end. And when I get home I want to live a humdrum monotonous existence with lots of routine work, lots of new 'things' that don't disappoint me too much, and occasional conducting jobs and 3 day walks – I want this for the next three or four years!

It doesn't seem an unreasonable desire![442]

Having arrived back in England on 5 May, later that year Gustav was travelling again, once again leaving Isobel behind at Great Easton, the family having needed to downsize from the

---

[438] Britten Pears Arts HOL/1/5/1/8/46 Letter from Gustav to Isobel Holst 22 February 1929.

[439] Britten Pears Arts HOL/1/5/1/8/47 Letter from Gustav to Isobel Holst 26 February 1929.

[440] Britten Pears Arts HOL/1/5/1/8/48 Letter from Gustav to Isobel Holst 12–14 March 1929.

[441] Presumably to water Isobel's garden.

[442] Britten Pears Arts, HOL/1/5/1/8/49 Letter from Gustav to Isobel Holst 12 April 1929.

large house at Brook End to The Cottage, Great Easton during the year as performances of Gustav's compositions had declined.[443] The Countess of Warwick's grand plans for Easton Labour College had come to nothing, as the quarter of a million pounds she had expected from trades union funding had been used to support the Coal Strike of 1927.[444]

In October 1929 Gustav had planned to go on another of his usual solitary visits, this time to Paris to hear the first French performance of *Egdon Heath*. The evening before his departure he issued a spur-of-the moment invitation to Imogen to join him. They wrote a joint postcard to Isobel from Paris, Imogen writing "We have just had a wonderful meal in an open-air restaurant, we have been drinking your health & wishing you were with us. B.L.I", with Gustav adding in parenthesis: "The meal in question is rather different to the ones we had near here in bye gone days!"[445] Their postcard was sent on the Friday before the Sunday afternoon concert, where the reception of Gustav's favourite composition was if anything even worse than the London premiere which Isobel had attended the previous year. The audience hissed in disapproval, Gustav's friends failed to convince him that hissing was a compliment in Paris and Gustav, usually at most a moderate drinker, downed three cocktails in quick succession before father and daughter went home to London on the evening train.[446] It was just as well that Isobel was not in the party.

Despite successful performances in Paris and London of Gustav's Humbert Wolfe songs in the next few months, Gustav was once more in a downward spiral: "He had sunk, once more, into that cold region of utter despair."[447] Walking and travelling continued to provide him with the solitude he needed to compose, and at this time Imogen was following in her father's footsteps by becoming an indefatigable traveller, which gave father and daughter an additional common ground in their voluminous correspondence. For example, in one of the 12 surviving letters Imogen wrote to her father in 1930, mostly whilst she was using her travelling scholarship, she described her recent visit to Budapest:

They've got an absolute genius for colour:– all the dull uninteresting things in the shops and streets & railway stations are painted bright blues & greens & oranges. Iso would have loved it.[448]

Meanwhile Isobel retained her dislike of letter-writing and her holidays were rare. She had dinner with Gustav, Imogen, Nora Day and Vally Lasker at the end of Gustav's school term in April 1930, after which Gustav set off for a two-week tour of the Netherlands. Gustav noted in his diary for 6 June that Isobel was motoring him to Chichester. This was for the first of the Whitsun music festivals to be held at Chichester, and as it turned out, the last that Gustav himself conducted. Isobel herself was due to be away for only two days in August, followed by 14 days in London. All three Holsts wrote to Vally Lasker on 5 September during a jolly pre-theatre dinner at The George pub in Hammersmith, with Gustav and Isobel both writing partly in broken German, in Isobel's case:

---

[443] Grogan, *Imogen Holst*, 62.

[444] *Life's Ebb and Flow*, 269–70.

[445] Britten Pears Arts HOL/1/5/1/8/50 Postcard franked 18.10.1929. Early in their married life Isobel and Gustav had "spent a fortnight in Paris, when a friend lent them a studio furnished with seven oil stoves and two broken-down wicker chairs that collapsed every time any one sat on them." I. Holst, *Gustav Holst*, 24, 140–1.

[446] Short, *Gustav Holst*, 284.

[447] I. Holst, *Gustav Holst*, 141.

[448] Britten Pears Arts HOL/1/5/2/23/21 Letter from Imogen to Gustav Holst 15 November 1930.

Liebe Vally

Wir sitzen in der Georg und trinken und essen zu veil! Es ist sehr heiss, und ich habe mein Deutsch alle vergessen and the long & short of it is I cant even collect my scattered brains to write my native tongue, but anyhow I feel that the world is a very good place! I may have different thoughts in the morning, but sufficient until the day etc etc. I hope you are having an excellent time & it will be very nice to see you on the 18th

B. L. Iso[449]

Isobel's main project for the year was renovations to The Cottage. Disappointingly, they were delayed, and the Noels invited the family to spend Christmas in Thaxted with them instead. As Imogen wrote to Gustav from Berlin on 10 December:

Iso has just written to say that the cottage won't be ready for Christmas. This is an awful blow for her. She suggests that I should go to Delia Greenwood's, and I've said "yes", anyhow for the first four or five days, and have asked her to deal with it for me.

It's fearfully nice of Miriam to have us at the Vicarage for Christmas. Will you be there too? Do hope you will.[450]

In March 1931 Imogen wrote a long letter to her mother from Florence, where she was nearing the end of a scholarship tour and had been buying decorative pottery for Isobel with money provided by Gustav for this purpose. Imogen's letter refers to Isobel suffering at home "with 'flu and a damp cottage and a series of snow storms" and asked whether she could come down to the cottage on her return "Or would you rather not have me there, if you're not straight yet? … Longing to see the cottage. Do take care of yourself, and be lazy sometimes & damn the consequences. Best love, Imo."[451] The cottage was Hill Cottage, Great Easton, where Isobel lived for around seven years spanning the death of her husband.[452] On her return home Imogen stayed for a while with her mother at Hill Cottage before returning to her professional life in London.[453]

Gustav was to return to America for a third time, in 1932. Despite a handsome fee, a planned duration of several months, and the fact that Imogen was now an adult with a musical life of her own, there is no surviving evidence that Gustav and Isobel contemplated making the visit together. Letters from Harvard University show that Isobel would have been more than welcome.[454] Gustav's hope to be able to save some of the fee may well have been a factor, recalling the joyful extravagance of their shared visit to America in 1923. His notebook shows that money matters were once again looming large, and he jotted down reminders such as "remit money home … don't keep big balance … bring home $ …" For the first time in his life he employed a professional agent, Duncan McKenzie, rather than relying on Isobel to provide publicity photos and keep unwanted visitors at bay. He wrote to McKenzie on 4 December 1931:

I thank you for your most helpful letter and should be delighted if you would be my agent and accept 20% commission for every engagement you get me. … I will conduct any work of mine with the

---

[449] Britten Pears Arts HOL/1/5/1/15/69 Letter from Gustav Holst and Isobel Holst to Vally Lasker.

[450] Britten Pears Arts HOL/1/5/2/23/26 Letter from Imogen Holst to Gustav Holst 10 December 1930. Miriam Noel was the wife of the Revd Conrad Noel.

[451] Britten Pears Arts HOL/2/8/1/9/5 Letter from Imogen Holst to Isobel Holst 14 March 1931.

[452] Telephone directory entries are in Isobel's name there for 1932–3, 1935–8.

[453] Grogan, *Imogen Holst*, 93–4.

[454] Mitchell, *Comprehensive Biography*, 527, 529, 532, 538, 539.

proviso that if 'The Planets' are wanted I must have all seven done or none. Although I am sincerely grateful to you for your offer yet I am also a little anxious. In fact I rather hope that you won't get me too many engagements! I am not as strong as I was and public engagements are best for me if they come singly.

Normally I lead a very quiet life and have to forgo much that would otherwise give me great pleasure. One great favor I would ask and this is to be quiet and alone before any public appearance.[455]

The evening before Gustav's departure for America in January 1932 he, Isobel and Imogen had dinner together before attending the London premiere of George Dyson's *The Canterbury Pilgrims*. Gustav and Isobel then spent the rest of the evening at the "Jolly Talgarth"[456] – Vally Lasker's home at 103 Talgarth Road, Hammersmith, where Gustav often spent the night. Jon Mitchell, Gustav Holst's most recent biographer, explains this unusual arrangement:

While this sleeping arrangement may appear to have been unorthodox and could raise some eyebrows, available evidence points to there having been no improper relationship between Holst and Vally Lasker. In addition to being a teacher, accompanist and amanuensis, Vally was also a hostess for St Paul's Girls' School, often giving food and lodging to the school's visitors. Still, Holst and Vally had developed a very close relationship and, possibly by his second trip to America in 1929 and certainly by his third in 1932, Vally had displaced Isobel (and, later, Imogen) as the person to whom he had the most written correspondence. This may have been due in part to professional concerns, but the fact remains that sometimes Holst's most personal and wittiest commentary was reserved for her. Yet, even if their marriage was not what it once had been, Holst and Isobel remained devoted to each other. There is nothing to prove otherwise.[457]

During this third American visit Gustav sent press cuttings (which he described as "junk") to Isobel for her to pass on. In a letter to her father from Hill Cottage, Great Easton on 7 February Imogen had read this "dope", and concluded that "Boston approves of you". She added "Iso is very much better. She sends love and says she is writing in a day or two."[458]

In financial terms Gustav's brief period of employing an agent worked well, and his third American visit more than broke even. He enjoyed his first weeks in America greatly. He was treated as a celebrity, and conducted three symphony concerts and four rehearsals. His interviews with journalists went well, and the resultant press coverage was positive. He wrote appreciatively about his agent: "What a good fellow is Duncan MacKenzie. He was most helpful when I was in New York."[459] Gustav was also able to spend the first night in 40 years under the same roof as his brother Emil, now the character actor Ernest Cossart. But Gustav became seriously ill with a duodenal ulcer whilst in America, and needed the outstanding care he received from his hosts, which included one of the doctors treating him using his own blood for a transfusion. Moreover, Gustav, "after leaving hospital ... developed a severe attack of home sickness". He might well have regretted Isobel's absence and his separation from her for the best part of half a year.

Nevertheless, despite Gustav's period of serious ill-health and the fact that in 1924 he had recuperated at Thaxted, his plans for the summer mostly involved being "alone in Talgarth

---

[455] Mitchell, *Comprehensive Biography,* 426–8.

[456] Paul Spicer, *Sir George Dyson: His Life and Music* (Boydell Press, Woodbridge, 2014), 176–7; Mitchell, *Comprehensive Biography*, 428.

[457] Mitchell, *Comprehensive Biography*.

[458] Britten Pears Arts HOL/1/5/2/23/24 Letter from Imogen Holst to Gustav Holst 7 Feb 1932.

[459] *Gustav Holst: Letters to W. G. Whittaker*, 115.

Road[460] except when my wife joins me from time to time."[461] Having been due to stay in London overnight the day after Gustav's arrival back in England, later in June 1932 Isobel was once again at home at Great Easton when Gustav, his brother Emil (visiting from America after many years there) and Imogen were on holiday in the Cotswolds together. They wrote a combined wedding anniversary postcard to her on 21 June, Gustav and Imogen both wishing she were with them, an echo of their joint message from Paris three years earlier, and Emil "expecting to see your new car enter the courtyard any minute."[462] Their wish was due to come true in August, when Gustav was expecting to be back in the Cotswolds for the weekend with Emil's daughter and his niece Valerie, an actress, as well as Isobel and Imogen.[463] Meanwhile in September 1932 Isobel extended her interest in Essex life by joining the Essex Archaeological Society.[464] The year ended with what was to become Isobel and Gustav's last Christmas together at Hill Cottage, Great Easton, followed by Gustav becoming seriously ill on Boxing Day followed by months of his being in and out of a nursing home.

Good Friday 1933 (14 April) saw another of Gustav's health crises. Vaughan Williams wrote to Vally Lasker on Isobel's behalf:

I heard just now from Mrs O'Neill that Gustav was not so well. So I rang up Ealing – he is better again & Dr Jones does not think he is in danger. There was a haemorrhage but it has now stopped and he is comfortable. The haemorrhage came on early this morning and he was taken to a nursing home in Ealing. Isabel has come up & is now stopping with Miss Jones.[465] So I think all is going well & they are ringing me up tomorrow morning. I promised to let you know as they cannot get you on the phone.[466]

Although Isobel from time to time wrote letters on her husband's behalf, thereby saving his neuritis-afflicted hand,[467] few of her autograph letters on his behalf have survived. They include three to Dora Herbert Jones starting with one dated 28 April 1933:

I am sure you will be very sorry to hear that my husband Gustav Holst is in a Nursing home, suffering from ulcerated stomach. He has been very ill indeed – he does not know how ill – & the Dr says his recovery will be very slow & there is no thought of his doing any work at all for the rest of the year.

He is greatly distressed at this & cant bear the idea of being out of everything & also he does not like disappointing people when he has undertaken to do things. However I am sure you will understand this.

He is hoping that, if he is well enough, you will allow him to come as an interesting – or rather interested invalid!

---

[460] ie at Vally Lasker's home, she presumably being away during the school summer holidays.

[461] *Gustav Holst: Letters to W. G. Whittaker*, 117.

[462] Britten Pears Arts HOL/2/8/1/9/4 Postcard from Gustav and Imogen Holst and Emil Cossart to Isobel Holst 21 June 1932.

[463] Gustav Holst: Letters to W. G. Whittaker, 117; Gustav Holst engagement diary 1932: "August 19 Fri In Oxford (Golden X Hotel) with Iso Imo Valerie".

[464] I am grateful to Michael Leach for his search of the Society's Transactions and for the reference to Volume xxi (new series) p.196, which records that Mrs. Gustav Holst joined the Society on the nomination of Mrs. Simcoe on 14 September 1932.

[465] Mabel Rodwell Jones.

[466] BL Ms MUS 1714/1/8, ff 27–8. Letter from Ralph Vaughan Williams to Vally Lasker.

[467] *Gustav Holst: Letters to W. G. Whittaker*, 77, 124.

However there is time to let you know later how he goes on.[468]

Isobel was also having a difficult time. Her new car did not last for long. As she wrote in a chatty letter from Great Easton to her friend Maja Kjöhler on 11 June 1933, she:

… had a motor accident in town[469] … & I hurt my arm & could not write for a few days & then having no car to get about in made things rather difficult & constant visits to Gustav etc. took up all my time. … I have to come up on Wed, first for the Dentist, then at 2.30 a police court case about the accident & then I shall rush over to see Gustav. … You will be glad to hear that G left the Nursing Home last Friday & he is having to stay in Ealing for a week under observation to see how he gets on when he is up, & then I am going to have him here for a week before he goes to Wales on the 23rd. I shall probably be in town on the 27th or 28th & I should love to look you up then to tell you all the news & hear all yours.

It has been a terrible time for us all during the last 3 months & I do hope poor old Gustav has at last got rid of his troubles – at any rate for a time.

He is not to do any work for the rest of the year & he is to rest a lot. Of course he hates that & is very depressed about it. … Imogen is having wonderful treatment for her arm but of course it will not remove the cause it will only ease the pain.

She is having her annual Hay Fever just now & is a perfect wreck! [470]

By July, however, Isobel had recovered sufficiently to join Gustav in a two-day visit to Balfour Gardiner, who asked Isobel beforehand about the restrictions in Gustav's diet.[471] In August 1933 father and daughter again holidayed together, sending Isobel at Great Easton a joint postcard of the Cloisters of Magdalen College Oxford, Gustav writing "We have had a lovely time together and send our love and hope you are not as hot as we are" and Imogen adding "This is just the right place for a heat-wave! Hope the mushrooms are not frying before they are picked."[472] Later that year, however, Gustav wrote to Imogen "I hope Iso is coming to London for a week from next Friday and that we shall paint the town a middle-aged red."[473] Gustav's diary records Isobel's expected arrival on the Friday and plans to go together to the "Russian ballet" on Saturday 9 September 1933 and to the matinée of a new play, "The Distaff Side", on Wednesday 13 September.

Gustav and Isobel's last prolonged separation was the result of neither a holiday nor work abroad, but of him being treated in the New Lodge Clinic in Windsor Forest for what became a terminal illness whilst she was suffering from another of her colds. As a result they saw each other neither on Christmas Day 1933 nor on New Year's Day 1934. Isobel and Imogen were due to spend Christmas together at Thaxted, and Gustav hoped that Imogen would "encourage her to lay up as much as possible and to shirk all duties."[474]

He wrote to Isobel from the clinic on Boxing Day:

---

[468] Britten Pears Arts HOL/1/5/3/3. Despite his illness Gustav, accompanied by Imogen, attended the Festival of Music and Poetry at Gregynog which Dora Herbert Jones organised in June.

[469] ie London.

[470] Britten Pears Arts HOL/1/5/3/1 Letter from Isobel Holst to Maja Kjöhler 11 June 1933.

[471] Lloyd, *Balfour Gardiner*, 188.

[472] Britten Pears Arts HOL/1/5/1/8 Postcard dated 6 August [1933].

[473] Mitchell, *Comprehensive Biography*, 425.

[474] Britten Pears Arts HOL/2/8/2/104/54 Letter from Gustav Holst to Imogen Holst 22 December 1933.

Dr Hurst has just brought me the verdict. They have found the ulcer and they hope to put me right in six weeks, no operation being necessary.

I am allowed to sit up in my room which is beautifully warm and there is a small library just outside so life is not too bad. I spent Xmas Day reading Jane Austin and Trotsky.

I hope your cold is gone or going and that Imogen is getting a real rest. If she is ever near Brook Green[475] she might look in and see if there are any parcels for me but it is not important. Ruthven is forwarding all letters here but I told him to keep parcels and to show them to you, Imogen, Vally or Nora and either of the two latter will let know if any have come.

Canon Fellowes[476] is coming to see me today and will probably take this and post it.

Greetings to all
BL
G.[477]

He wrote to Isobel again on 1 January 1934:

Thanks for letter and please thank Imogen for hers. It is good to know that your cold is going and that you are running no risks in this filthy weather. And it is exciting news that Imogen is really composing. I thought she would be only arranging.

Would you tell her that my visiting hours are 2–7 and if she could let me know the times of arrival and departure of her trains at Windsor by Friday morning at the latest (or else telephone to the office on Friday morning) the car shall fetch her both ways. Would the 4.47 from Windsor to Paddington give her time to catch the 6.30 from Liverpool Str? If so that would allow time for a little tea here.[478]

Re Me. The doctor told me today that the bleeding is gradually decreasing. The normal experience is four weeks on strict diet (hourly milky 'feeds') followed by two weeks on eggs and fish etc with a little walking. So I must reckon on being here until the beginning of February. Term will have begun before then so it's no use making any plans yet but if I'm allowed to travel I hope to come home every now and then.

Everything seems to be taking its normal course so we must just wait patiently a little longer.

I shall look forward to seeing you in about a fortnight when you are quite fit and the fogs have gone. If you spend a night at Vally's ask her a few days beforehand as I fancy she is having rather a lot of visitors. Glad you like 'Brazilian Adventure'[479]. I'm thinking of sending you 'Boomerang' which Mabel gave me at Xmas.

BL
G.[480]

On 31 January Gustav was still in the nursing home when he wrote to Imogen in an upbeat mood:

Iso has just left – we had a lovely time together. And Balfour[481] came on Tuesday and was in grand form. It's all right about March 3. … An Idea! Couldn't we persuade Iso to come? I'd sleep at my old inn and turn up for meals![482]

---

[475] ie St Paul's Girls' School.

[476] A minor canon of St George's Chapel Windsor and an authority on Tudor church music, who lent Gustav a Bible around this time.

[477] Britten Pears Arts HOL/1/5/1/8/52 Letter from Gustav to Isobel Holst 26 December 1933.

[478] Imogen's diary records that she intended to visit on 17 January.

[479] A book by Peter Fleming first published in 1933.

[480] Britten Pears Arts HOL/1/5/1/8/53 Letter from Gustav to Isobel Holst 1 January 1934.

[481] Balfour Gardiner.

[482] Britten Pears Arts HOL/2/8/2/104/56 Letter from Gustav to Imogen Holst 31 January 1934.

A week or so later his health was still in the balance. He wrote again to Imogen on 8 February:

> I'd love to come to Eothen next month but there is very little hope. And even less hope about March 3. I suggest Iso and you go to Oxford and if by some strange chance I am able to go at the last moment, you two women can quarrel about which one is to sleep out![483]

On 21 February 1934 Gustav left the nursing home to stay nearby with Mabel Rodwell Jones in Ealing.[484] He was a little stronger but fundamentally unhealed. He had resolved that if he was not better by then he was going to discharge himself anyway and try once again to live his own version of a "restricted life" whilst in addition he was "going to try quacks – Iso and I discussed it in this place of all places."[485]

Gustav was just about well enough to attend the March event referred to in his letters to Imogen – a concert at the Oxford Assembly rooms which included a performance of one of Imogen's folksong arrangements. It was to be the last concert Gustav ever attended.[486] On 15 March he wrote to Vally Lasker to say that he had had "another blow", and his blood count was still deemed too low. He added "I'm telling Isobel to ring you up … if she wants you to put her up."[487]

Two months later Gustav entered another nursing home to prepare for surgery, aware that this might be a matter of "kill or cure".[488] In April Imogen, who was herself convalescing at Champneys Nature Cure Resort, assumed that Isobel was preoccupied with her annual spring cleaning at home.[489] A couple of weeks later Isobel was suffering herself – "down with arthritis in the leg but hopes to come [to visit Gustav] on Thursday".[490] She was not fully recovered when she visited Gustav, who reported to Imogen that "Iso is up. She looked done up yesterday but I hear she is better today – she is coming to see me this afternoon."[491] It was, however, Gustav's "missus Isobel" who wrote to his good friend of over 20 years W. G. Whittaker – a visitor at the Holsts' home since their days in Barnes – and he responded with a well-received letter about fellow musicians, including Handel and JS Bach.[492] When the operation had finally been scheduled, on Bank Holiday Monday 21 May Gustav wrote what was to be his last letter to Imogen, who had visited him three weeks previously:

---

[483] Britten Pears Arts HOL/2/8/2/104/57 Letter from Gustav to Imogen Holst 8 February 1934.

[484] Gustav Holst diary entry for 21 February 1934.

[485] Britten Pears Arts HOL/2/8/2/104/58 Letter from Gustav Holst to Imogen Holst 11 February 1934.

[486] Grogan, *Imogen Holst*, 113.

[487] Britten Pears Arts HOL/1/5/1/14/92 Letter from Gustav Holst to Vally Lasker 15 March 1934.

[488] Short, *Gustav Holst*, 322–323.

[489] Imogen wrote to Gustav: "…I'm wondering how poor Iso is getting on with her spring-cleaning without enough water to go round." Britten Pears Arts HOL/1/5/2/23/45 Letter from Imogen Holst to Gustav Holst 23 April 1934.

[490] Britten Pears Arts HOL/2/8/2/104/60 Letter from Gustav Holst to Imogen Holst 6 May 1934.

[491] Britten Pears Arts HOL/2/8/2/104/62 Letter from Gustav Holst to Imogen Holst.

[492] *Gustav Holst: Letters to W. G. Whittaker,* 124.

Iso will be here and will keep you posted with the latest news. Enclosed is just to warn you of what is coming … Is there any chance of seeing you next Sunday if it's allowed which it will be if all goes well. Iso will be at Mabel's.[493]

All was not well. A poignant card dated 23 May 1934 from Isobel to Dora Herbert Jones, who was organising another music and poetry festival at Gregynog in June, updated her on Gustav's state of health:

My husband wanted me to let you know that he was having an operation this morning. It is safely over, altho it was a major one & he will not be out of danger for three days. It took three hours, & the shock to the system has been very great, which will make convalescence a very slow affair. I will let you know later how he goes on.[494]

Two days later Gustav died. As he had predicted, Isobel was with him. Gustav failed to recognise her when he came round from the anaesthetic.[495] Imogen was there too,[496] and telephoned Vaughan Williams with the news. The latter wrote to Isobel and Imogen straight away:

My very dearest love to you both. I know you don't want me to say more & I know that you know that he has it & you have it.

My only thought is now which ever way I turn what are we to do without him – every thing seems to have turned back to him – what would Gustav think or advise or do. …

I longed to come straight over, & see you when dear Imogen telephoned me this morning – & you know you have only got to say 'come' & I will come at once.[497]

Either Isobel or Imogen did ring Gustav's closest friend. He came. On 28 May Gustav's friend Dr George Bell, Bishop of Chichester, conducted his funeral, which Imogen described in her thank you letter to him as "perfect in every way."[498] On 31 May Bell's appreciation of Gustav was published in *The Times*, and on 1 June Isobel wrote an affectionate letter to the Bishop from a hydro in Matlock, Derbyshire, to ask permission for her husband's ashes to be buried in Chichester Cathedral:

Imogen is helping me with the letters & I think yours must be among them, because I cannot find it.

I want to thank you for the very beautiful way you read the service for dear Gustav and for your article in the Times of yesterday.

Do forgive me that I did not speak to you last Monday – I could not trust myself & thought it better to go away.

He always loved you & your wife & his visits to you & if it is at all possible I should love his ashes to rest in the Cathedral.

I am really glad now that he has passed on, because if he had lived he would have been an invalid & he would have been most unhappy.

I was with him to the end & his going out was so peaceful & beautiful, and he suffered no pain.

Again thank you, thank you for everything

---

[493] Britten Pears Arts HOL/2/8/2/104/61 Letter from Gustav Holst to Imogen Holst 20 May 1934. As the Holsts had no London home in the 1930s Gustav and Isobel both spent time staying with Mabel Rodwell Jones in West London, quite near the clinic.
[494] Britten Pears Arts HOL/1/5/3/3. The postcard was addressed from 2 Elm Crescent, Ealing.
[495] Short, *Gustav Holst*, 326.
[496] Information from Gustav Holst's death certificate.
[497] *Letters of Ralph Vaughan Williams 1895–1958*, ed Hugh Cobbe (Oxford, 2008) no 247.
[498] Lambeth Palace Library Bishop Bell Papers 208 f 205.

Isobel Holst[499]

Why did Isobel choose Chichester Cathedral for her husband's final resting place over Thaxted, where Gustav had enjoyed memorable music-making during the Whitsun Festivals and she had continuing ties? On the one hand, her husband's row with the vicar, Conrad Noel, which led to him moving the Festivals away from their Thaxted origin, had long since healed. Gustav had even spent Christmas 1931 at Thaxted vicarage as Noel's guest, and it was Noel who witnessed Gustav's signature on the commissioning contract for his Hammersmith. On the other, the radical reputation of Thaxted church and its vicar, inflamed by the practice of processing with the Host from the sacrament of the eucharist despite the express prohibition of the local bishop in 1919,[500] continued in 1934, when Conrad Noel wrote with pride that "the Thaxted worship … scandalises the 'ratepayer' and attracts many in the town itself and many pilgrims from all quarters … We preach the Christ who all through His life stressed the value of the common meal, the bread and wine joyously shared among His people, the mass as prelude to a New World Order in which all would be justly produced and equally distributed. … all this involves politics, and we are often rebuked for mixing politics with religion …"[501] Perhaps the main reason was as stated by Isobel in her letter to Bishop Bell, that she wanted Gustav's ashes to rest close to the friends with whom he had enjoyed spending time. Having collaborated with John Masefield and George Bell in the production of the pioneering and at the time controversial Mystery Play of *The Coming of Christ* at Canterbury in Whitsuntide 1928, Gustav's allegiance to George and Henrietta Bell continued when George Bell moved to become Bishop of Chichester.[502] The affection was reciprocated, with the new Bishop sending an early invitation to Gustav and the Whitsuntide Singers to celebrate Whitsun 1930 at Chichester.[503]

The service for the interment of Gustav's ashes, held on Sunday 24 June 1934, was indeed conducted by Bishop Bell at Chichester, incorporating music by both Vaughan Williams and Holst. Isobel clearly felt she had made the right choice, as Imogen wrote in another thank you letter to the Bishop:

Apart from the sheer beauty of the service, there was such conviction about it – it was so very much a beginning instead of an end, and any suggestion of finality would have been utterly impossible.

You will know how very, very grateful my mother and [I] feel to you for all that you have done, and how there are no words in which to try and thank you.[504]

Isobel also wrote to Vaughan Williams and his wife Adeline from the Matlock Hydro on 3 June:

---

[499] Lambeth Palace Library Bishop Bell Papers 208 f 206.

[500] *Uplifting the Son of Man as the God of Justice in our midst* (Church Publishing Company, Thaxted, 1919), 6–7.

[501] Epilogue by Conrad Noel to the history of Thaxted written by Isobel's friend, Ethel Simcoe, *A Short History of the Parish and Ancient Borough of Thaxted* (W. Hart & Son, Saffron Walden, 1934), 135–6.

[502] Lambeth Palace Library Bishop Bell Papers 154, ff 276–7, private letter from Gustav to George Bell.

[503] Lambeth Palace Library Bishop Bell Papers 155, ff 3–4, letter dated 1 January 1930 from Bishop Bell to Gustav, and ff 5–6, letter dated 6 January from Gustav to Bishop Bell.

[504] Lambeth Palace Library Bishop Bell Papers 208, f 215v–216.

Thank you so much for your beautiful letter & for all that you have done for us always. One cant write about these things, but I would like you to know that dear Gustav died quietly & peacefully like a little child, knowing nothing about it. I was with him all the time & he suffered no pain after the operation.

It was a very severe operation & he could never have recovered sufficiently to work & enjoy life & I know he did not wish to live unless he could do that, so I am thankful he was spared all the pain & disappointment of recovery.

Imogen was wonderful – She adored her father & they were so much to each other in every way & she took charge of all business & saw to the funeral arrangements & thought of everything & then insisted on my coming here at once.

She left me no loophole of escape because she booked my room & bought my railway ticket.

I was glad to come away from everybody I know for a time & I am slowly getting through the hundreds of letters I have received.[505]

Again, Bless you & thank you
Yours affectionately
Isobel[506]

---

[505] Almost none of which have survived.
[506] BL Ms MUS 1714/1/8, f 156.

Chapter Eight
Life after Gustav

Isobel Holst with two dogs (Britten Pears Arts HOL/2/11/5/21)

How did Isobel live her life after her husband's death? Between them, Gustav, Imogen and Ralph Vaughan Williams provided for her materially. Gustav had written to Imogen on 21 December 1933:

You are not mentioned in my will partly because Iso will let you have anything you want, but chiefly because the one thing I want to leave you is too intimate to be allowed in a legal document.

I send you my deepest gratitude for all the joy and pride you have brought me. And my best wish for you is that you shall one day have a son or daughter who will be to you what you have been to me.[507]

What this meant in practical terms was that Gustav's will made provision that the income from the royalties, which was limited to only 4 per cent of their capital value, that would have been £36 a year, should go to Isobel, and the rest should be accumulated and the capital would pass to Imogen when Isobel died. The royalties were valued at £960 in 1934, and the whole estate at about £8,000–9,000. They would not have been enough to support Isobel and through successive deeds of variation Imogen chose to accept only a small percentage of her father's estate for herself, diverting the rest to her mother.[508]

Imogen's friend Rosamund Strode developed a theory that Gustav's will was restrictive because:

Isobel was what you might call a 'big-spender' if she had the chance, and I certainly know she used to, as an old lady, she used to take a taxi up to London, and she'd blow a lot of money at Harrods, and Floris, and expensive Knightsbridge shops because she enjoyed high living, but didn't really have the means most of her life. And it's possible that this rather restricting-looking Will was done precisely with that in mind. … if she'd been left everything absolutely she might easily have gone through the lot.[509]

During the two years after Gustav's death Imogen visited her mother more often, including to "go through books" with her in July 1934 and accompanying her to a musical performance of *The Rivals* in November 1935. In June 1935 they even went to Paris for the weekend together.

Isobel spent most of the following 30 years in Essex, for the first few years of her lengthy widowhood remaining at Hill Cottage, Great Easton, which until 1938, like some of her other previous homes, was not connected to the main water supply.[510] She maintained her interest in Essex history, including for several years her membership of the Essex Archaeological Society.[511] Barbara Simcoe recalled Isobel being her mother Ethel's "best woman friend", and that "she and Mum used to go tearing off to the churches and things".[512]

When Ethel Simcoe arranged a historical pageant in aid of Great Sampford church Isobel was an enthusiastic participant as a yokel, dressed in breeches with a red scarf round her neck

---

[507] Britten Pears Arts HOL/2/8/2/104/53. This letter was written two days before Gustav was due to have preparatory X-rays before surgery, as he explained in a further letter to Imogen on 22 December HOL/2/8/2/104/54.

[508] Grogan, *Imogen Holst*, 112, 114.

[509] Britten Pears Arts HOL/5/2/13 Transcript of RS/Len Haswell's taped conversation 23 June 1988. Len Haswell, who gives the impression of trying to avoid being drawn into speculation, replied: "If one doesn't have a great deal of money, and one is fond of ones wife, one would think of her rather than ones children."

[510] Britten Pears Arts HOL/4/5/1/2 Harrison family papers, partially dated letter (Sunday May 22) Isobel Holst to Toby [Harry Hughes Harrison].

[511] I am grateful to the Society's Deputy Librarian, Andrew Smith, for the reference to Isobel's presence on the 1935–6 membership list, which included her address at Hill Cottage, Great Easton, Dunmow.

[512] Britten Pears Arts HOL/5/2/15 Full transcript of RS/Barbara Simcoe's taped conversation 16 July 1988.

and brandishing a beaker of beer. Imogen, who provided the music for the pageant,[513] joined her at the celebration of Conrad Noel's silver jubilee as Vicar of Thaxted in September 1935.[514]

Vaughan Williams remained thoughtfully supportive, corresponding with both Isobel and Imogen. In summer 1934 he encouraged Adrian Boult to arrange for one of the BBC concerts to be devoted to Gustav's music, and include the Scherzo (H192) of a Symphony which Gustav had worked on in 1933–1934, and completed shortly before his death.[515] When Adrian Boult replied positively to the suggestion, it was to Isobel that Vaughan Williams directed him for the subsequent agreements:

I am telling Isobel what you say & asking her to write to you. It is of course she and not I who have control over Gustav's music.[516]

The first performance of Gustav's Scherzo took place at the Queen's Hall, London, on 6 February 1935, with Adrian Boult conducting the BBC Symphony Orchestra. June 1935 saw the first Whitsun Festival after Gustav's death. As part of the celebrations, on the Monday Vaughan Williams conducted his own Mass in Chichester Cathedral, the venue for several of the festivals during Gustav's lifetime and where he was now buried. Vaughan Williams thought it sad that Imogen was not present, but wrote to her after the event to report that he "thought Isobel distinctly better".[517]

On Saturday 6 March 1937 Isobel received a rare share of the limelight when she, together with Vaughan Williams, was presented to Queen Mary at the opening ceremony of the new Holst music room which was built at Morley College as a lasting memorial to her husband.[518] Queen Mary chose the date herself, and it was inconvenient for Imogen, who agreed to make a fleeting visit to play one of Holst's compositions on the piano, but not to stay to be presented to the Queen because of her work commitments. Fortunately Isobel – who once again had been suffering from flu – responded to the Principal's invitation enthusiastically, mentioning her wish

to present to the Memorial Room a baton which was given to my husband by Masefield after he had done the music for the latter's play 'The Coming of Christ' in Canterbury Cathedral. It has an inscription on it & I should love Morley to have it.[519]

On 10 July 1937 Isobel had a less pleasant experience when she suffered a burglary at Hill Cottage. Two local newspapers covered her response to the 19-year-old offender's crime with

---

[513] Britten Pears Arts HOL/5/2/15 Full transcript of RS/Barbara Simcoe's taped conversation 16 July 1988.

[514] "Thaxted Jubilee: The Rev. Conrad Noel 25 years as vicar", *Essex Chronicle*, 27 September 1935. I am grateful to Michael Goatcher for this information.

[515] J. N. Moore ed., *Music and Friends: Seven decades of letters to Adrian Boult* (London, 1979), 116–117.

[516] British Library MS Mus.1714/1/8, ff. 101–102, Letter from Ralph Vaughan Williams to Adrian Boult, 19 August 1934.

[517] Britten Pears Arts HOL/2/7/7/67 Letter from Ralph Vaughan Williams to Imogen Holst, 14 June [1935].

[518] *The Times*, 12 March 1937.

[519] Correspondence in Morley College Library, for access to which I am indebted to Elaine Andrews. Although the Holst Music Room is still in regular use at Morley College, his baton appears not to have survived the WWII bombing.

the heading "Gustav Holst's Widow's kind gesture". The young burglar had struck whilst Isobel had gone to Thaxted one Saturday afternoon, and had taken a bank safe containing a shilling from a drawer in her sitting-room, a 10 shilling note from a drawer in her dressing table and a pair of binoculars. The defendant, who pleaded guilty, stated that he was down and out, with no work and no trade, and had knocked at the house several times to ask for some bread. Having agreed to promise to join the Army, after which his period of probation would be cancelled, and to return the 10 shilling note to Mrs Holst, the police superintendent reported that "he understood that Mrs. Holst desired to present the 10/- note to the accused"[520] – a kind gesture indeed.

Imogen spent much of August and September 1937 writing her biography of her father. She recorded that she was "especially grateful to Dr. R. Vaughan Williams and my mother for their advice and criticism" in writing the book. Its publication in 1938 must have been a significant milestone for all three of them.

One of only two surviving letters from Isobel to her elder brother Harry (Toby), written from Great Easton on 30 April 1938, four years after Gustav's death, provides insight into her life as a widow:

Forgive my delay in answering your letter as I have only just got back from a Motor Tour with Imogen,[521] & the pile of letters waiting for me was appalling.

I should very much like to see you & Clara again & in about a fortnight I shall have a little spare time & then I shall be staying in town every Tuesday night until the end of the month. Would it suit you if I ran over one Tuesday afternoon? I could ring up & settle when it would be convenient to you. Imogen will be away those nights & she lends me the flat. It is a one room flat with a Divan bed & I garage the car quite near.

Don't ever risk coming here without warning as I am away a great deal & I shut up the cottage which is quite small & I have no maid. Ive got a very busy time just now as I belong to several society's, Essex Archaeological Society, Essex Agricultural Soc:, I do transport work – taking lecturers to remote W.I.[522] societys where there are no buses, etc, etc, I also have to look after the car & do most of the gardening, – I only have an old man of 75 once a week, & with my weekly visits to town the week's slip by at a most alarming rate. Some people think that if you live in the country you just sit & twiddle your thumbs & long for something to turn up!

I shall like to hear about Graham[523] & his wife & daughter.

Ive had a very trying & expensive time with arthritis in my spine & that is why I come to town once a week for treatment. I'm much better now but last year I crawled about with the aid of a stick & thought I should be like that for the rest of my life! Well, let me know if my suggestion is any good to you.

If not, I will arrange to stay a weekend in town & come over then. I know your house, because one Sunday afternoon last year when I was up for the weekend I ran over to see you & no one was at home.

I had no card with me & not even a pencil & paper, & I meant to write when I got back but I didn't.

I am the world's worst letter writer – I hate it & never write unless I can help it.

I hope you & Clara are both in good health & not too depressed at the state of the world at present!

---

[520] *Chelmsford Chronicle*, 16 July 1937, 5; *Essex Newsman*, 17 July 1937.

[521] Isobel would have been the driver.

[522] Women's Institute. Thaxted had its own branch.

[523] Harry's son Graham was born in 1906 in Chiswick so was a similar age to Imogen, and they were to die in the same year. He was elected to the Chartered Institute of Patent Agents in 1937 and listed in the Institute's Transactions for 1943–4 as c/o Pollak, Mercer & Tench, London. In September 1965, when he was granted probate for his late mother's estate, he was a chartered patent agent.

>Imogen & I had planned a holiday in Vienna at Easter but of course it was quite impossible.[524]
>More when we meet
>Affectionately yours
>Isobel.[525]

The explanation for Isobel and her brother having so much news to catch up on was more than Isobel's reluctant letter-writing. Harry had continued in his engineering career, and was a telegraph apparatus worker by 1911, when he, his wife Clara Caroline and five-year-old son Graham Alfred, were living in a 6 room house in Chiswick. It seems likely that his travels to Chicago via New York in 1920 and from Lisbon to Southampton in 1934 were connected to his work, whilst Clara stayed at home in Liverpool, their main home from 1917, when he started to work for the Automatic Telephone Manufacturing (ATM) Company Limited there. He had a successful career before being compulsorily retired before the age of 60 during the hard times of the thirties, and in 1932 was awarded an honorary MEng degree by Liverpool University. He was the author of a number of books, including *Model Steam Turbines: How to design and build them* (nd, 1904), *Engineering Mathematics Simply Explained* (nd, 1905), *An Introduction to the Strowger System of Automatic Telephony* (1924),[526] and *The Elements of Telephone Transmission* (1927). In the preface to this last work he proudly acknowledged that his son, "G. A. Harrison of King's College, Cambridge" had read through the manuscript.

According to Isobel's nephew Graham, writing to Imogen many years later, in 1980, despite the previously close relationship of both Isobel and Gustav with his father, contact was infrequent in later years, a fact which he attributed to his mother:

>My mother, Clara Caroline Fraser, was the eldest of a family of nine, the father being Hugh Fraser of Inverness. They were an uncompromising family, particularly the women. As it turned out my mother and father were not ideally suited to one another. My father was in some respects an idealist and a scholar in a limited sense. My mother was intensely practical and very down-to-earth. Such opposite characteristics must, however, have provided a strong attractive force because they were engaged for thirteen years – mainly because of the necessity for my father to maintain his family until his mother died. This was a cause of my mother's resentment against the Harrisons and in fact she wanted to break the engagement. However, they were eventually married in 1905 and although my father and yours remained good friends, the two families did tend to drift apart.[527]

Around 1939 Isobel moved house to Little Barn, Park Road, Little Easton, about a mile away from Great Easton.[528] In the 1939 Register, compiled just after the outbreak of war, Isobel was recorded as living there with Katherine Hecht, a singer. Isobel and Imogen were joint holders of the copyright in Gustav's unpublished compositions.[529]

During WWII Isobel remained in north Essex. Whilst sheltered from the horrors of the blitz bombings of London, it was sufficiently close to the capital to attract its share in the fear and alarm of war. On 26 August 1940 one of the German hurricane aircraft flying over Debden

---

[524] Europe was on the verge of WWII.

[525] Britten Pears Arts HOL/1/5/3/4. A second letter from Isobel to Toby, dated 22 May (no year) proposes a time and date to meet – "I shall come by car & I know the way."

[526] By which time he was MIEE and MIRSE.

[527] Britten Pears Arts HOL/4/5/1/2 Harrison family papers Graham Harrison Notes on the Harrison Family.

[528] Telephone directory entries are in Isobel's name there for 1939 and 1941–2.

[529] Britten Pears Arts HOL/1/5/3/6 Letter from Ralph Vaughan Williams to Vally Lasker ?1939.

airfield crashed into one of the corn fields surrounding Thaxted. On 25–26 February 1942 Imogen paid a "flying visit to my home in Essex … as my mother was being turned out of her house." Thousands of trees on the previously grand Easton Lodge estate where Gustav and Isobel had benefited from the hospitality and patronage of the late Countess of Warwick[530] were destroyed to create the Little Easton airfield, where in July 1943 the US Air Force took up residence.

Isobel was now in her 60s. Conrad Noel's granddaughter, Sylvia Heath *née* Putterill, recalled doing some work on a local chicken farm at the beginning of the war and on the first morning being put to work on the chaff machine in a barn "and there turning the handle of the machine was Isobel! Dressed appropriately in dungarees as befitted a farm hand!"[531]

By 1946, and probably before, Isobel moved to 5 Westbury House, Stortford Road, Great Dunmow, where she lived until 1955.[532] Whilst only a few miles away from her previous Essex homes, Westbury House was in the centre of Dunmow, which is a town rather than a village, and about 6 miles from Thaxted. In 1985 the daughter of one of her friends and companions wrote:

> … my mother moved to Dunmow in about 1940 I suppose and it was then the two ladies met – Mrs. Holst was of course living in Dunmow at that time.
>
> My mother lived in a rather lonely house on the outskirts and the bombing made her, and us her daughters, very nervous for her safety. So she moved in with Isobel and acted as companion and general dog's body for several years. I'm afraid I cant remember whether she actually moved with Isobel to Thaxted … I am fairly certain she had her own little pad of some sort but spent a great deal of her time with Isobel whose increasing deafness together with a mastectomy (followed eventually by a further mastectomy) meant she really needed a good deal of help and companionship. This Imogen could not possibly give though she was unstinting in her care and concern.[533]

In 1949 Isobel and Imogen, as well as Vaughan Williams, attended the unveiling of a plaque at Gustav's birthplace in Cheltenham. Imogen was writing her study of *The Music of Gustav Holst* in the late 1940s, and following the book's publication, in February 1952 Isobel and Imogen presented the majority of Gustav's original manuscript scores of his own compositions – 35 bound volumes – to the British Library.[534] In summer 1952 Ralph Vaughan Williams and his soon-to-become second wife Ursula were planning to stay with Isobel at the Imperial Hotel, probably for the Three Choirs' Festival.[535]

Benjamin Britten, who had driven Imogen to the station to see her mother in Great Dunmow and friends at Thaxted over Christmas 1952, drove Imogen to and from her mother when she visited her for the Easter weekend in 1953, and commented on "how young Iso looked and how nice she'd made the house." On the way there Britten had asked Imogen why her mother lived in Dunmow, and Imogen responded by talking about Arthur Caton, the Thaxted weaver who had known all three members of the Holst family for several decades

---

[530] She died in 1938.

[531] Letter from Sylvia Hughes to Michael Goatcher postmark 3 June 2015.

[532] Telephone directory entries are in Isobel's name there for 1946 and 1948–54.

[533] Britten Pears Arts, letter dated 1 October 1985 from Mrs (Jane) Mary Tomlinson to Mrs H Lilley.

[534] The certificate of receipt to Mrs Isobel and Miss Imogen Holst is at Britten Pears Arts HOL/2/7/21/1, 16 February 1952.

[535] Letter from Ralph Vaughan Williams to Alice Sumsion, 27 July 1952.

and kept more of an eye on Isobel than her daughter, who lived about 80 miles away, was able to do.[536]

Isobel herself, despite her modest means, for many years supported the Aldeburgh Festival founded by Britten, Peter Pears and Eric Crozier. When Aldeburgh's Jubilee Hall, the main venue for the early years of the Festival, underwent extensive renovation in 1959–1960, Isobel was one of the guarantors, as well as one of the much larger number of Jubilee Hall subscribers.[537] Imogen spent much of 1951 abroad, and on her return spent several months living with her mother in Dunmow, travelling by bus, train and on foot to Aldeburgh on Wednesday evenings to take the rehearsals for the Aldeburgh Festival Choir.[538] Isobel's consistent support for the Aldeburgh Festival coincided with her daughter's moving to Aldeburgh in September 1952 and her increasingly active role in the Festival's organisation from 1953. At the end of July 1953, with the Festival over for another year, Britten, Peter Pears and Imogen detoured to Thaxted to see Isobel on their way back to Aldeburgh from the Decca recording studios in Hampstead. Imogen wrote in her diary:

We stopped for tea at Westbury House:– the sun was shining and none of the neighbours had got their radios on and Iso was at the top of her form – they both enjoyed it and it was lovely and peaceful.[539]

Imogen's visits to Thaxted were rare during this busy stage of her life. She managed, however, a 10-day visit at the end of June 1954, when Britten was away, and at the end of September Isobel went to stay in Aldeburgh for four days, with Imogen making two further visits to Thaxted in October and at Christmas.[540]

Vaughan Williams continued to demonstrate his affectionate support for Isobel, mentioning her as one of only two personal recipients of financial support from the trust fund he set up in 1956.[541] Although it was very much Imogen rather than Isobel who promoted Gustav's works and kept the memory of his music alive, when in December 1956 Vaughan Williams sponsored a concert of Gustav's lesser-known works at the Royal Festival Hall in London, the 80-year-old Isobel as well as Imogen planned to attend.[542]

Around 1955 the royalties from Gustav's works started to increase, chiefly as recordings proliferated. Isobel was able to move to her last home of her own at Weaverhead Cottage, close to the centre of Thaxted.[543] The house – which Isobel owned, and which was the only home to be owned rather than rented by her, Gustav or Imogen – is set at an angle to the lane, giving it a fine view of the church she loved. It was built by Bertram and Constance Hawker, sister of Lord Noel-Buxton, so was yet another connection with Conrad Noel and his

---

[536] Grogan, *Imogen Holst*, 230, 260–261.

[537] Aldeburgh Festival Programme (1960). I am grateful to Michael Goatcher for this reference and for information from the Festival Programmes from 1953–1969.

[538] Wilfrid J Wren, *Voices by the Sea: The story of the Aldeburgh Festival Choir* (Lavenham, 1981), 25.

[539] Grogan, *Imogen Holst*, 282.

[540] Britten Pears Arts HOL/2/9/19 Imogen Holst engagement diary for 1954.

[541] Letter from Ralph Vaughan Williams to the Committee of the Ralph Vaughan Williams Trust, 29 October 1956. He suggested a fund of £250 for Mrs Holst, and by far his largest donation was a guarantee of £1500 for the concert of Holst's music.

[542] J. N. Moore ed., *Music and Friends*, 163.

[543] Telephone directory entries there for 1955, 1957–8, 1960, 1961–4, 1968 and 1969; Grogan, *Imogen Holst* 345.

family.[544] It is also close to Church House, Arthur Caton and Kate Butters' home, and Rosamund Strode believed that Arthur, as well as Isobel's Trustees, had been instrumental in persuading her to buy it, noting that "he was marvellous at looking after Isobel".[545] It was from Weaverhead Cottage that Isobel signed her last will in January 1957. Her previous Essex homes had been several centuries old, which gave her full range for her renovation and decorating schemes.[546]

Imogen, who visited her there in October 1958 whilst Benjamin Britten, for whom she was still devotedly working, was abroad, was conscious of the infrequency of her visits but did little to rectify this. The relationship between daughter and mother was dutiful rather than close. Not only did Imogen follow her father into a musical career, she also adopted some of his tastes and mannerisms, including a lack of domesticity and, unlike her mother, never learning to drive. Isobel clearly enjoyed cooking and baking, and played a leading role in catering for community events in Thaxted, whilst Imogen almost prided herself in only being able to cook eggs. According to Barbara Simcoe, "Iso told me that she and Imogen could never live together." Rosamund Strode agreed:

> I'm sure that's absolutely true; I only saw them in the house, you know, at the end of little visits, and I always thought that it looked as if the visit had been long enough … But if they both realised that, that's not so bad is it.[547]

Despite having such similar nicknames, Iso and Imo had developed increasingly different interests, and Imogen's devotion to her father further emphasised their differences. Her attitude towards her now elderly mother was apparent to her close friend and assistant Rosamund Strode, who observed that Imogen "simply failed to realize quite how much Caton did in caring for Iso, characteristically parking the situation in a far corner of her busy mind because 'she didn't want to get too involved about it'. …" Rosamund also experienced at first hand that Imogen "could be dismissive to an embarrassing degree of her mother's gestures of affection – especially gifts of food and clothes."[548] Food and clothes were two of the things which Isobel did best.

Isobel became a familiar figure in the Thaxted shops, sometimes wearing a green eye shade. She still had the pre-war Morris 8 car which had also served as the Arts Department car at Dartington Hall in Devon, where Imogen had worked from 1942 to 1951, at a time when petrol was scarce and the Department did not have a car of its own. When she could no longer drive it herself Dorothy Ives, a retired district nurse, drove it for her.[549] Long-standing Thaxted pillar of the community Peter King, a former pupil of Arthur Caton's partner Kate Butters, helped her in various ways and noted her chattiness and, particularly, her kindness.[550]

---

[544] Information from Michael Goatcher.

[545] Britten Pears Arts HOL/5/2/6 Full transcript of RS/Barbara Simcoe's taped conversations 6 November 1985.

[546] Britten Pears Arts HOL/5/2/4 Notes on RS's taped conversation with Arthur Caton 28 August 1985.

[547] Britten Pears Arts HOL/5/2/6 Full transcript of RS/Barbara Simcoe's taped conversations 6 November 1985.

[548] Grogan, *Imogen Holst*, 358–9.

[549] Information in this paragraph from Michael Goatcher.

[550] Conversation with the late Peter King.

By her late 80s Isobel's eyesight was fading and her handwriting deteriorated. As she explained in a post-Christmas letter to Rosamund Strode in 1959: "I am getting very blind & have to use a magnifying glass which is very awkward." Imogen had been with her over Christmas for a fleeting two-day visit.[551] Imogen had her own health problems, leading to an operation to remove both her ovaries in 1960. She asked Britten to write to her mother when she was safely through the operation. For his pains, Britten received a typically blunt reply from Isobel:

I have been worried for a long time about her [Imogen's] health because I do think she is doing too much – too many jobs, & too much uncomfortable travelling – working against time, which is so wearing especially for a woman. However it is her choice and she loves her work, so what can one do?[552]

Isobel continued her semi-independent existence despite declining health. Imogen wrote to Britten in April 1962:

For the last 2 days I've been with my mother: – she's getting a bit shaky and has been alone for 2½ months, but the Lord has provided a new companion who is coming just before Easter, so it will be wonderful to start a new life without those particular ostinato crises![553]

It was in 1962 that Isobel and Imogen parted with the best portrait of Gustav, donating Millicent Lisle Woodforde's painting of him to the National Portrait Gallery. The following year, in 1963, Isobel was well enough to attend the unveiling of the blue plaque at her former home in Thaxted, The Steps, by Sir Adrian Boult, accompanied by Imogen and Ursula Vaughan Williams, herself a widow since the death of her husband in 1958.

In September 1963 Isobel's brother Harry died at the age of 89, but there is no evidence of sustained contact between the two during their later lives. An obituary in *Electronics and Power*[554] includes the following pen portrait which gives an insight into Harry's personality:

His interests were catholic, and outside his work and professional interests he showed keen enthusiasm for music, which he practised as a playing member of various orchestras. He will be remembered as a quiet, unassuming, jaunty figure, confident, approachable and ever-sympathetic.

In 1964 Imogen retired from her post as Britten's music assistant and devoted much of her time to promoting her father's music. Her activities included conducting two of Gustav's operas, *Savitri*, and *At the Boar's Head*, in Barnes. Isobel did not attend, but Clare Mackail, whom Gustav had taught at St Paul's Girls' School and who had participated in the first Whitsun Festival at Thaxted in 1916, wrote enthusiastically to her about Imogen's performance – testimony to a lasting friendship on both sides.[555] Isobel wrote affectionately, but in very shaky handwriting, to her daughter from Thaxted on 30 March 1965:

Dearest Imo
    I am still gloating over all your lovely presents – especially the Book which I am hoping to get someone to read to me.

---

[551] Britten Pears Arts HOL/2/15/3 Letter from Isobel Holst to Rosamund Strode 28 December 1959.

[552] Grogan, *Imogen Holst*, 362.

[553] Grogan, *Imogen Holst*, 367.

[554] January 1964, p 25.

[555] Grogan, *Imogen Holst*, 377. Claire Mackail's father, John William Mackail, was a close friend and the official biographer of William Morris.

I do hope you are feeling better & enjoying the sunny days we are having we had all the doors and windows open yesterday & I sat in the garden for hours and Heidi[556] got plenty of exercise chasing butterflies

No more now as my eyes are giving out

Much love and many thanks for giving me such a happy Birthday

Take care of yourself and don't forget how much you mean to everyone who knows you ISO[557]

As she entered her tenth decade, Isobel was becoming frailer. In July 1966 she suffered a fall. Imogen returned to Thaxted, staying at Weaverhead Cottage for the next few weeks rather than – as she usually did – at her friend Arthur Caton and Kate Butters' house, and visiting her mother daily at a nursing home in Cambridge.[558] Imogen arranged a new companion to take care of her before returning to Aldeburgh. Isobel managed to write a shorter birthday postcard to "Dearest Imogen" in 1967, signed off with much love.[559] Isobel remained fortunate in the strong friendships she had maintained over the years. Gustav's former pupil Clare Mackail wrote one of her many letters to Imogen in 1967:

… so much of the happiness & beauty of my youth has been through you and Gustav & Iso, and one can look back with inexpressible gratitude to that wonderful 'golden age' of music and work & laughter.[560]

A photograph of Isobel with Kate Butters taken around this time shows Isobel with her eye shade and a walking stick, with Kate in support.[561] In addition to the selfless assistance of these loyal neighbours, Isobel was increasingly dependent on her paid companions – Mrs Rooney in 1967, succeeded by Mrs Paloch in 1967–1968. Sylvia Heath also recalls her mother, Barbara Putterill, going to sit with Isobel in the evenings around this time.[562] Barbara Simcoe, who was a few years younger than Imogen, also enjoyed staying overnight at Weaverhead Cottage whenever she could after her own mother died. She enjoyed being able to sleep in what theoretically was Imogen's bedroom there, recounting that "everywhere upstairs there were books and biscuits, flowers – everywhere there were Thaxted colours." Barbara Simcoe was full of admiration for Isobel at this stage of her life, when she had a lot to put up with and her arthritis was particularly troublesome at night. Despite everything, Isobel continued to wear make up until the end of her life, and "never seemed to go grey".[563]

Although her daughter had been increasingly active in arranging her financial affairs, Imogen felt able to write in response to a letter from their solicitor, Robert Lucas, in September 1967 asking whether her mother still drew her own cheques that "She is still able to do this if someone with her holds the paper still and helps her to sign."[564]

---

[556] Described by Rosamund Strode as "that rather horrible little dachshund" Britten Pears Arts HOL/5/2/6 Full transcript of RS/Barbara Simcoe's taped conversations 6 November 1985.

[557] Britten Pears Arts HOL/2/8/2/106.

[558] Grogan, *Imogen Holst*, 388.

[559] Britten Pears Arts HOL/2/8/2/106.

[560] McGee, *Barely Clare*, p 19.

[561] Britten Pears Arts HOL/2/11/6/40 Photograph of Isobel Holst and Kate Butters.

[562] Letter from Sylvia Hughes to Michael Goatcher (n.d. May 2015).

[563] Britten Pears Arts HOL/5/2/6 Full transcript of RS/Barbara Simcoe's taped conversations 6 November 1985.

[564] Britten Pears Arts, letter dated 22 September 1967 from Imogen Holst to Robert Lucas.

Around this time Isobel gave her one and only newspaper interview. Unreliable in many respects, it is interesting for her tale of what she might have wished to have been true:

She was educated very largely by her widowed mother, who started a girls' finishing school outside London. Her mother was a wonderful linguist and played the organ and piano beautifully. She recalls her father as a most handsome man of independent means, who died in his late thirties[565]

Isobel's days of being able to tour the Essex countryside looking at historic churches were well and truly over. On 8 July 1968 Imogen wrote in response to an invitation from one of Isobel's friends:

Very many thanks for your kind letter; generous of you to suggest that Iso should go to the ceremony on Monday but I'm afraid I don't think it would be advisable, her sight and hearing and memory are all much worse than when she went to the meeting in Dunmow School. She would see and hear so little of what's going on, she might not be able to concentrate. Also the journey to Colchester is much longer.[566]

Despite increased support from her companion, and the tactful support of their solicitor,[567] Isobel's health was clearly deteriorating further. Clare Mackail, who by then had sustained her friendship with the Holst family for almost five decades, concluded a letter to Imogen in 1968 by sending "love to Iso (when you communicate)". In the autumn and winter of 1968–1969 Imogen arranged for Isobel to move into Stow Lodge Hospital, Onehouse, Stowmarket. This elegant former workhouse, whilst nearer than Thaxted to Imogen's own home in Aldeburgh, was still around an hour's drive away, and at first glance was a rather odd choice. Isobel's place in the hospital had been found by Dr John Agate,[568] a dedicated and renowned geriatrician who "pioneered the concept that those patients deemed old (then over 65) deserved as good a quality of life as possible, expert medical care to ensure this, and above all, respect".[569] Dr Agate was a member of the Aldeburgh Festival Choir and a friend and doctor to Imogen, who dedicated her song "Out of your sleep arise and wake", written in 1968, to him.

Imogen was able to visit her mother more frequently towards the end of her life, and Isobel retained Weaverhead Cottage until her death.[570] Imogen was in Thaxted on 2 April 1969 when she gave Robert Lucas two photographs of Gustav's music room at The Steps together with an autograph manuscript from the original sketches for *The Perfect Fool*, "as a token of gratitude for all his help."[571] Imogen's diary for Sunday 13 April 1969 records Isobel's last few days of illness. Imogen's plans for the rest of that week are mostly crossed out, including

---

[565] Interview by fellow Thaxted resident Pam Croome for the *Saffron Walden Weekly News*, c. early April 1968. I am most grateful to Michael Goatcher for his copy of this article.

[566] Britten Pears Arts HOL/5/2/23 Partial transcript of RS/Ann Burns *née* Crittall taped conversation 26 April 1991.

[567] Britten Pears Arts letter dated 3 May 1968 from Imogen Holst to Robert Lucas: "… We can never repay you for the help and encouragement which you give to my mother."

[568] Grogan, *Imogen Holst*, 393.

[569] Obituary of Dr John Agate CBE in *The Independent*, 20 November 1998.

[570] I am very grateful to Michael Goatcher for the photo, inscribed on the back "Christmas 1965", so taken before then.

[571] ERO T 2155 Box 1 Copy note written to Robert Lucas by Imogen Holst describing photographs showing Gustav Holst's music room at Thaxted.

the possibility of visiting her mother on her way back from Thaxted[572] on Wednesday 16 April. Instead, Imogen's diary for that day simply noted "Iso died."[573] Isobel was 93, and the death certificate records her occupation as "Widow of Gustav Holst, Musician", and the primary causes of her death as bronchopneumonia and cerebral thrombosis and the secondary cause as senility.[574] Five people attended the funeral at Ipswich Crematorium five days later, with Imogen the only relative present. In accordance with Isobel's wishes none of the mourners – the others being Imogen's friend Rosamund Strode, Isobel's daily help, the woman who 'came in to sleep in the house' and their Thaxted taxi driver – wore black.[575]

Unlike Imogen, who is buried close to Benjamin Britten and Peter Pears in Aldeburgh Churchyard, Isobel Holst has no gravestone. She joined those whom Vaughan Williams commemorated in his canticle *Let us now praise famous men*: "some there be which have no memorial, who have perished as though they have never been." This was in accordance with the wishes she had expressed in her will of 1957, "that my funeral shall be as simple as possible and without flowers, that my body be cremated and the ashes scattered, and that no memorial stone or inscription be erected." The net probate value of Isobel's estate was £1798 3s 10d – not a great amount in 1969. Isobel left most of her modest estate to Imogen, with pecuniary legacies to her friends Winifred Sumner[576] and Ethel Simcoe,[577] with £100 to the vicar of Thaxted for the repair and maintenance of the roof of Thaxted Parish Church. Fittingly for a woman who had done much to support her musician husband, and who had shared with him in the early years of their marriage the struggle to make ends meet, Isobel's final request in her will was that if Imogen predeceased her, the residue of her estate should be directed to the Musicians' Benevolent Fund.

In its request for simplicity and bequest to the vicar of Thaxted, Isobel's will is reminiscent of some late mediaeval English wills. This may have been a conscious reflection on her part. One of her collection of books, a present from Gustav, was the Revd Edward L. Cutts' *Scenes & Characters of the Middle Ages*,[578] which drew on the texts of some of these wills.

---

[572] Imogen had a room in Arthur Caton's house in Thaxted.
[573] Britten Pears Arts HOL/2/9/34 Imogen Holst's engagement diary for 1969.
[574] Her death certificate wrongly records her year of birth as 1877 rather than 1876.
[575] Grogan, *Imogen Holst*, 393–394.
[576] A Little Easton resident who predeceased Isobel, dying in 1962.
[577] Another long-term Thaxted resident and widow and author of *A short history of ... Thaxted* (1934).
[578] Published by Daniel O'Connor, London, 1922. I am most grateful to Sybil King for letting me see Isobel's copy of this book.

Epilogue
An Equal Partner?

Drawing of Isobel by Clare Mackail (Holst Victorian House)

This has been an attempt to draw what can be discovered about Isobel's life out of the shadows. It partly confirms the impression that the extent to which the Venn diagram of the lives of Isobel, Gustav and Imogen overlapped was at times small as they each pursued their own work and interests. Perhaps Isobel wished things had been different. In the newspaper interview the year before she died she gave the interviewer the impression that "Mrs. Holst has spent a good deal of her life travelling with her husband all over the world and it is abundantly clear, when talking to her, how fully she shared his life and entered into all his activities."[579]

Nevertheless, set in the context of the age in which they lived, Isobel and Gustav's relationship was strikingly egalitarian. Several of his letters underline the extent to which Gustav relied on Isobel for advice, as well as for practical support, particularly in the early stages of his career. He was also appreciative of how hard Isobel herself worked.[580] Although fewer letters written by Isobel have survived, and apparently none written by her to Gustav,

---

[579] *Saffron Walden Weekly News*, c. early April 1968.
[580] See for example, *Gustav Holst: Letters to W. G. Whittaker*, 77.

her letters to Vally Lasker reveal a woman with a quirky sense of humour similar to that of her husband.

Isobel Holst, and the role she played in supporting the work of her famous husband, was not misremembered in the sense that some of the women researched by Ann Oakley were.[581] Perhaps in accordance with her own wish when her daughter Imogen was writing one of the first biographies of Gustav, much of Isobel's life was unrecorded and, like her final resting place, is thus unmarked. Apart from the small number of references to her in successive biographies of Gustav, Isobel Holst became one of the wives forgotten by history.

In July 2000 Rosamund Strode, who was working on the *Dictionary of National Biography* (DNB) entry on Imogen Holst and knew Isobel only in her later life, corresponded with John Warrack, who had sent her his draft entry on Gustav for the New DNB. Rosamund provided the following background information about Isobel:

Her great talent was as a home-maker, she was a good cook and a good needlewoman with an excellent eye for colour, and had a flair for furnishing the many houses in which the family lived. The Harrison family was certainly artistic and musical to some degree, but I don't know the extent of their attainments. Like many people who become isolated through deafness she was, in her later years at any rate, a determined person and at some points verged on being "difficult", though I fully understand why! Does this help? I think she was 'mysterious' at the time when Imogen wrote her 1938 biography because she did not want to get dragged in too far – she must, of course, have read the book through before it ever got published and may, for all I know, have stipulated that she was to be largely kept out of it.

Isobel died on 16 April 1969, having been at the large geriatric hospital near Stowmarket under the care of the County Geriatrician, a good friend to Imogen.[582] I quite agree that it is difficult to find out much about her (Isobel's) background, when I knew her she was already in her late 70s and beginning to go deaf. She ended up pretty immobile, not only deaf but almost blind as well, hence the need for her to be cared for properly, and Stowmarket was a good deal nearer to Aldeburgh than Thaxted for Imogen, who never learned to drive.[583]

Ten years previously, Rosamund Strode had responded to a request for some details about Isobel with the following comments, prefacing them with the observation that "even her only child [Imogen] … knew very little of her mother's early life."

She was born Emily Isobel Harrison on 26 March 1877, the only girl (and second child) in a family of three. Imogen's cousin described the father as 'a jack-of-all-trades' who ended up as a baker – he thought. We have not been able to discover the name of either parent but I believe the mother was rather an invalid and much devolved on Isobel. It seems that the father was to some extent artistic (he has been described as 'painting unsuccessful water-colours') and the mother must have been musical for she gave piano lessons.

Isobel Harrison met Gustav Holst when she joined the Hammersmith Socialist Society Choir, which he conducted, in 1897. They married on 22 June 1901, and Imogen (12 April 1907 – 9 March 1984) was their only child.

After their marriage, Isobel Holst did not concern herself with her husband's activities, but concentrated on providing him with a comfortable, well-run home. She played the cello a little but from an anecdotal recollection of my mother's (who was a pupil at St Paul's Girls' School during Holst's

---

[581] Oakley, *Forgotten Wives*, 13.
[582] John Agate: a good amateur bass singer and married to a musician.
[583] Britten Pears Arts HOL/4/5/1/2 Harrison family papers: Letter from Rosamund Strode to Dr John Warrack, 13 July 2000.

years teaching there) I suspect that her standard of musicianship was none too great! At that time – during World War I – Isobel apparently tried playing double bass in the school orchestra.

The Holsts lived in various west London houses while Imogen was at school, leasing a succession of cottages/houses in the area near Thaxted, Essex, from c. 1916 onwards. Essex became the family's home from 1925 (after that Gustav Holst commuted, staying overnight in London with friends when necessary) and she made a busy life for herself, concentrating on whichever house they were in at the time. She had a real gift for home furnishing, and an eye for antiques and country furniture.

In the mid-nineteen fifties Isobel moved to her last home (the only one to be owned by the family) – Weaverhead, Thaxted, where she stayed until the autumn of 1968 when, as a very old lady, by now very deaf and losing her sight, she became a resident at Stow Lodge Hospital, Stowmarket, where she died, aged ninety-two, on 16 April 1969.[584]

Imogen, who did not always appreciate the role her mother played in supporting her father, or indeed herself, towards the end of her own life went to some length to explain the question why her mother was "often absent from his travels abroad". The interviewer, John Morrison, clearly touched a raw nerve, and Imogen's impassioned response deserves quoting at length:

She was absent from the travels abroad that were purely musical ones. And which linked up with his need for walking in solitude … in order to think about his compositions. Now my mother as you know from pictures and what I've written in my books, she was with him in Berlin, in 1903 – you've got the picture; she was with him in Ann Arbor, in 1923, you've got the picture and all that sort of thing. He had that four months abroad … [in 1929, when he went to Italy] that was planned on money that had been given to him, by friends collecting for him to have a long, long holiday, when the right moment came, and it was planned as a working holiday but not with any responsibilities. And that is the sort of thing that any composer might hope to have before he died; he was only five years off his death when he had it – it was the first time ever – and he joined it up with meeting musicians abroad, going to concerts, going to opera a bit, and, with looking at beautiful places, and walking, alone. And that would not have been the right sort of foreign tour for my mother to go. She had the home to keep, she was not a walker, ever – you get that in the letters in Heirs and Rebels that he's walking her off her feet in 1903; you see, my father was a very good walker and she, poor dear, had rheumatic feet so that wouldn't have done. Now my father, you couldn't ask a man who wants solitary walks for his composition, to go abroad with a wife who can't walk, when he goes from place to place; where they'd have hired cars, and been driven and that sort of thing, it just doesn't go together. So that it may seem very odd and that's one of the many things that worries me that when I'm dead, there won't be any one to argue against complete misunderstanding. Now those letters to Whittaker which Michael [Short] edited so marvellously … in this book there is … a letter from my father to Whittaker, one August, saying that 'I'm here alone' – this is from London – 'my wife looks in on me from time to time'. Now, a critic, when that book was published – I don't think I've got this press cutting, I wish I'd kept it – wrote, 'One can feel the loneliness'. Well, poor man, he didn't know better, but you see, August had always been my father's composing month, because of his school term; everybody knew that. Everybody knew that he had to be alone, and when I had friends at school, I used to go and stay with them in August – didn't invite them; I invited them for an occasional weekend in Thaxted but I wouldn't dream of it. He was having a solitary August in London, writing – of course, going every day to his sound-proof room – and that was understood by all of us; that was part of his working life. But how can you educate the journalists? And you see, especially that phrase with the tongue in the cheek saying 'my wife looks in on me from time to time' well to begin with, there's this thing of referring to each other as 'my wife' which he and Vaughan Williams do practically all the way through Heirs and Rebels, which shocked me as it shocked John – that's one of his questions. When I was writing my first biography, which was my first book and I was very ignorant, I took a lot of trouble to ask people what I didn't understand.

---

[584] Britten Pears Arts HOL/4/5/1/2 Harrison family papers, Letter from Rosamund Strode to Dr D Benson, 13 August 1990.

And that was one of the things: why did these two who knew each other so well, refer to each other as 'your wife' and 'my wife'? It was the way people talked in those days, and it changed in about the twenties, by which time of course I was calling my parents 'Gussie' and 'Iso', and the whole of life was changing that way. But, that's very difficult to understand. Now to go back to this letter to Whittaker, 'my wife looks in on me from time to time', 'my wife' could, by then, have been referred to as 'Isobel', I think it was sufficiently late, but you see, the tongue in the cheek is absolutely audible to me because it gives that impression, to a very close friend, Whittaker, of one's own wife, coming along to see whether one's got enough socks and that sort of thing – you know, all those things – and it being their way of enjoying each other's company; they'd have gone out for a meal, somewhere, and heard the news, and everything and he'd have gone on composing and she'd have gone back to Thaxted, or wherever it was in Essex. And the inverted commas around 'my wife looks in on me from time to time' audibly in that kind of mood and that kind of way he was talking to a real close friend. Now I can't possibly go into all that every time there's a doubtful phrase in any of these letters to close friends. The things between the lines are so well known to the writer and the receiver of the letter, and must seem so strange to the journalist reader. But I do think, Michael [Short] – that depressed me enormously when I read that, you see; well, I thought, 'I give up trying, it's no good, I can't possibly make people understand about my father's life and how he lived'. You see, of course, obviously the journalist would love it; 'the loneliness can be felt', you see, the scandal, and all that. What I would ask you, Michael dear, if there should be a second impression of that marvellous book of letters, if you'd give me exactly a line and a half of the bottom of my Introduction to it as a PS, and I can actually mention it, because it would be an example of the sort of difficulty.[585]

Despite her early socialism, as well as the generosity and kindness for which she was often remembered, from at least 1907 onwards (following Imogen's birth), Isobel enjoyed luxuries when she could afford them, such as shopping for culinary treats for herself and others at Fortnum and Mason's, and almost "always had someone helping in the house". At The Steps that included Hubert Adams, Gustav's manservant for four and a half years, who lived in, as did Carol Drane and several of the helpers at Weaverhead Cottage towards the end of Isobel's life. Discussing Imogen and Isobel's attitude to paid help with Barbara Simcoe, Rosamund Strode commented that:

… one of the things that Imogen never talked about was any kind of domestic help because it conflicted with their Socialist ideals. But it was quite obvious that they did have someone but she just didn't talk about them.

Isobel's practice of using paid help was considered normal for most of the period spanning her life. She was, however, a considerate employer, as well as rarely seeming to be afraid of speaking her own mind, including voicing unsolicited opinions. According to Barbara Simcoe[586] she was very critical of Miriam Noel, considering that:

she wasn't a good Vicar's wife – she never visited … and of course she used to impose on her char-ladies, as they were called in those days – it was a big Vicarage to run, and they only had sixpence an hour – they had the Green Study upstairs and they had a fire up there and they used to carry a coal-skuttle up – coal and things – it was a dreadful old house to run …

Iso always treated her people very well and liberally. … She may have been critical but she was very good to her staff. Yes. Coral stayed with her all those times; it was only when she became older

---

[585] Britten Pears Arts HOL/5/2/29 Transcript of Imogen Holst replying to questions by John Morrison, recorded 19–20 April 1980. The tape ends at this point.
[586] In contrast, Ann Burns née Crittall assumed that "Miriam Noel would have been a great friend of hers". Britten Pears Arts HOL/5/2/23 Partial transcript of RS/Ann Burns née Crittall taped conversation 26 April 1991.

that she had to have somebody there, sort of pseudo companion and she was critical of them because they hadn't got the same things in common … she was very good to all her people … Conrad[587] used to take the coal from these women if he passed them on the stairs; he was an invalid … he was what we used to call 'a perfect gentleman'. Also a practising Christian – he felt it was wrong.[588]

The stepdaughter of one of Isobel's loyal friends, whose memories of Isobel were mostly from before 1947, however, recalled another side of her:

I think she was very sort of muted – she wore a mute most of the time. From force of habit; I mean, Gussie was the person who mattered, and he was worshipped by Imogen, and by Iso, and so Iso rather thought of herself as a 'second eleven', you know.[589]

Isobel used to talk to Barbara Simcoe about Vally Lasker, who outlived both Isobel and Gustav and died in 1978. A few years later Rosamund Strode asked Barbara whether Iso "[got] on all right with those sort of people or do you think she was a little put out by the people who helped Holst … Thaxted was such a long way from his London activities …" Barbara and Rosamund agreed that Isobel didn't seem to mind, and got on with her own affairs.[590]

Were Isobel and Gustav Holst equal partners in a marriage of two independent hearts and minds? This is a question which Rosamund (RS) seems to pose in an interview with Len Haswell (LH) in 1988 in which she made a number of leading remarks:

RS: But that was in my time of knowing Imo, because her mother, with this pleasure she got out of houses, she was permanently on the move. And Imo told me when I had her to lunch one Sunday, I said rhubarb, and she said 'How lovely, I love rhubarb and so did my mother and we always planted it wherever we were – we never had any of it because you have to leave it in three years before you can eat it, and we were always moved by then!' She was one of those.
LH: Yes.
RS: So I'm not surprised that Gustav took refuge in his music-room at St Paul's – stayed there, you know? But I think they worked out a perfectly amenable sort of existing.
LH: It's a pity, because we haven't anyone still living who did know them.
RS: I don't want to go into total relationships; they obviously – I think they got on with each other, they didn't seem to avoid each other, but he had absolute requirements which Isobel understood, and Imo makes that quite clear on a tape from a man who asked some fairly impertinent questions – or was about to – and she shut the door on that, as you can imagine; and said her mother had never really got the credit that was due to her for understanding that this is what Gustav needed. And I think she did. I'm sure she didn't make a fuss. She must have had a shock or two; because Imo said that she got the table nicely got up – put flowers in the middle – and he swept them aside and spread out his music on it, you know, and that's a shock to a bride, who thinks she's making a nice little home.
LH: Yes, it would be.
RS: Having got over that shock and also the fact that he needed school holidays – because that's an exhausting business, teaching, after all – and travelling in, constantly taking trains to and fro, for of course there were trains in those days – to Thaxted, which had its own station.

---

[587] The vicar of Thaxted.

[588] Britten Pears Arts HOL/5/2/15 Full transcript of RS/Barbara Simcoe's taped conversation 16 July 1988.

[589] Britten Pears Arts HOL/5/2/23 Partial transcript of RS/Ann Burns née Crittall taped conversation 26 April 1991.

[590] Britten Pears Arts HOL/5/2/6 Full transcript of RS/Barbara Simcoe's taped conversations 6 November 1985.

LH: It's no good speculating, is it?[591]

Unlike Alice Elgar, Isobel did not help her husband with several thousands of pages of his scores.[592] Unlike Jelka Delius, she did not identify texts which her husband could set to music. Unlike Ursula Vaughan Williams, Isobel did not spend her early years of widowhood writing her late husband's biography. It was Ralph Vaughan Williams who once said that Isobel was "born out of her time" and that 20 years later she could have had a good career in interior decorating and furnishing.[593] In 1982 Imogen, then aged 75, was interviewed by the veteran broadcaster and music critic John Amis, who had known her for 35 years. Amis commented that Imogen had no attachments, so far as he knew, but that he would never "dream of bringing up a subject like that". He did, however, ask Imogen about her mother, which makes the interview unusual. Imogen repeated to Amis the story, well-known from her biographies, of Isobel singing in her father's first choir as his youngest soprano. She added: "They were both very good amateur actors. My mother could take off anyone and did, brilliantly."[594]

Shortly before her own death in March 1984, Imogen was interviewed for a television programme about her father. This included her longest and most appreciative tribute to her mother:

She had a very very kindly personality. She was *very* practical. She could cook *superbly*. She came from a family in Fulham, local, to Hammersmith, who were hard up, and there was nothing she couldn't do to make a home comfortable. And that was one of the things that my father appreciated so much, the practical side of someone who was kindly, understanding about his wanting to be alone and quiet when he was composing, of course, and being a *superb* cook and a *superb* manager, managing to live very well on a *very* small income as it was to begin with.[595]

During Isobel's long life, and often in difficult circumstances, her independence of mind and spirit shone through. Whilst she excelled at homemaking, cooking and dressmaking, her early active involvement with the Hammersmith Socialist Society, her voluntary ambulance driving for the Green Cross during WWI, and her embracing of country life in Thaxted and its surrounds show a woman who, like her husband, continued to develop new interests for most of her life. Perhaps above all, she understood and accommodated her husband's need to be alone to walk and to explore and to compose. Isobel's obituary in *The Times* paraphrased Imogen in writing that Isobel had been "kind and generous", and "brought into his life grace and ease and comfort."[596] That obituary might be Isobel's only lasting memorial, but they are good words by which to be remembered.

---

[591] Britten Pears Arts HOL/5/2/13 Transcript of RS/Len Haswell's taped conversation 23 June 1988.
[592] *Daily Telegraph* obituary 10 April 1920.
[593] Grogan, *Imogen Holst*, 18–19.
[594] John Amis interview with Imogen Holst, BBC, 23 July 1982. I am deeply indebted to Michael Goatcher for sharing his copies of Holst-related interviews with me.
[595] *Contrasts*, broadcast by Central Television on 28 May 1984, producer Jim Berrow.
[596] *The Times*, 19 April 1969.

Appendix 1
The family tree of Isobel Holst *née* Harrison

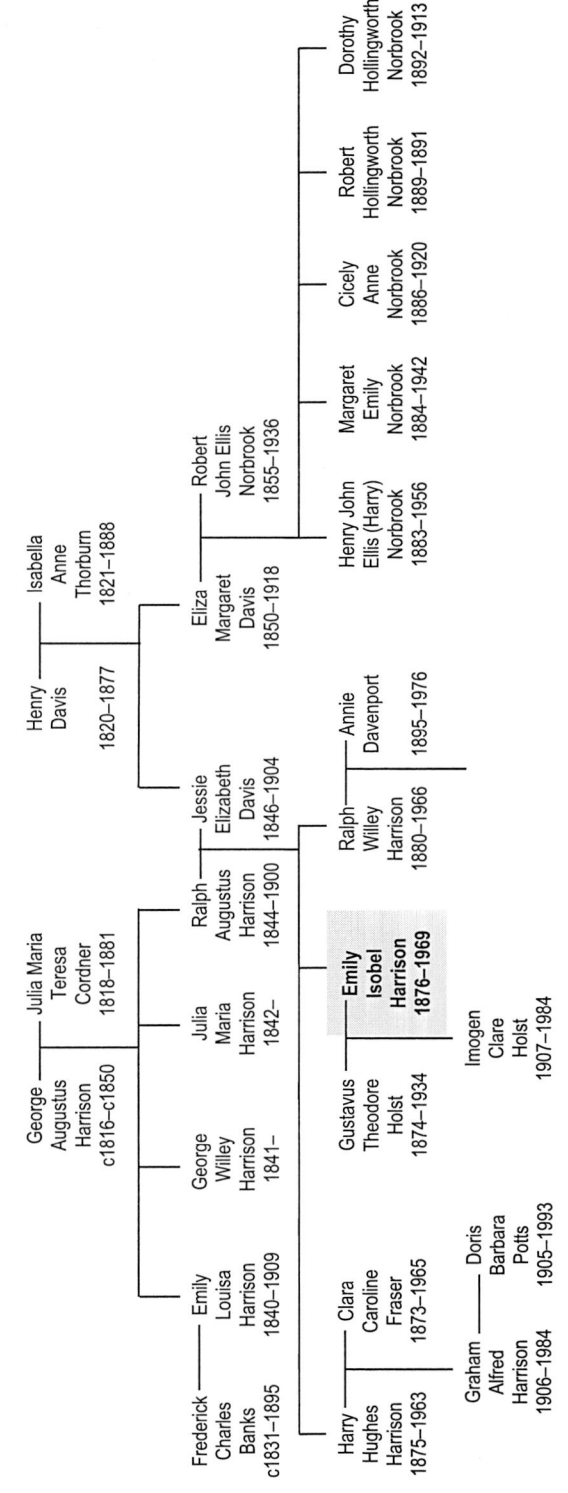

Appendix 2
Isobel Holst's key dates and home addresses

26 March 1876	Emily Isabel Harrison born at 1 Myddleton Terrace, Finsbury Road, Wood Green.
1881 census	Living at 87 Beaconsfield Road, Tottenham.
1891 census	Living at Alexandra House, High Street, Tottenham.
31 May 1892	Confirmed at St Alban's, Fulham (address: 55 Roxwell Road, West London)
1895 or 1896	Meets Gustav von Holst at the Hammersmith Socialist Society.
5 Feb 1898	Sings first performance of Holst's composition *Two Brown Eyes*.
15 July 1900	Isobel's father Ralph Augustus Harrison dies aged 56.
22 June 1901	Marries Gustav von Holst at Fulham Register Office.
1901	Following marriage, moves with Gustav to rooms at 162 Shepherds Bush Road near Hammersmith.
1903	Delayed honeymoon in Germany.
6 Nov 1904	Isobel's mother Jessie Elizabeth Harrison *née* Davis dies aged 58.
1904 to 1907	Isobel and Gustav living at 31 Grena Road near Richmond, then at No. 23 until 1908.
12 April 1907	Daughter Imogen born.
Summer 1908	Move to 10 the Terrace, Barnes.
1910–11	Isobel's portrait painted by Millicent Lisle Woodforde.
Summer 1913	Move to 10 Luxemburg Gardens, Brook Green.
Summer 1914	Isobel stays at Ashford home of James Brown, who paints her portrait.
1914–17	Rent thatched cottage at Monk Street, Thaxted, Essex.
1917–25	Move to "The Steps" in the centre of Thaxted.
1917	Imogen starts boarding school.
1917–18	Volunteers with Green Cross in the Women's Reserve Ambulance.
1917–18	Stays with James Brown and his family at Dunstable House, Richmond, when in London.
29 Sept 1918	Attends first orchestral performance of Gustav's *Planets* Suite.
Nov 1918–June 1919	Gustav away on YMCA duty in Salonica.
30 June 1919	Isobel and Gustav reunited at Thaxted.
July 1922	Move into London home at 32 Gunterstone Road, Barons Court (until 1925).
April–June 1923	Accompanies Gustav on visit to America.
March–Dec 1924	Gustav suffers nervous breakdown and he recovers "Alone in Thaxted".
1925	Gustav and Isobel give up London home and move to Brook End, Easton Park (until 1929).
1929	Move from Brook End to The Cottage, Great Easton (until c. 1931).
c. 1931	Move to Hill Cottage, Great Easton, where Isobel lives (until c. 1938).
1933	Motor accident whilst driving.
25 May 1934	Gustav dies with Isobel at his side.
6 March 1937	Presented to Queen Mary at the opening of the Holst music room at Morley College.
c. 1939	Moves to Little Barn, Little Easton.
c. 1942	Moves to 5 Westbury House, Stortford Road, Great Dunmow (until 1955).
c. 1955	Moves to Weaverhead Cottage, Thaxted (until 1968/9).
Late 1968	Moves into Stow Lodge Hospital, Onehouse, Stowmarket.
16 April 1969	Dies at Stowmarket.

Bibliography

Manuscript sources

Ashmolean Museum Oxford, Print Collection, Pissarro Archive
Letter from James Brown to Mrs Lucien Pissarro

British Library
Add Ms 45893	Hammersmith Socialist Society Minute books 1890–1896
Add Ms 45894	Hammersmith Socialist Society Papers vol. IV
Add Ms 57876	Gustav Holst MSS vol xiv 1910
Add Ms 57953	Gustav Holst letters to Ralph & Adeline Vaughan Williams (1903)
Add Ms 61951	Gustav Holst letters to Linetta Palamidessi de Castelvecchi (1901)
MS Mus 158	Letters from Vaughan Williams to Gustav Holst
MS Mus 1714/1	Vaughan Williams letters

Britten Pears Arts
HOL/1/5/1/7 Letters from Gustav Holst to Frances R Gray 1918–1928
HOL 1/5/1/8 Letters from Gustav Holst to Isobel Holst 1908–1933
HOL 1/5/1/13 Letters from Gustav Holst to Maja Kjohler 1907–1920s
HOL/1/5/1/14 Letters from Gustav Holst to Vally Lasker 1912–1934
HOL/1/5/1/16 Letter from Gustav Holst to Kathleen Long
HOL/1/5/2/1–22 Letters from Clifford Bax and Frances Gray to Gustav Holst
HOL/1/5/2/23 Letters from Imogen Holst to Gustav Holst
HOL/1/5/3/1 Letters from Isobel Holst to Maja Kjöhler 1906–1933
HOL 1/5/3/2 Letters from Isobel Holst to Vally Lasker 1913–1923
HOL 1/5/3/3 Letters from Isobel Holst to Dora Herbert Jones 1933–1934
HOL/1/5/3/4 Letters from Isobel Holst to Toby (Harry) Harrison 1938 & "22 May"
HOL/1/5/3/6 Letter from Ralph Vaughan Williams to Vally Lasker ?1939
HOL/1/6 Gustav Holst engagement diaries 1912–1934
HOL/1/7 Gustav Holst notebooks 1913–1934
HOL/2/6/1 Imogen Holst scrapbook May 1926-Aug 1928
HOL/2/7/1 Letters from Imogen Holst c. 1919–1973
HOL/2/7/7/67 Letter from Ralph Vaughan Williams to Imogen Holst, 14 June [1935]
HOL 2/8/2/104 Correspondence from Gustav Holst to Imogen Holst 1918-early 1930s
HOL/2/8/2/106 Correspondence from Isobel Holst to Imogen Holst 1965–1967
HOL/2/9 Imogen Holst engagement diaries 1930–1984
HOL/2/15/10 Five architectural drawings by George Harrison
HOL/4/5/1/2 Harrison family papers (Imogen Holst's notes)
Letter dated 22 September 1967 from Imogen Holst to Robert Lucas
Letter dated 3 May 1968 from Imogen Holst to Robert Lucas
Letter dated 1 October 1985 from Mrs (Jane) Mary Tomlinson to Mrs H Lilley

Britten Pears Arts transcripts and notes of interview recordings
HOL/5/2/4 Notes on RS's taped conversation with Arthur Caton 28 August 1985
HOL/5/2/13 Transcript of RS/Len Haswell's taped conversation 23 June 1988

HOL/5/2/15 Full transcript of RS/Barbara Simcoe's taped conversation 16 July 1988
HOL/5/2/17 Transcript of RS/Lady Helen Asquith's taped conversation 31 August 1988
HOL/5/2/23 Partial transcript of RS/Ann Burns *née* Crittall taped conversation 26 April 1991
HOL/5/2/26 Partial transcript of Stephen Wilkinson talking to Imogen Holst in Aldeburgh 3 February 1984
HOL/5/2/29 Transcript of Imogen Holst replying to questions by John Morrison, recorded 19–20 April 1980

Essex Record Office
ERO C/E 2/81 1918 Electoral Register for Saffron Walden (Parish of Thaxted)
ERO D/F 35/8/308 documents relating to Monk Street Property belonging to S. L. Bensusan Esquire 1924
ERO T 2155 Box 1 Copy note written to Robert Lucas by Imogen Holst describing photographs showing Gustav Holst's music room at Thaxted

Lambeth Palace Library
Bishop Bell Papers volumes 153, 154, 155, 208

London Metropolitan Archives
P77/ALB/011 Saint Alban, Fulham Register of confirmations 1892–1907
P77/ALB/063 St Albans Relief Committee Register of clothes and loan blankets 1894–1913

Morley College Library
Letters from Isobel and Imogen Holst

Westminster City Archives
CML/212, letter to Edwin Evans from Gustav Holst, 28 April 1924

Printed sources

Sushila Anand, *Daisy: The Life and Loves of the Countess of Warwick* (Piatkus, London, 2008).
Rosemary Ashton, *Thomas & Jane Carlyle: Portrait of a Marriage* (Chatto and Windus, London, 2001).
Howard Bailes, *Once a Paulina* (James & James, London, 2000).
Lawrence Barker, *In Search of Mars*, Essex record office blog. co.uk, posted 23 June 2014.
Clifford Bax, *Inland Far* (London, Heinemann, 1925).
M. E. Bulkley, *The Feeding of School Children* (London, G. Bell and Sons, 1914).
Richard Capell, "Gustav Holst: Notes for a Biography (I)", The Musical Times, 1 December 1926, 1075.
Richard Capell, "Gustav Holst: Notes for a Biography (II)", The Musical Times, 1 January 1927, 17.
Jessie Coleridge-Taylor, A memory sketch, or personal reminiscences of my husband, genius and musician S. Coleridge-Taylor (John Crowther, Bognor Regis, 1943).
Edward L. Cutts, *Scenes & Characters of the Middle Ages* (Daniel O'Connor, London, 1922).
Mabel Potter Daggett, *Women Wanted: the story written in blood red letters on the horizon of the Great World War* (George H. Doran, New York, 1918).

Helen Dore, *William Morris* (Pyramid Books, London, 1990).

Chris Fletcher, "Gustav and Isobel", Holst Birthplace Trust Newsletter, Issue 28, May 2010.

Alain Frogley and Aidan J Thompson eds., *Cambridge Companion to Vaughan Williams*, (Cambridge University Press, 2013).

Alan Gibbs, *Holst Among Friends* (Thames Publishing, London, 2000).

J. Bruce Glasier, *William Morris* (Longmans, London, 1921).

Harvey Grace, "Gustav Holst – Teacher", The Musical Times (August 1934), 689-696.

Chris Green, "Imogen Holst – a study in commitment", Norfolk and Suffolk Life (February 2019).

Christopher Grogan ed., *Imogen Holst: A Life in Music* (Boydell Press, Woodbridge, Revised Edition 2010).

Fritz Hart, "Early memories of GH", R.C.M. Magazine 39/2 (pp 43–52) and 39/3 (pp 84–9).

Raymond Head, review of *Gustav Holst: The Man and His Music by Michael Short*, Tempo New Series, no. 176 (Mar., 1991), pp 57–8.

Gustav Holst: Letters to W. G. Whittaker, ed. Michael Short (Glasgow, 1974).

"Gustav Holst's Widow's kind gesture", *Chelmsford Chronicle*, 16 July 1937, 5; Essex Newsman, 17 July 1937.

Andrew Heywood, "Gustav Holst, William Morris and the Socialist Movement", *Journal of the William Morris Society*, XI(4) 39–47, Spring 1996.

Imogen Holst, *Gustav Holst: A Biography* (2nd ed., OUP, 1969).

Imogen Holst, Gustav Holst 1874–1934: a guide to his centenary (Cambridge Music Shop, 1974).

Imogen Holst, *Gustav Holst at Thaxted*, first published 1966.

Imogen Holst, *Holst* (Faber & Faber, The Great Composers Series, 2nd ed. 1981).

Imogen Holst, *Holst* (Novello short biographies, 1972).

Imogen Holst, *A Scrap-book for the Holst Birthplace Museum* (Holst Birthplace Museum Trust, 1978).

Imogen Holst, *A Thematic Catalogue of Gustav Holst's Music* (Faber, London, 1974).

Imogen Holst and Ursula Vaughan Williams, eds. *Heirs and Rebels: Letters Written to Each Other and Occasional Writings on Music*, by Ralph Vaughan Williams and Gustav Holst (Oxford University Press, London, 1959).

Imogen Holst interview with Alan Blyth for Gramophone September 1974, reprinted by James McCarthy, Gramophone, 12 April 2013.

Imogen Holst, *The Music of Gustav Holst*, third revised edition (Oxford University Press, 1986).

Charles Kay, "The Marriage of Samuel Coleridge-Taylor and Jessie Walmisley", *Black Music Research Journal*, Vol. 21(2), Autumn 2001, pp 159–177.

Laura Kinnear, "Theodore von Holst", *Holst Birthplace Trust Newsletter*, Issue 59 (February 2018), p 2.

J.W.S. Litten, *The Marquis d'Oisy – Aesthete, Exotic and Enigma* (Anglo-Catholic History Society, 2014).

Stephen Lloyd, *H. Balfour Gardiner* (Cambridge University Press, 1984).

Tim McGee, *Barely Clare: The little-known life of Clare Mackail* (2020).

Jon C. Mitchell, A Comprehensive Biography of Composer Gustav Holst, with Correspondence and Diary Excerpts: Including His American Years (Lewiston, N.Y.: E. Mellen Press, 2001).

The Outlying Portions of the Easton Lodge Estate Essex (London, 1919).

J. N. Moore ed., *Music and Friends: Seven decades of letters to Adrian Boult* (London, 1979).

Morley College, *Magazine*.

William Morris, *Chants for Socialists* (The Socialist League, London, 1892).

"Mrs. Isobel Holst, Widow of the Composer." *The Times* (London), no. 57539 (April 19, 1969).

Ann Oakley, *Forgotten Wives: How Women Get Written Out of History* (Policy Press, Bristol, 2021)

Hugh Ottaway, "Review: Holst for the Young", *The Musical Times*, vol. 115, no. 1575 (May, 1974), p 392.

J. Putterill, *Thaxted Quest for Social Justice* (Precision Press, Marlow, 1977).

Paul Rusiecki, *The Impact of Catastrophe: The people of Essex and the First World War (1914–1920)* (Essex Record Office, Chelmsford, 2008).

St. Alban's Fulham, *Parish Magazine*, vol. 1, no 3, 18 March 1895

Michael Short, *Gustav Holst: The Man and his Music* (Oxford University Press, 1990; republished by Circaidy Gregory Press, 2014).

Ethel Simcoe, *A Short History of the Parish and Ancient Borough of Thaxted* (W. Hart & Son, Saffron Walden, 1934).

Paul Spicer, *Sir George Dyson: His Life and Music* (Boydell Press, Woodbridge, 2014).

Martin Stott, "A garden party at Kelmscott house ... would be pleasant", *William Morris Society Magazine* (Spring 2017), pp 10–15.

Sir Richard Terry, *On Music's Borders* (T. Fisher Unwin, London, 1927).

"Thaxted Jubilee: The Rev. Conrad Noel 25 years as vicar", *Essex Chronicle*, 27 September 1935.

Three on Holiday at Rye 1913: A Group of Post Impressionists Lucien Pissarro, James Bolivar Manson, James Brown, Catalogue with an Introduction by Malcolm Eastman (1980).

Philippa Tudor, "Gustav Holst and the Whitsun Festival in Dulwich 1920", *Dulwich Society Journal* (205, summer 2020), 29–34.

Philippa Tudor, "Millicent Lisle Woodforde and her paintings of the Holsts' home at 10 The Terrace Barnes", Holst Birthplace Museum website, July 2013.

Philippa Tudor, "The composer and the critic: Gustav Holst and Edwin Evans", *The Musical Times* (vol. 117, no. 1937, Winter 2016, pp 71–86.

Uplifting the Son of Man as the God of Justice in our midst (Church Publishing Company, Thaxted, 1919).

Ralph Vaughan Williams, 'Gustav Holst: An Essay and a note', in *National Music and other essays*, 2nd ed. (Oxford, 1987).

Letters of Ralph Vaughan Williams 1895–1958, ed Hugh Cobbe (Oxford, 2008).

Frances, Countess of Warwick, *Life's Ebb and Flow* (London, Hutchinson, 1929).

Wilfrid J Wren, *Voices by the Sea: The story of the Aldeburgh Festival Choir* (Lavenham, 1981)

Sound recording

John Amis interview with Imogen Holst, BBC, 23 July 1982

Television

Central Television Broadcast May 1984, Producer Jim Berrow

Typescripts

Thomas Armstrong, *Vally Lasker*: address given at her funeral service in St. Peter's Church, Kensington Park Road, on 18th April, 1978.

Theodore von Holst, Matthias Ralph Bromley von Holst (1886–1956) typescript notes May 2015.

Dr Vaughan Williams on "Gustav Holst", Extracts from a Lecture at Morley College on 20th January 1953. (supplied by Michael Goatcher)

INDEX

Agate, John, 113, 116
Allen, Hugh, 60, 89
Armstrong, Thomas, 44
Asquith, Helen, 77, 78, 79, 80
Balfour Gardiner, Henry, 8, 42, 43, 44, 49, 50, 56, 64, 65, 73, 79, 82, 88, 97, 98
Barnes, 36, 39, 40, 41, 42, 43, 44, 111
Bax, Clifford and Arnold, 42, 43, 44, 49, 63
Beames, Jessie, 47, 50, 59
Beames, Jessie and May, 46
Bell, George, 89, 100, 101
Bell, Henrietta, 89, 101
Bensusan, Samuel Levy, 45, 65
Boult, Adrian, 56, 62, 65, 105, 111
Britten, Benjamin, 9, 108, 109, 110, 111, 114
Brook End, Easton Park, 81, 82, 85, 88, 93
Brook Green, 33, 44, 98
Brown, James, 45, 46, 55
Brown, Sebastian, 42, 45, 55
Buckton, Alice, 41
Butters, Kate, 10, 110, 112
Capell, Richard, 34, 75
Carlyle, Thomas, 2
Castelvecchio, Elisina Palamidessi di, 29
Caton, Arthur, 10, 76, 82, 83, 108, 110, 112
Clarion, The (Socialist newspaper), 22, 23, 25
Coleridge-Taylor, Samuel and Jessie, 8
Coles, Cecil, 42, 55
Cossart, Ernest. *See* Holst, Emil von
Cranham, 18
Daggett, Mabel Potter, 54
Day, Nora, 47, 52, 57, 58, 62, 77, 80, 84, 91, 92, 93, 98
Delius, Frederick, 2, 4
Delius, Jelka née Rosen, 5–8, 120
Drane, Carol, 118
Dulwich, 32, 46, 60, 62, 76
Elgar, Carice, 3, 4
Elgar, Caroline Alice née Roberts, 2, 8, 120
Elgar, Edward, 2, 4
English Folk Dance Society, 76, 83
Essex Archaeological Society, 96, 104, 106
Evans, Edwin, 78
Eyles, Hannah, 10

Fenby, Eric, 7
Glasier, John Bruce, 20
Gotch, Nancy, 48
Gray, Frances Ralph, 35, 53, 67, 84, 91
Hammersmith Socialist Choir, 14, 18, 21, 24, 116
Hammersmith Socialist Club, 23
Hammersmith Socialist Society, 16, 18, 19, 21, 22, 48, 53, 55, 116, 120
Hardy, Thomas, 88, 89
Harrison, George Augustus, 12
Harrison, Graham Alfred, 17, 31, 106, 107
Harrison, Harry Hughes, 11, 14, 17, 18, 19, 20, 21, 26, 28, 31, 106, 107, 111
Harrison, Jessie Elizabeth née Davis, 11, 13, 26, 31, 113
Harrison, Ralph Augustus, 11, 12, 17, 26, 113
Harrison, Ralph Willey, 12, 31
Hart, Fritz, 16, 21, 22, 28, 33
Harvey, Lily, 71, 86
Head, Raymond, 9
Heath, Sylvia, 75, 108, 112
Hecht, Katherine, 107
Hill Cottage, Great Easton, 94, 95, 96, 104, 105
Holst, Adolph von, 14, 26, 29
Holst, Clara von, née Lediard, 14
Holst, Emil von, 8, 14, 55, 95, 96
Holst, Gustav
   Cotswolds Symphony, 29
   Egdon Heath, 88, 93
   Hecuba's Lament, 64, 91
   Hymn of Jesus, 70
   Perfect Fool, The, 75, 113
   Planets Suite, The, 56, 62, 69, 75, 78
   Savitri, 39, 59, 75, 111
Holst, Imogen, 8, 14, 17, 24, 25, 29, 35–37, 39–51, 54, 56, 59, 61, 62, 64, 65, 68, 70, 71, 75, 76, 81, 83–85, 87–102, 93, 103–14, 107, 115–20
Holst, Mary Thorley von, née Stone, 15
Holst, Mathias (Max) von, 15, 68
Holst, Nina von, 15, 28, 58, 68
Holst, Thorley von, 15, 75

Ives, Dorothy, 110
James Allen's Girls' School, 32, 42
Jelken, Rosa. *See* Delius, Jelka *née* Rosen
Jones, Dora Herbert, 96, 100
Jones, Mabel Rodwell, 42, 58, 60, 64, 74, 79, 80, 83, 85, 91, 96, 98, 99, 100
Joseph, Jane, 50, 60, 61, 62, 69, 80, 92
Kelmscott House, 16, 17, 18, 19, 20, 21
King, Peter, 110
Kjöhler, Maja, 33, 36, 38, 69, 97
Lasker, Vally, 43, 47, 50, 52, 57, 58, 59, 60, 67, 68, 71, 74, 78, 79, 80, 84, 88, 91, 92, 93, 95, 96, 98, 99, 116, 119
Lidbury, Austin, 75
Long, Kathleen, 90
Lucas, Robert, 112
Mackail, Clare, 41, 48, 111, 112, 113, 115
Mackail, John William, 48
Marx, Eleanor, 20
Masefield, John, 89, 101, 105
Merry, Frank, 24
Monk Street Cottage, 45, 46, 47, 49, 51, 52
Morley College, 34, 35, 39, 41, 45, 47, 50, 55, 63, 66, 76, 79, 105
Morris, William, 14, 16, 18, 20, 22, 24
Morrison, John, 9, 117
Newman, Anna *née* Lediard, 39
Newman, Mary, 39
Noel, Conrad, 56, 70, 72, 75, 83, 101, 105, 108, 109, 119
Noel, Miriam, 94, 118
Noel-Buxton, 1st Lord, 76, 109
Norbrook, Eliza *née* Davis, 13, 26
Norbrook, Harry, 13
Norbrook, Robert, 13, 26
Nutting, Dulcie, 58
Oakley, Ann, 2, 116
Paycocke's, Essex, 76, 86
Pears, Peter, 109, 114
Pissarro, Lucien, 45
Purcell, William and Frances, 1
Putterill, Barbara, 112
Putterill, Jack, 83
Scholes, Percy, 55, 62, 65
Sheppey, Isle of, 32, 36
Short, Michael, 8, 9, 117
Simcoe, Barbara, 28, 55, 71, 73, 76, 86, 90, 104, 110, 112, 118
Simcoe, Ethel, 55, 104, 114
St Paul's Girls' School, 33, 35, 41, 43, 44, 47, 48, 51, 53, 63, 65, 68, 70, 71, 76, 77, 79, 80, 82, 83, 84, 95, 111, 116, 119
Stow Lodge Hospital, Stowmarket, 113, 116
Strode, Rosamund, 9, 48, 76, 80, 104, 110, 114, 116, 118, 119
Sumner, Winifred, 114
Terry, Richard, 57, 61, 63, 64, 87
Thaxted, 9, 40, 45, 47, 48, 50, 55, 59, 68, 69, 70, 71, 72, 75, 76, 77, 78, 79, 81, 83, 90, 94, 95, 97, 101, 106, 108, 109, 110, 111, 113
The Steps, Thaxted, 51, 55, 64, 76, 111, 113, 118
Vaughan Williams, Adeline, 26, 27, 33, 45
Vaughan Williams, Ralph, 23, 25, 26, 27, 29, 30, 32, 33, 36, 44, 55, 65, 70, 73, 78, 83, 96, 100, 101, 103, 105, 106, 108, 109, 114, 117, 120
Vaughan Williams, Ursula, 108, 111, 120
Walker, Emery, 16, 18, 19
Warwick, Frances (Daisy), Countess of, 81, 82, 93, 108
Weaverhead Cottage, 86, 109, 112, 113, 117, 118
Westbury House, Great Dunmow, 108, 109
Whitsun music festivals, 47, 48, 79, 93, 101, 105
Whittaker, William Gillies, 68, 72, 74, 77, 78, 81, 99, 117
Wilkinson, Stephen, 10
Woodforde, Millicent Lisle, 40, 111